# The Law of Self-Defense in North Carolina

# The Law of Self-Defense in North Carolina

John Rubin

1996

INSTITUTE *of* GOVERNMENT
The University of North Carolina at Chapel Hill

THE INSTITUTE OF GOVERNMENT of The University of North Carolina at Chapel Hill is devoted to teaching, research, and consultation in state and local government.

Since 1931 the Institute has conducted schools and short courses for city, county, and state officials. Through monographs, guidebooks, bulletins, and periodicals, the research findings of the Institute are made available to public officials throughout the state.

Each day that the General Assembly is in session, the Institute's *Daily Bulletin* reports on the Assembly's activities for members of the legislature and other state and local officials who need to follow the course of legislation.

Over the years the Institute has served as the research agency for numerous study commissions of the state and local governments.

Michael R. Smith, DIRECTOR
William A. Campbell, ASSOCIATE DIRECTOR

FACULTY

| | | |
|---|---|---|
| Stephen Allred | Robert L. Farb | Janet Mason |
| A. Fleming Bell, II | Joseph S. Ferrell | Richard R. McMahon |
| Frayda S. Bluestein | Cary M. Grant | Laurie L. Mesibov |
| Mark F. Botts | Milton S. Heath, Jr. | David W. Owens |
| Joan G. Brannon | Cheryl Daniels Howell | John Rubin |
| Anita R. Brown-Graham | Joseph E. Hunt | John L. Saxon |
| Margaret S. Carlson | Kurt J. Jenne | Roger M. Schwarz |
| K. Lee Carter, Jr. | Robert P. Joyce | John B. Stephens |
| Stevens H. Clarke | Jeffrey S. Koeze | Thomas H. Thornburg |
| Anne S. Davidson | Patricia A. Langelier | A. John Vogt |
| Anne M. Dellinger | David M. Lawrence | Michael L. Williamson |
| James C. Drennan | Charles D. Liner | |
| Richard D. Ducker | Ben F. Loeb, Jr. | |

Cover illustration: *Untitled (683)*, by Michael Brady. Prismacolor on paper, 1983.

*To my parents*

# Summary Table of Contents

# Detailed Table of Contents

# Figures

# Preface

As a practicing lawyer I often had to learn new areas of law. Always, it seemed, I had too little time to do so. Few things eased my burden more than a good secondary source. Good ones did a lot of the work for me, gathering relevant cases, explaining the law, and highlighting potential problems. That is what I have aimed for here. I hope this book will be a useful resource in one small area of criminal law, the law of self-defense.

I have tried to do two basic things: set out the prevailing law in North Carolina and employ a systematic approach to analyzing defenses involving defensive force. The two do not always mesh. At times I have imposed my own sense of order when the law may not be so orderly. The book should provide readers with enough information to draw their own conclusions.

The specific contents of the book were determined largely by the decisions of the North Carolina appellate courts. This must be so because the law of self-defense consists largely of court-made law. Still, I have tried to organize the discussion according to what I would want to know before entering the courtroom. What exactly are the rules governing the use of defensive force? What evidentiary issues are likely to come up? What should instructions to the jury look like? The book does not discuss trial tactics, but it does discuss the law that determines the answers to these questions.

More people than I can list patiently listened to my meanderings about the topics covered in this book and had useful ideas. I want to thank in particular those who read all or part of earlier drafts (Robert Farb, Benjamin Sendor, Alexander Charns, Stevens Clarke, William Crumpler, David Lawrence, and James Williams); Marjorie Hudson, who tirelessly edited the manuscript; and Carol Offen, Michael Brady, Daniel Soileau, and the many other Institute of Government staff who contributed to the book's production. Above all, I want to thank Jane Perkins, my wife and also a lawyer, for her constant support and insight.

Perhaps the best thing about writing a book is being the one who decides what goes in it. Thus any errors are my own. I welcome comments about the book's scope, organization, and content. Comments may be sent to me at the Institute of Government, CB # 3330, Knapp Building, The University of North Carolina at Chapel Hill, Chapel Hill, North Carolina 27599-3330. Or, I can be reached by e-mail at rubin.iog@mhs.unc.edu.

Chapel Hill                                                      John Rubin
Spring 1996

# The Law of
# Self-Defense in
# North Carolina

# 1 Introduction

# 1   Introduction

❧❧❧   Early in this century Justice Holmes observed that the law of self-defense has had "a tendency to ossify into specific rules without much regard for reason."[1] Those words retain their sting today. The law of self-defense often seems a thicket of rules, qualifiers, and exceptions, neither intuitive nor easily explained.

To complicate matters, self-defense is one of several different defenses concerning the use of defensive force. The law recognizes defense of another, defense of property, and defense of habitation, among others. In his two-volume treatise on defenses, Robinson refers to this family of defenses as *defensive-force defenses*.[2] However inelegant this term may seem, it is an apt way to refer to such defenses and will be used throughout this book.

Defensive-force defenses share several common attributes. They comprise a fairly self-contained subset of the larger class of *justification* defenses—that is, defenses that authorize, or *justify*, conduct that the law otherwise would consider wrongful. They concern a threat of harm to a particular interest, such as oneself, other persons, and property. And, they allow the use of force or the taking of some other defensive action to protect against the threatened harm.[3] Yet, despite their similarities, each defensive-force defense has tended to develop its own specialized rules.

---

1. Brown v. United States, 256 U.S. 335, 343, 41 S. Ct. 501, 502, 65 L. Ed. 961, 963 (1921).

2. 2 Paul H. Robinson, Criminal Law Defenses 69 (1984).

3. *See infra* § 2.1 (discussing basic principles of defensive force).

## § 1.1   Purpose of Book

The purpose of this book is to lay out, in as orderly a fashion as possible, the existing, criminal-law rules in North Carolina on self-defense and other defensive-force defenses.[4] Its goal is not to offer a simple, easy-to-use alternative to the current state of the law. Even if such a model could be constructed, it would not necessarily serve the intended consumers of this book—primarily, lawyers and judges—who must have a working command of the law as it currently exists. Still, this book aims to do more than recite mere boilerplate. It attempts to cut through the mass of cases on defensive force and highlight the dominant themes in North Carolina law. It also probes the rationale behind the various rules on defensive force, identifies inconsistencies and ambiguities, and considers ways to rationalize and streamline the law.

With this overall purpose, the book considers

- the general requirements for employing defensive-force defenses;
- the distinguishing characteristics of each defensive-force defense;
- the availability of such defenses against different criminal charges;
- the types of evidence that the defense and prosecution may offer;
- the circumstances in which the defendant is entitled to jury instructions on defensive force or dismissal of the state's case; and
- the required components of instructions to be given to the jury.

This book concentrates on North Carolina law. For those interested in a more general discussion of defensive-force defenses, several good treatises are available.[5] Also, the *American Law Reports* (A.L.R.) contain an array of annotations on various aspects of defensive force that include extensive citations to the law of other states.

---

4. This book does not deal with North Carolina's civil-law rules on defensive force, although similarities undoubtedly exist between the criminal and civil law in this area. *See generally* CHARLES E. DAYE & MARK W. MORRIS, NORTH CAROLINA LAW OF TORTS 119–25 (1991).

5. *See* WAYNE R. LaFAVE & AUSTIN W. SCOTT, JR., SUBSTANTIVE CRIMINAL LAW (1986); MODEL PENAL CODE AND COMMENTARIES (American Law Institute 1985); PAUL H. ROBINSON, CRIMINAL LAW DEFENSES (1984); ROLLIN M. PERKINS & RONALD N. BOYCE, CRIMINAL LAW (3d ed. 1982).

## § 1.2  Using Substantive Rules at Trial

Much of this book is about the substantive rules of defensive force—the limitations on the use of deadly force, for example, or the circumstances in which one person may come to the defense of another. These substantive rules address a wide range of conduct that takes place outside the courtroom. Lawyers and judges, however, must understand how these rules develop and apply in the relatively narrow confines of a criminal trial. The substantive rules primarily come into play at three junctures. They affect determinations concerning

- the *admissibility of evidence* that is offered by the defense or prosecution;
- the *sufficiency of the evidence* to warrant submitting to the jury the defense raised by the defendant and the offense charged by the state; and
- the *wording of instructions* to the jury.

Chapters 7 and 8 consider at length questions relating to the admissibility of evidence, sufficiency of evidence, and wording of instructions. It is useful to consider these topics briefly at the outset, however, because of their importance to the discussion of the substantive law in earlier parts of the book.

### (a)  Admissibility of Evidence

The first principle of evidence is that evidence must be relevant to be admissible.[6] The substantive rules on defensive force necessarily play a part in determining the relevancy of evidence, and thus its admissibility, because they serve to define the issues in the case.

For example, in a defensive-force case the jury must consider whether the defendant reasonably believed that he or she was facing some threat of harm and used a reasonable amount of force in response. The presence of these substantive issues opens up lines of inquiry that

---

6. Rule 402 of the North Carolina Rules of Evidence states this general principle of admissibility. It provides that "[a]ll relevant evidence is admissible" except as provided by federal or state constitutions, state statutes, or the rules of evidence themselves. Rule 401 gives the basic definition of relevancy: "'Relevant evidence' means evidence having any tendency to make the existence of any fact that is of consequence to the determination of the action more probable or less probable than it would be without the evidence."

might otherwise be irrelevant, such as inquiries into whether the victim had been violent in the past. The courts have often found such evidence to be relevant because it bears on the reasonableness of the defendant's perceptions and actions in the encounter under consideration.[7] Other rules of evidence may affect the admissibility of such evidence, but the substantive rules of defensive force provide for its basic relevance.

### (b) Sufficiency of Evidence

The court makes two determinations about the sufficiency of evidence in a defensive-force case. One, the court determines whether the evidence is sufficient to warrant submitting instructions to the jury on the *defense* asserted by the defendant. A defendant relying on a defensive-force defense has the burden of producing, or coming forward with, sufficient evidence in support of that defense. If the defendant meets this burden of production, the court must submit instructions to the jury explaining the defense. Two, the court determines whether the evidence is sufficient to warrant submitting to the jury the *offense* charged by the state. In all criminal cases, the state bears the burden of producing sufficient evidence to support submission of the charges to the jury. In cases in which the defendant raises a defensive-force defense, the prosecution also may need to produce evidence that the defendant did not have the right to use defensive force. If the defendant's evidence in support of the defense is sufficiently strong, the prosecution's failure to produce countervailing evidence may result in dismissal or nonsuit of the charges.[8]

These inquiries into the sufficiency of the evidence necessarily implicate the substantive rules of defensive force. Such rules determine the issues on which the defendant and prosecution must produce evidence. Appellate decisions on the sufficiency of the evidence, in turn, flesh out the meaning of the substantive law of defensive force. For example, under the substantive law, a person may use defensive force only if the person reasonably believes that he or she must defend against some threat of harm. To obtain instructions on defensive force, the defendant must produce evidence showing the reasonableness of that belief. Case law addressing the sufficiency of the evidence on rea-

---

7. *See infra* § 7.2 (discussing evidence relating to victim's character and conduct).

8. *See infra* § 8.2(c) (discussing defendant's burden of production) and § 8.2(d) (discussing prosecution's burden of production).

sonableness, in turn, provides a gauge of the circumstances that do and do not show a defendant's actions to be reasonable.

It is important to keep separate, however, decisions involving requests for defensive-force instructions and decisions involving motions for dismissal or nonsuit. When a court denies instructions on defensive force, it essentially concludes that the evidence in support of the defendant's claim of defensive force is so weak that a rational jury, if instructed on the claim, *would* necessarily reject it. When a court denies a motion for dismissal or nonsuit of the state's case, it finds only that a rational jury *could* reject the defendant's claim of defensive force and convict the defendant of the charged offense. Consequently, appellate cases finding that the evidence of defensive force did not warrant dismissal or nonsuit may have little bearing on whether similar evidence would warrant instructions on defensive force.

It also is important to distinguish the *burdens of production* borne by the defendant and prosecution from the ultimate *burden of persuasion*. The burdens of production apply only when the trial court is assessing the sufficiency of the evidence and is determining the issues to submit to the jury. Once the court submits the case to the jury, those burdens are no longer significant. In general, the prosecution bears the burden of persuading the jury of the defendant's guilt beyond a reasonable doubt. As part of its burden of persuasion in a defensive-force case, the prosecution must prove beyond a reasonable doubt that the defendant did not have the right to use defensive force. For the sake of brevity, this book sometimes states that a defendant claiming the right to use defensive force must have satisfied this rule or that rule. Before the jury, however, the prosecution actually bears the burden of proving that the defendant did not comply with the rules on defensive force.[9]

### (c) Wording of Instructions

Perhaps the most direct contact between the substantive rules of defensive force and the trial of defensive-force cases is in the wording of instructions to be given to the jury. Although trial courts have some leeway in how to word jury instructions, the instructions must adequately explain the substantive law on the use of defensive force. Further, the instructions must explain the particular principles of defensive force supported by the evidence. For example, in a case in which the evidence

---

9. *See infra* § 8.2(b) (discussing prosecution's burden of persuasion).

supports both self-defense and defense of habitation, the trial court must adequately explain the substantive law relating to both defenses.[10]

## § 1.3   Outline of Contents

A book of this kind, which aspires to provide a comprehensive treatment of a complex subject, runs the risk of being as inaccessible as the subject it attempts to treat. The following outline of the contents of the book may help the reader find his or her way to appropriate sections.

Chapter 2 describes the principles common to all defensive-force defenses. It begins by discussing the exculpatory nature of defensive-force defenses generally and the fundamental principles underlying the defenses—namely, necessity, proportionality, and fault (§ 2.1). The chapter then offers a three-step approach for determining whether a particular defense is available. It identifies the various kinds of harm a person would be justified in using force to prevent, considers the defenses that do and do not permit *deadly* force, and introduces the four-part test articulated in *State v. Norris*[11] (referred to throughout the book as "the *Norris* test"), which embodies the main rules on the use of defensive force in North Carolina (§ 2.2).

Chapters 3 through 5 focus on the substantive elements of the various defensive-force defenses. Together, these three chapters attempt to cover the circumstances in which the law permits a person to use defensive force. Chapter 3, by far the longest chapter of the book, analyzes the right to kill in self-defense. The length of that chapter reflects not that claims of defensive force are more appropriately made in homicide than in other criminal cases, but simply that homicide cases have drawn more of the appellate courts' attention and have generated a body of law central to analyzing the use of defensive force in other contexts. Chapter 3 begins by discussing the two doctrines that may arise in homicide cases: perfect and imperfect self-defense (§ 3.1). It then analyzes in detail the elements of the *Norris* test and the circumstances in which a person may rely on perfect and imperfect self-defense. For perfect self-defense to apply, the defendant must meet all of the *Norris* elements. In essence, the defendant must have an *honest* and *reasonable* belief in the need to defend himself or herself from harm, the first two elements of the *Norris* test (§ 3.2); must not be the

---

10. *See infra* § 8.4 (discussing required components of jury instructions on defensive force).

11. 303 N.C. 526, 279 S.E.2d 570 (1981).

*aggressor*, the third element of *Norris* (§ 3.3); and must not use *excessive force*, the fourth element (§ 3.4). For imperfect self-defense to apply, the defendant must meet the first two *Norris* elements and must not be an aggressor with murderous intent. The chapter closes by discussing whether North Carolina imposes a duty to retreat in addition to the requirements of *Norris* (§ 3.5).

Chapter 4 deals with variations on self-defense—situations that either do not involve killing in defense of oneself or are sufficiently distinctive to warrant separate treatment. It discusses the use of deadly force in self-defense when the force does not result in the death of the attacker (§ 4.1); self-defense against sexual assaults, such as rape and sexual offense (§ 4.2); the right to use nondeadly force to defend against mere bodily harm or offensive physical contact (§ 4.3); the differences between the rules of self-defense within the home or business and self-defense elsewhere (§ 4.4); and self-defense cases involving battered persons (§ 4.5).

Chapter 5 discusses defensive-force defenses that do *not* necessarily involve defense of oneself. The chapter discusses the right to prevent the commission of crime and detain offenders, which technically is not a defensive-force defense but involves similar principles (§ 5.1); the right to defend another person, which rests on both crime prevention and defensive-force principles (§ 5.2); the right to use force to defend real and personal property, including evicting trespassers (§ 5.3); defense of one's home, or "habitation," a doctrine distinct from both defense of self and defense of property (§ 5.4); and the limited circumstances in which one may use force to defend oneself and other interests against law-enforcement officers (§ 5.5).

Chapters 6 through 8 focus on issues that may arise in criminal trials involving claims of defensive force. Chapter 6 considers the applicability of defensive-force defenses against certain types of charges. Although defensive-force defenses provide an appropriate basis for defending against most homicide and assault charges, the availability of such defenses may not be as clear in other criminal cases. The chapter considers whether defensive-force defenses are available against felony murder (§ 6.1), involuntary manslaughter (§ 6.2), and specialized assault and other nonhomicide charges (§ 6.3).

Chapter 7 discusses evidentiary issues that commonly arise in defensive-force cases. Many of the cases are concerned with the admissibility of evidence about the character and prior conduct of the parties to the conflict. Such evidence includes opinion and reputation testimony about the parties' character, evidence of "prior bad acts," criminal convictions, and threatening statements. The chapter discusses the admissibility of each of these types of evidence when offered about the defendant (§ 7.1) and when offered about the victim (§ 7.2). The last section of the chapter discusses the admissibility of evidence about the defendant's state of mind, including expert testimony (§ 7.3).

Chapter 8 describes the burdens that the defense and prosecution bear in defensive-force cases and the required components of instructions to the jury on the rules of defensive force. The chapter first notes the lack of any "burden" on the defendant to plead or otherwise give notice of whether he or she intends to rely on a defensive-force defense (§ 8.1). It then considers the different burdens of proof applicable in defensive-force cases: the defendant's burden of producing sufficient evidence to warrant instructions on defensive force; the prosecution's burden of producing sufficient evidence to avoid dismissal or nonsuit; and the prosecution's burden of persuading the jury beyond a reasonable doubt that the defendant did not properly exercise the right to use defensive force (§ 8.2). Although for the sake of brevity this book often states that a defendant must meet certain requirements to use defensive force, ultimately the prosecution has the burden of proving that the defendant did *not* meet those requirements. Chapter 8 also considers the presumption of malice that may arise in homicide cases and how evidence in support of a defensive-force defense serves to rebut any such presumption (§ 8.3). The concluding section of the book discusses in general the required components of instructions to the jury on defensive force (§ 8.4).

# 2   Principles of Defensive Force

# 2   Principles of Defensive Force

❦❦❦   Like most jurisdictions, North Carolina recognizes several defensive-force defenses. Some, such as defense of another and defense of property, the courts typically regard as distinct doctrines. Others, such as nondeadly force in self-defense, are sufficiently different from other defensive-force defenses to warrant separate treatment in this book. Each is considered on its own terms in Chapters 3 through 5. It is useful at the outset, however, to isolate the principles common to all of these related defenses.

## § 2.1   Basic Principles

### (a) The Exculpatory Nature of Defensive-Force Defenses

In the parlance of criminal-law theory, the various defensive-force defenses fall into the class of defenses known as *justifications*. Such defenses authorize, or *justify*, conduct that otherwise would be considered wrongful.[1] Thus a person may strike or even kill another if the person meets the legal requirements for using defensive force. In most instances the person would be guilty of no crime.[2]

---

1. *See generally* George P. Fletcher, Rethinking Criminal Law 759 (1978). Other justification defenses include the necessity defense, under which a person may violate the literal terms of the criminal law to avoid a greater evil, and defenses based on the defendant's special authority (such as a parent's responsibility for the care of a child or a law-enforcement officer's authority to enforce the law), under which the defendant may use reasonable force in carrying out his or her responsibilities. *See generally* 1 Paul H. Robinson, Criminal Law Defenses 83–86 (1984). These other justification defenses are beyond the scope of this book.

2. An "imperfect" variation of self-defense and other defensive-force defenses also exists. It is the one form of defensive-force defense that is not fully exculpatory, serving only to mitigate criminal liability. *See generally* § 2.2(c) *infra*.

This academic explanation, however, does not reflect the wide appeal of self-defense and other defensive-force defenses. Exalted expressions on the subject can be found throughout the jurisprudence of this state. In an 1877 case the North Carolina Supreme Court opined that the defendant, drawn into combat to defend himself, was driven by "the very instinct and constitution of his being."[3] Fifty years later, in a 1927 opinion, the court pronounced, "The first law of nature is that of self-defense."[4] Again in 1989 the court characterized self-preservation as a "primal impulse" and "an inherent right of natural law."[5] These statements cannot be dismissed as just flowery rhetoric. They reflect an abiding commitment to the right to defend oneself, one's property, and other interests recognized by the law.[6]

### (b) Necessity, Proportionality, and Fault

The right to use defensive force rests on three fundamental principles: necessity, proportionality, and fault. Although the specific rules governing the use of defensive force vary somewhat with each jurisdiction, these three principles are constant.[7]

First, the defendant's use of force must be *reasonably necessary* to avert some harm.[8] To take a simple example, A is entitled to push B if it is reasonably necessary to prevent B from pushing A.

---

3. State v. Turpin, 77 N.C. 473, 477 (1877).

4. State v. Holland, 193 N.C. 713, 718, 138 S.E. 8, 10 (1927).

5. State v. Norman, 324 N.C. 253, 259, 378 S.E.2d 8, 12 (1989).

6. Expressions such as those recited in the text can be found in connection with several different defensive-force defenses. *See, e.g.,* State v. Lee, 258 N.C. 44, 46–47, 127 S.E.2d 774, 776 (1962) ("As an incident to the indubitable right to acquire and own property, . . . a person . . . has the legal right to defend and protect it."); State v. Maney, 194 N.C. 34, 36, 138 S.E. 441, 442 (1927) (defendant, who defended wife from attack, acted in accordance with "primary law of nature" and from "highest impulse and instinct"); State v. Gray, 162 N.C. 608, 613, 77 S.E. 833, 835 (1913) ("A man's house, however humble, is his castle, and his castle he is entitled to protect against invasion.").

7. *See* Richard A. Rosen, *On Self-Defense, Imminence, and Women Who Kill Their Batterers*, 71 N.C. L. Rev. 371, 378–79 & nn.12–18 (1993) (surveying authorities on self-defense and discussing the three fundamental principles underlying the right of self-defense).

8. The types of harm that the various defensive-force defenses allow a person to prevent are discussed generally in § 2.2(a) *infra*.

Second, the amount of force used by the defendant against another person must be *proportional* to the harm threatened by that person. Continuing with the above example, A ordinarily may not shoot B even if it is necessary to prevent B from pushing A; the reason is that shooting B is not proportional to the harm threatened by B.

Third, the defendant must not be *at fault* in the conflict. Thus, if A pushes B first, provoking B to push back, A forfeits the right to defend against B's push. Having started the conflict, A may not use further force even if such force is reasonably necessary and proportional.

At least in this pristine form, these principles reflect no more than what a parent might tell a child about fighting: don't be the one to start it (fault), don't hit unless you have to (necessity), and don't overdo it (proportionality). This book returns to these general principles when considering the specific rules governing defensive-force defenses in North Carolina. The principles help explain both the purpose of those rules and how they should be applied in gray areas.

## § 2.2 A Three-Step Approach

While the theoretical underpinnings of defensive-force defenses are fairly straightforward, the specific rules governing such defenses often seem painfully complex. This section offers a three-step approach for analyzing how defensive-force defenses operate in North Carolina and for determining whether a defendant may rely on a particular defense. The three steps are as follows:

- *Identify the harm to be prevented.* Does the particular defense cover the harm that was, or reasonably appeared to be, threatened? If not, the defense is inapplicable. See § 2.2(a).
- *Determine the propriety of deadly force.* Does the defense permit the use of deadly force or does it allow only nondeadly force? If the defendant used deadly force in the encounter, he or she ordinarily would gain no legal benefit from a defense allowing only nondeadly force. See § 2.2(b).
- *Apply the* Norris *test.* Did the defendant act in conformity with the specific rules governing the defense? This third step primarily involves an assessment of whether the defendant satisfied the four-part test in *State v. Norris*.[9] The test consists of an *honest belief* requirement; a *reasonable belief* requirement;

---

9. 303 N.C. 526, 279 S.E.2d 570 (1981).

an *aggressor* requirement; and an *excessive force* requirement. Although *Norris* dealt with a homicide case involving a claim of self-defense, its four-part test embodies the essential elements of most defensive-force defenses recognized in North Carolina. See § 2.2(c).

The first two steps described above are essentially screening devices for determining whether a particular defense is available. The *Norris* test, designated above as the third step of the analysis, actually contains the bulk of the requirements on the use of defensive force. Figure 1 reflects the first two steps, listing the defensive-force defenses recognized in this state, describing the type of harm covered by each defense, and indicating the propriety of deadly force. Figure 2 sets out the basic components of the *Norris* test, which are generally applicable to all of the defensive-force defenses.[10]

### (a) Identifying the Harm to Be Prevented

In assessing whether a particular defense is available to a defendant, the place to begin is with the *harm* covered by the defense. Each defensive-force defense permits a person to use force to prevent a particular threat of harm. When the harm is not present (or at least does not reasonably appear to be present), the defense does not apply.[11]

For example, a person may rely on defense of property when the harm posed is some loss of, damage to, or encroachment on the property. When the threat of harm is loss of life or great bodily injury, a person has the right to kill in self-defense (assuming the other elements of the defense are satisfied).[12] When the threat is mere bodily harm or offensive contact, a person may use only nondeadly force in self-defense. Self-defense against a sexual assault requires just that— a threat of sexual assault—while defense of another person simply involves a harm threatened against someone other than oneself. Certain

---

10. A more detailed chart, Figure 3, describes how each *Norris* element operates in homicide cases and appears on pages 33–34 in connection with the discussion of killing in self-defense.

11. *See generally* 1 Robinson, *supra* note 1, at 84–85 (1984) (defensive-force defenses are usually categorized according to the interest threatened).

12. The harm triggering the right to kill in self-defense is often referred to as the threat of *imminent* death or great bodily injury. The concept of *imminence*, which is more an outgrowth of the principle of necessity than of the type of harm threatened, is discussed in § 3.2(d) *infra*.

**Figure 1. Distinguishing Characteristics of Defensive-Force Defenses**

| | Description of Defense | Type of Harm Posed | Is Deadly Force Permitted? |
|---|---|---|---|
| (1) | Killing in self-defense (perfect and imperfect) | Death or great bodily injury | Yes |
| (2) | Deadly force in self-defense (not resulting in death) | Death or great bodily injury | Yes |
| (3) | Self-defense against sexual assault | Sexual assault | Yes |
| (4) | Nondeadly force in self-defense | Bodily harm or offensive physical contact | No |
| (5) | Self-defense within home or business | One of harms in (1)–(4), posed in home or business | Yes, if one of harms is (1)–(3); no, if harm is (4) only |
| (6) | Crime prevention (including detention of offender) | Commission of certain crimes | Yes, if to prevent dangerous felony; no, if to prevent nondangerous felony or misdemeanor; no, if to detain offender except in special circumstances |
| (7) | Defense of another | One of harms in (1)–(6), posed to another person | Corresponds to (1)–(6) |
| (8) | Defense of property (real or personal) | Damage to, loss of, or encroachment on property (including trespass) | No |
| (9) | Defense of habitation | Forcible entry into habitation by one who intends to cause death or great bodily injury or commit felony | Yes |
| (10) | Defensive force against law-enforcement officer | (a) One of harms in (1)–(9), posed by "unknown" officer | Corresponds to (1)–(9) |
| | | (b) Unlawful arrest or other unlawful conduct | No, unless threat of additional harm is posed |
| | | (c) Excessive force | Depends on harm posed |

## Figure 2. The *Norris* Test, in General

| Element | Description |
| --- | --- |
| 1. The Honest Belief Requirement | Defendant must have actually, or *honestly*, believed in the need to defend himself, herself, or some other interest from a threat of harm. |
| 2. The Reasonable Belief Requirement | Defendant's belief must have been *reasonable* in light of the circumstances as they appeared to him or her at the time. |
| 3. The Aggressor Requirement | Defendant must not have been the *aggressor* in the encounter or, if the aggressor, must have withdrawn from the encounter. |
| 4. The Excessive Force Requirement | Defendant must not have used *excessive force*, that is, more force than was or reasonably appeared to be necessary in the circumstances. |

defensive-force defenses require both a threat of harm and some other circumstance. Thus self-defense within the home or business requires that some harm be posed *and* that the conflict occur within one's home or place of business.

When more than one harm is or reasonably appears to be threatened, a defendant may rely on more than one defensive-force defense to justify his or her use of force. The various defensive-force defenses recognized in North Carolina are by no means mutually exclusive.[13] For example, an assailant may act in such a way as to threaten harm to both the defendant and other persons. The defendant's use of force would be justified both by self-defense and defense of another, assuming the defendant complied with the other requirements of those defenses.

Isolating the type of harm covered by each defensive-force defense is a useful analytical tool, as it helps to differentiate the defenses. Figure 1 lists the types of harm associated with each defensive-force defense. (The type of harm covered by each defensive-force defense is discussed further in the section dealing with that defense.) As a general

---

13. *See infra* § 3.2(b)(2) (discussing multiple threats of harm), § 8.4(c) (discussing trial court's duty to instruct jury on multiple defenses when supported by the evidence).

rule, however, a threat of harm need not actually exist for a person to be entitled to use defensive force. It is sufficient if it *appears* to the person that some harm is threatened and the person's belief is *reasonable*. This result flows from the apparent necessity doctrine, which is reflected in the first two elements of the *Norris* test. For example, for a person to kill in self-defense, *Norris* requires that the person honestly and reasonably believe that he or she is faced with death or great bodily injury. The effect of this formulation is that a threat of death or great bodily injury need not actually exist as long as it *reasonably appears* that such a harm is threatened.[14]

## (b) Determining the Propriety of Deadly Force

Once the appropriate defensive-force defense is identified in light of the kind of harm threatened, it then must be determined whether that defense permits a defendant to use *deadly* force. If a defense allows the use of deadly force, then *a fortiori* it permits nondeadly force as well. Certain defenses, however, sanction only the use of *nondeadly* force. A nondeadly-force defense ordinarily does not aid a defendant who uses deadly force in an encounter.[15]

### (1) Rationale for Limitations

The limitations on the use of deadly force are an outgrowth of the proportionality principle, one of the three basic principles underlying the right to use defensive force.[16] The proportionality principle operates to prohibit a person from using deadly force to prevent relatively

---

14. *See infra* § 3.2(a) (discussing how apparent necessity doctrine, embodied in first two elements of *Norris* test, applies to defendant's perception of threat of harm). In certain cases involving defensive force against law-enforcement officers, apparent necessity principles may not completely apply. *See infra* §§ 5.5(b), (c).

15. In some cases, a defendant may benefit from both a deadly-force and a nondeadly-force defense. *See infra* § 3.3(b)(3) (if defendant justifiably uses nondeadly force against assailant and assailant responds with deadly force, defendant may use deadly force without being considered aggressor in conflict), § 4.3 (when evidence supports right to defend against death or great bodily injury *and* bodily harm or offensive physical contact, defendant is entitled to jury instructions on both rights).

16. *See generally* § 2.1(b) *supra* (discussing basic principles of defensive force).

minor kinds of harm.[17] For example, the North Carolina courts have held that a person may not use deadly force to prevent the loss of personal property. Deadly force is disallowed in such cases because the harm inflicted on the person taking the property is not *proportional* to the harm threatening the property owner. If by using nondeadly force the property owner cannot prevent the property from being taken, he or she must suffer the loss. Defense of property and certain other defenses thus can be categorized as nondeadly-force defenses.[18]

Whether a particular defense permits the use of deadly force is discussed further in the section dealing with that defense (see also Figure 1, page 17). Two principles generally apply in all cases, however. First, it is the apparent and not the actual threat of harm that generally determines whether deadly force is permissible. For example, if John is stealing Mary's property, but does so in a manner that makes Mary reasonably believe that she will suffer death or serious bodily injury, Mary would have the right to use deadly force to defend herself. The propriety of Mary's actions would depend not on the rules regulating defense of property but on the rules governing the right to kill or use other deadly force in self-defense.[19]

---

17. *See, e.g.,* State v. Hunter, 315 N.C. 371, 373–74, 338 S.E.2d 99, 102 (1986) (deadly force not permitted to protect against mere bodily harm or offensive physical contact); State v. Clay, 297 N.C. 555, 562–63, 256 S.E.2d 176, 182 (1979) (to same effect); State v. Lee, 258 N.C. 44, 46–47, 127 S.E.2d 774, 776 (1962) (person has right to use force to prevent injury to or loss of personal property, but human life must not be endangered or great bodily harm inflicted); State v. Morgan, 25 N.C. 186, 193 (1842) (person may not kill or cause great bodily injury to prevent a mere trespass; such force is justified only to save life or limb, prevent a great crime, or accomplish a necessary public duty). *See also* FLETCHER, *supra* note 1, at 870 (discussing rationale for such limitations); 2 ROBINSON, *supra* note 1, at 81–82 (similar discussion).

18. Some North Carolina opinions state that deadly force is "excessive as a matter of law" when used to prevent the loss of property and other relatively minor kinds of harm. *See, e.g., Hunter,* 315 N.C. at 373–74, 338 S.E.2d at 102. These statements suggest that the restrictions on deadly force arise out of the fourth element of the *Norris* test, which prohibits the use of "excessive force." *See infra* § 2.2(c) (discussing *Norris* test generally). It does not appear, however, that the excessive-force element of *Norris* is addressed to situations in which the defendant's use of deadly force is disproportional in the sense described in the text. Rather, by virtue of the proportionality principle, the limitations on deadly force are an inherent part of each defensive-force defense. This issue is of some importance in understanding how to apply the excessive-force element of *Norris. See infra* § 3.4(b) (discussing excessive-force element in detail).

19. This principle is an outgrowth of the apparent necessity doctrine, which is

Second, a defendant's right to use deadly force does *not* depend on whether the person attacking the defendant is using deadly force; a defendant's rights depend on the harm that he or she reasonably believes to be threatened.[20] Thus a defendant has the right to use deadly force against an assailant when the defendant reasonably believes that the assailant's conduct would result in the defendant's own death (assuming the other elements of self-defense are satisfied). Deadly force likewise may be used by a defendant when he or she reasonably believes that an assailant will inflict great bodily injury. Other threats of harm, such as sexual assault, also are sufficiently serious to trigger a defendant's right to use deadly force in response. Although the attacker's use of deadly force may bolster the defendant's claimed need to use deadly force in response, it is not a prerequisite.[21]

---

part of the first two elements of the *Norris* test. *See infra* § 3.2(a) (discussing application of apparent necessity doctrine to defendant's perception of harm).

20. *See, e.g.,* State v. Jones, 299 N.C. 103, 107, 261 S.E.2d 1, 5 (1980) (person has the right to use deadly force in defense of habitation, even if intruder is not armed with deadly weapon, where person reasonably apprehends death or great bodily harm to himself, herself, or occupants or reasonably believes assailant intends to commit felony); State v. Spaulding, 298 N.C. 149, 156–57, 257 S.E.2d 391, 395–96 (1979) (defendant did not see weapon and victim did not actually make show of deadly force; critical issue, however, was reasonableness of defendant's apprehension); State v. Pearson, 288 N.C. 34, 40, 215 S.E.2d 598, 603 (1975) (person entitled to use deadly force where death or great bodily harm is possible; assailant need not have been using deadly force or deadly weapon); State v. Hill, 141 N.C. 769, 771, 53 S.E. 311, 311 (1906) (assault on defendant need not have been with deadly weapon for person to kill in self-defense; fierceness of assault, position of parties, and difference in relative size or strength can show that defendant reasonably believed that he was in danger of death or great bodily harm).

21. In some cases, including some of those cited in the previous note, courts have stated generally that a defendant may use deadly force only when acting to repel a *felonious assault* or an *attack with murderous intent* or an *assault with deadly force. See, e.g., Hunter,* 315 N.C. at 373–74, 338 S.E.2d at 101–02; *Pearson,* 288 N.C. at 39–40, 215 S.E.2d at 602–03. Those terms have become synonyms, however, for conduct sufficient to raise a reasonable apprehension of death or great bodily injury or some other harm sufficient to warrant deadly force in response. Construing the opinions otherwise would mean that a person would be required, in the heat of the moment, to determine whether an attack constituted a felonious assault, or the attacker had the intent to kill, or the attacker's conduct met the legal definition of deadly force.

### (2) Meaning of "Deadly Force"

In *State v. Pearson,* the North Carolina Supreme Court defined *deadly force* as "force intended or likely to cause death or great bodily harm."[22] A few points are worth noting about this definition.

First, the harm actually inflicted by the defendant does not necessarily determine whether a defendant's force is defined under the law as deadly or nondeadly. On the one hand, force may be *deadly* within the meaning of *Pearson* even if no injury is actually inflicted. For example, if Mary intentionally fires a gun at John's chest, but misses, she nonetheless will have used force "intended or likely to cause death or great bodily harm."[23] If Mary were only trying to prevent John from taking her property—a defense allowing only nondeadly force—her shooting at John would be improper. On the other hand, if Mary simply pushes John, and he falls over backward and suffers great bodily injury, she will not have used deadly force because her pushing of John would not constitute force "intended or likely to cause death or great bodily harm."[24]

Second, the *Pearson* definition of *deadly force* avoids potentially troublesome questions about whether the defendant's specific purpose was to kill. In *State v. Clay,* for example, the defendant argued that the force she used in self-defense should be considered deadly only if she acted with the intent to kill. According to the defendant, the evidence showed that she shot the victim but not that she intended to kill him. The court rejected the defendant's argument, finding that the defendant's force (shooting) was likely to cause death or serious bodily injury and therefore constituted deadly force.[25] (Of course, the prosecution may still have to prove that the defendant acted with the intent to kill if

---

22. 288 N.C. at 39, 215 S.E.2d at 602. *Accord Hunter,* 315 N.C. at 373, 338 S.E.2d at 102; State v. Clay, 297 N.C. 555, 563, 256 S.E.2d 176, 182 (1979).

23. *See* MODEL PENAL CODE AND COMMENTARIES § 3.11 cmt. 2 (American Law Institute 1985) (reaching similar conclusion under similar definition of *deadly force*).

24. *Pearson,* 288 N.C. at 39, 215 S.E.2d at 602 (defining *nondeadly force* as force "neither intended nor likely" to cause death or great bodily harm). It would therefore seem to follow that Mary would have the right to rely on a defense allowing only nondeadly force even though John suffered great bodily injury. *Cf. infra* §§ 3.2(b)(3), (4) (discussing whether defendant must believe in need to use specific level of force when defending against threat of death or great bodily injury).

25. 297 N.C. at 561, 256 S.E.2d at 181.

the defendant is charged with an offense, such as first-degree murder, that requires an intent to kill.)

A lingering question is whether the threat to use a deadly weapon constitutes *deadly force*. For example, suppose John is still trying to steal Mary's property and, in an effort to prevent the theft, Mary points a gun at John and then fires a warning shot into the air. Would the pointing of the gun or firing of the warning shot constitute deadly force and therefore deprive Mary of the ability to rely on defense of property, a defense allowing only nondeadly force? *State v. Clay*, discussed above, does not resolve the issue. Although the court held there that the defendant acted improperly by using a deadly weapon to ward off a simple assault, the evidence showed that the defendant used a weapon in a deadly manner: namely, she fired a shotgun *at* the victim and hit him in the leg. To paraphrase the *Clay* opinion, "under the circumstances of its use" the weapon was an instrument likely to cause death or serious bodily injury.[26] The decision does not resolve the issue of whether a threat to use a deadly weapon constitutes deadly force.

It appears that the only North Carolina cases directly addressing the issue are from the nineteenth century. In *State v. Yancey*, decided in 1876, the court held that the defendant could threaten another person with a deadly weapon to defend his personal property even though the defendant would not have had the right to use the weapon against the person. There, the defendant drew his knife and threatened to cut the person who had taken the defendant's property unless the person released it.[27] Although the sheer age of *Yancey* might suggest that it is unreliable authority, it appears to remain good law. A number of commentators have cited the decision with approval, concluding that the threatened use of a deadly weapon does not constitute deadly force.[28] The Fourth Circuit Court of Appeals has reached the same conclusion

---

26. *Id.* at 563, 256 S.E.2d at 182.

27. 74 N.C. 244, 245 (1876) (threatened use of deadly weapon is permissible in defense of personal property although actual use of deadly weapon would not be). In so ruling, the court disregarded an even earlier case suggesting the opposite conclusion. *See* State v. Myerfield, 61 N.C. 108, 111–12 (1867) (defendant could not threaten to use deadly weapon to prevent trespass).

28. Rollin M. Perkins & Ronald N. Boyce, Criminal Law 1157 & n.29 (3d ed. 1982) (citing *Yancey* with approval); Model Penal Code and Commentaries, *supra* note 23, § 3.11 & cmt. 2 (citing *Yancey* with approval). *See also* 1 Wayne R. LaFave & Austin W. Scott, Jr., Substantive Criminal Law 651 (1986) (threat to use deadly weapon does not constitute deadly force).

under federal law.[29] And more recent cases in North Carolina assume without discussion that pointing a gun at another person or firing warning shots does not necessarily constitute deadly force.[30]

### (c) Applying the *Norris* Test

Identifying the appropriate defensive-force defense in light of the kind of harm threatened and determining whether the defense allows the use of deadly force are only the first two steps. It then must be determined whether the specific rules governing the particular defense are satisfied. For the most part, those rules are embodied in the four-part test set forth in *State v. Potter*[31] and *State v. Norris*,[32] both of which involved a killing allegedly in self-defense. Although the two opinions described the test in somewhat different terms,[33] they each articulated four main elements. For the sake of convenience, this book ordinarily refers to the four-part test as the *Norris* test or the *Norris* elements, after the latter case.

In *Norris*, the court held that the law "excuses a killing altogether if, at the time of the killing, . . . four elements existed." Those elements, as set out in *Norris*, are

(1) it appeared to defendant and he believed it to be necessary to kill the deceased in order to save himself from death or great bodily harm; and

(2) defendant's belief was reasonable in that the circumstances as they appeared to him at the time were sufficient to create such a belief in the mind of a person of ordinary firmness; and

---

29. United States v. Black, 692 F.2d 314, 317–19 (4th Cir. 1982) (threatened use of deadly weapon against correctional officer does not constitute deadly force).

30. *See* State v. Ataei-Kachuei, 68 N.C. App. 209, 213–14, 314 S.E.2d 751, 754 (defendant who allegedly fired warning shots in air and inadvertently struck victim was entitled to instruction on right to detain offender, a defense allowing only nondeadly force under the circumstances), *rev. denied*, 311 N.C. 763, 321 S.E.2d 146 (1984); State v. Polk, 29 N.C. App. 360, 361–62, 224 S.E.2d 272, 273 (1976) (defendant who fired shots to scare attacker was entitled to instruction on right to defend against bodily injury or offensive physical contact, a nondeadly-force defense).

31. 295 N.C. 126, 244 S.E.2d 397 (1978).

32. 303 N.C. 526, 279 S.E.2d 570 (1981).

33. *Potter* described the first element as belief in the need "to shoot," 295 N.C. at 143, 244 S.E.2d at 408, while *Norris* described the first element as belief in the need "to kill." 303 N.C. at 530, 279 S.E.2d at 572. The appropriate phrasing of the first element has been the subject of several cases, discussed in §§ 3.2(b)(3) and (4) *infra*.

(3) defendant was not the aggressor in bringing on the affray, *i.e.*, he did not aggressively and willingly enter into the fight without legal excuse or provocation; and

(4) defendant did not use excessive force, *i.e.*, did not use more force than was necessary or reasonably appeared to him to be necessary under the circumstances to protect himself from death or great bodily harm.[34]

Although phrased in terms of a killing in self-defense, the rules embodied in the *Norris* test have wider application. At least in general terms, the rules are the same regardless of the defensive-force defense at issue. A condensed version of the test, generally applicable to all defensive-force defenses, is as follows:

1. The defendant must actually, or *honestly*, believe in the need to defend against some threat of harm;
2. The defendant's belief must be *reasonable* in the circumstances;
3. The defendant must not be the *aggressor* in the encounter; and
4. The defendant must not use *excessive force*.

The principal difference in these requirements, from one defense to another, is in the harm that the defendant must perceive. For example, in the context of self-defense against sexual assault, the *Norris* elements would be modified to reflect that the defendant must believe in the need to prevent a sexual assault rather than death or great bodily injury.

The *Norris* test also may lead to a different result depending on whether the defendant is charged with murder or some other offense. In cases involving murder charges, the courts distinguish between *perfect* and *imperfect* defensive-force defenses. The *perfect* label signifies that the defendant has satisfied all of the elements of the *Norris* test and is entitled to acquittal.[35] To claim the benefit of an *imperfect* form of a defensive-force defense, the defendant must satisfy only the first two elements of *Norris*—that is, he or she must have an honest and reasonable belief in the need to defend against some threat of harm. Also, the defendant must not be an aggressor with murderous intent. Compliance with these more limited requirements has the effect of mitigating

---

34. 303 N.C. at 530, 279 S.E.2d at 572.

35. Actually, the defendant need not prove that he or she complied with the requirements of *Norris*; the burden is ultimately on the prosecution to persuade the jury that the defendant violated one or more of the requirements. *See infra* § 8.2(b) (discussing prosecution's burden of persuasion in defensive-force cases).

murder to manslaughter. Although *Norris* discussed the idea of an imperfect defense in the context of self-defense, a defendant charged with murder may be able to rely on imperfect versions of other defensive-force defenses, such as imperfect defense of another.[36] In nonhomicide cases, however, imperfect defensive-force defenses have not been recognized by the North Carolina courts. In such cases, defendants must meet all of the *Norris* elements, and then the result is acquittal.[37]

The next three chapters explore the meaning of the four *Norris* elements as well as the differences between *perfect* and *imperfect* defenses. The bulk of the analysis is contained in Chapter 3, which deals with killing in self-defense. Chapters 4 and 5, dealing with other defensive-force defenses, contain a more limited discussion of *Norris*, intended only to highlight how the principles embodied in the test apply to those defenses.

Two further observations about the *Norris* test can be made here, however. First, although the test is now the benchmark for analyzing defensive-force cases, it should be viewed less as a break with prior law than as an attempt at synthesis. Many of the concepts embodied in the test can be found in earlier decisions of the North Carolina Supreme Court.[38] What was new about *Potter* and *Norris* was the four-step approach to analyzing the use of defensive force, which the courts had not specifically employed in previous cases. As will be seen in later chapters, the test has both simplified the analysis of defensive-force cases and created its own problems of interpretation.

---

36. *See infra* § 5.2(a)(1) (defense of another). The North Carolina courts may be unwilling to allow a defendant to rely on imperfect defense of habitation, despite earlier indications to the contrary. *See infra* § 5.4(a) (defense of habitation). Whether a defendant may rely on an imperfect defensive-force defense in a felony murder case is discussed in § 6.1(a) *infra*.

37. *See infra* § 4.1 (discussing potential differences in the application of the *Norris* elements in homicide and nonhomicide cases).

38. *See, e.g.,* State v. Jackson, 284 N.C. 383, 390–91, 200 S.E.2d 596, 601 (1973) (person may kill in self-defense if reasonably necessary even if not actually necessary); State v. Woods, 278 N.C. 210, 217–18, 179 S.E.2d 358, 363 (1971) (when person uses excessive force in self-defense and kills, person is guilty of voluntary manslaughter); State v. Pollard, 168 N.C. 116, 121–22, 83 S.E. 167, 170 (1914) (when person unlawfully assaults another and then kills in progress of fight, person is guilty of manslaughter though it may have been necessary to kill to save person's own life); State v. Matthews, 78 N.C. 523, 534 (1878) (defendant could kill if he reasonably believed assailant intended to kill him or cause enormous bodily harm).

Second, the test articulated in *Norris* continues to evolve and cannot be applied formulaically. On the one hand, certain parts of the test are not absolute requirements. For example, if read literally, the first element of *Norris* requires a defendant to have "believed it necessary to kill." Recently, however, the supreme court has indicated that a belief in the need to kill is not essential for a killing to be justified in self-defense.[39] On the other hand, the *Norris* test omits certain requirements. For example, the supreme court has held that a person may kill in self-defense only when the threat of death or great bodily harm is or reasonably appears to be *imminent*, although this term appears nowhere in the *Norris* test itself.[40]

---

39. *See infra* § 3.2(b)(4).
40. *See infra* § 3.2(d).

# 3　Perfect and Imperfect Self-Defense

# 3   Perfect and Imperfect Self-Defense

❦❦❦   Two doctrines apply to homicide cases in which the defendant claims to have killed in self-defense: perfect and imperfect self-defense. Because of the interrelationship of the two doctrines, they are treated together.

## § 3.1  Killing in Self-Defense

A person's ability to rely on a particular defensive-force defense depends first on the harm that the person was trying to prevent.[1] Both perfect and imperfect self-defense deal with the same threat of harm. When a person kills to avoid death *or* great bodily harm, the threat of either harm being sufficient, the person may be able to invoke one or both of these defenses.[2]

---

1. *See supra* § 2.2(a).

2. *See* State v. Mosley, 213 N.C. 304, 308–09, 195 S.E. 830, 833 (1938) (error to instruct jury that defendant must reasonably believe he or she is about to be killed; instruction also must include reference to reasonable belief in great bodily injury); State v. Waldroop, 193 N.C. 12, 16, 135 S.E. 165, 166–67 (1927) (to same effect); State v. Matthews, 78 N.C. 523, 534 (1878) (to same effect). The supreme court has held that a serious *mental injury* may satisfy the serious injury element of the offense of assault with a deadly weapon inflicting serious injury. *See* State v. Everhardt, 326 N.C. 777, 779–81, 392 S.E.2d 391, 392–93 (1990) (assaults by husband on wife were "psychologically torturous in nature, calculated to inflict mental or emotional injury rather than bodily injury"; serious injury element satisfied by serious mental injuries suffered by wife). The courts may be unwilling, however, to allow a person to use deadly force to *prevent* a serious mental injury. *Cf. infra* § 4.5 (discussing self-defense cases involving battered persons).

A person's right to use defensive force, in defense of self or other interests, also depends on application of the rules set forth in *State v. Norris*.[3] The four-part *Norris* test requires in essence that

1. the defendant actually, or *honestly*, believe in the need to defend against some threat of harm;
2. the defendant's belief be *reasonable* in the circumstances;
3. the defendant not be the *aggressor* in the encounter; and
4. the defendant not use *excessive force*.

The difference between perfect and imperfect self-defense lies in the particular elements of the *Norris* test that must be satisfied and the effect of doing so. A defendant charged with homicide who meets all of the *Norris* elements is entitled to acquittal on the ground of perfect self-defense.[4] Ultimately, the burden is on the prosecution to persuade the jury that the defendant did not act in perfect self-defense. It is therefore more accurate to say that the defendant loses the benefit of perfect self-defense if the prosecution proves beyond a reasonable doubt that the defendant did not comply with one or more of the four requirements of the *Norris* test.[5]

Imperfect self-defense reduces murder to voluntary manslaughter; it does not result in acquittal. The stated rationale for this result is that imperfect self-defense "displaces" the element of malice required for first- and second-degree murder, thus reducing the crime to manslaughter.[6] To claim imperfect self-defense the defendant must meet only the first two requirements of the *Norris* test: that is, the defendant's belief in the need to defend himself or herself must be both *honest* and *reasonable*. The defendant need not meet either the third or fourth requirement (the *aggressor* or the *excessive force* requirement), subject to one qualification: the defendant must not be an aggressor with murderous intent. As with perfect self-defense, it is the prosecution's burden to

---

3. 303 N.C. 526, 530, 279 S.E.2d 570, 572 (1981). The *Norris* test is discussed generally in § 2.2(c) *supra*.

4. *Id.* at 530, 279 S.E.2d at 572–73; *accord* State v. Bush, 307 N.C. 152, 158–59, 297 S.E.2d 563, 568 (1982).

5. *See infra* § 8.2(b) (discussing prosecution's burden of persuasion in defensive-force cases).

6. State v. Wilkerson, 295 N.C. 559, 579, 247 S.E.2d 905, 916 (1978). *See also Norris*, 303 N.C. at 531, 279 S.E.2d at 573 (when first two elements of test are met, person has not acted "without justification or excuse," which is element of murder in the first or second degree). Whether a defendant may rely on imperfect self-defense in felony murder cases is discussed in § 6.1(a) *infra*.

prove that the defendant did not act in imperfect self-defense. Only if the prosecution proves beyond a reasonable doubt that the defendant did not act in accordance with the first or second element of *Norris*, or that the defendant was the aggressor with murderous intent within the meaning of the third element, does the defendant lose the right of imperfect self-defense.

In recent cases, defendants have claimed that the rules governing imperfect self-defense should be modified. Defendants have focused, in particular, on the difficulty of distinguishing the second and fourth elements of the *Norris* test (the *reasonable belief* and *excessive force* requirements). Although the supreme court has been unwilling to change the basic rules of imperfect self-defense, it has attempted to draw a clearer distinction between elements two and four. That development is taken up later in this chapter in § 3.4.

Each of the *Norris* requirements is discussed in depth below. Figure 3 on pages 34–35 boils that discussion down to a quick summary describing the basics of each *Norris* requirement and flagging the major problems of interpretation.

## § 3.2 The Honest-and-Reasonable-Belief Requirement

*It appeared to defendant and he believed it to be necessary to kill the deceased in order to save himself from death or great bodily harm.*

—State v. Norris

*Defendant's belief was reasonable in that the circumstances as they appeared to him at the time were sufficient to create such a belief in the mind of a person of ordinary firmness.*

—State v. Norris

### (a) Purpose of the Honest-and-Reasonable-Belief Requirement

The conditions quoted above represent the first two elements of the *Norris* test. A defendant must satisfy both conditions to claim the right of perfect or imperfect self-defense.[7] Before analyzing how each element has been interpreted, however, it is important to understand

---

7. 303 N.C. at 530, 279 S.E.2d at 572–73. The four-part *Norris* test is discussed generally in §§ 2.2(c), 3.1 *supra*.

## Figure 3. *Norris* Issues in Homicide Cases

### In General

**The *Norris* Test:** In *State v. Norris*, 303 N.C. 526, 530, 279 S.E.2d 570, 572–73 (1981), the court articulated a four-part test for analyzing a person's right to kill in self-defense. In essence, the test requires that (1) the defendant have an *honest* belief in the need to protect himself or herself from death or great bodily injury; (2) the defendant's belief be *reasonable* in the circumstances; (3) the defendant not be the *aggressor* in the encounter; and (4) the defendant not use *excessive force*. See §§ 2.2(c), 3.1.

**Perfect and Imperfect Self-Defense:** In homicide cases the North Carolina courts recognize a *perfect* and *imperfect* version of self-defense (and other defensive-force defenses). If the defendant satisfies all four elements of the *Norris* test (or, more accurately, if the prosecution fails to disprove at least one of the elements beyond a reasonable doubt), the defendant is entitled to acquittal on the ground of *perfect* self-defense. If a defendant satisfies the first two elements of the *Norris* test and is not an aggressor with murderous intent, he or she is entitled to rely on *imperfect* self-defense, which reduces murder to manslaughter. See §§ 2.2(c), 3.1.

### Elements 1 and 2: The Honest-and-Reasonable-Belief Requirement

**Element 1:** The first element of *Norris* is subjective. The defendant must *honestly*, or actually, believe that he or she (a) is threatened with death or great bodily injury and (b) must protect himself or herself from the threatened harm. See § 3.2(b)(1).

> Note on "Need to Kill": Until recently, it has been unclear in homicide cases whether the defendant must believe in the "need to kill." The supreme court now appears to hold that a defendant must believe it necessary to protect himself or herself from death or great bodily injury but does not have to believe in the need to use a specific level of force, such as killing. The amount of force used by a defendant remains critical, but under element four, discussed below. Questions still linger, however, about whether jury instructions on the first element may be phrased in terms of whether the defendant believed it necessary to "kill" to avoid death or great bodily injury. See § 3.2(b)(3, 4).

**Element 2:** Under the second element of *Norris*, the defendant's belief must be *reasonable*. The test of reasonableness is a combination of subjective and objective factors. The jury must determine whether, in the circumstances as they appeared to the defendant (the subjective part), a person of "ordinary firmness" would have formed a similar belief (the objective part). See § 3.2(c).

**Imminence:** The first two elements of *Norris* also require that the defendant honestly and reasonably believe that the threat of death or great bodily injury is imminent. In North Carolina, *imminent* means "immediate" or "about to" happen. See § 3.2(d).

> Note on Battered Persons: In most cases the imminence requirement does not affect whether it was or was not reasonably necessary for the defendant to defend himself or herself. In certain cases, particularly those involving battered persons, the requirement may undercut a claim of self-defense. See § 3.2(d).

*continued on next page*

## Figure 3. *Norris* Issues in Homicide Cases (continued)

### Element 3: The Aggressor Requirement

**In General:** North Carolina recognizes two types of aggressors: those with murderous intent and those without. Aggressors with murderous intent forfeit the right of both perfect and imperfect self-defense if they kill without complying with the applicable rules on withdrawal. Aggressors without murderous intent forfeit the right of perfect, but not imperfect, self-defense if they kill without complying with applicable withdrawal rules. See § 3.3(a).

> NOTE ON MEANING OF "AGGRESSOR": As used in the law of self-defense, *aggressor* has special meaning. Although the courts have not precisely described what would make a person an aggressor, the case law appears to establish certain basic criteria. (Whether a person who meets these criteria would be considered an aggressor *with* murderous intent, or *without*, is discussed separately below.) Ordinarily, the person's actions must (a) create the necessity for his or her use of force; (b) occur in the current encounter; (c) be without legal excuse or provocation; and (d) be aggressive and willing. See § 3.3(b).

**Aggressor with Murderous Intent:** An aggressor *with* murderous intent is one who brings on a conflict with the intent to take life or inflict serious bodily injury. Such an aggressor regains the right of self-defense either when the encounter is concluded *or* when he or she clearly withdraws from the encounter. See § 3.3(c).

**Aggressor without Murderous Intent:** An aggressor *without* murderous intent is one who brings on a conflict by (a) assault or battery, (b) mutual willingness to fight, or (c) language or conduct calculated and intended to bring about a fight. Each of these categories concerns behavior that is a criminal offense in itself—i.e., assault or affray—or a close analog of a criminal offense. Such an aggressor regains the right of perfect self-defense either when the encounter is concluded *or* when he or she attempts to withdraw from the encounter and signifies this intent to his or her adversary. See § 3.3(d).

> NOTE ON WITHDRAWAL: Some North Carolina cases suggest that a defendant who is an aggressor without murderous intent need not withdraw if the person assaulted resorts to deadly force so suddenly that the defendant cannot withdraw without risk of death or great bodily injury. Other cases indicate, however, that withdrawal is required even in these circumstances. See § 3.3(d)(2).

### Element 4: The Excessive Force Requirement

**In General:** A person who uses excessive force but otherwise complies with the *Norris* test may rely on imperfect self-defense. *Norris* defines *excessive force* as more force than "necessary or reasonably necessary" to avert the threatened harm. See § 3.4(a).

**Confusion with Element 2:** The courts have struggled with how to distinguish the second element of *Norris* from the fourth, as both elements consider the reasonableness of the defendant's perceptions and actions. See § 3.4(b). The supreme court appears to have refined the first element of the *Norris* test, the honest belief requirement, as a way of distinguishing the second and fourth elements. The first element no longer requires a belief in the need for a specific level of force (see discussion of element one, above), so the second element no longer considers whether a reasonable person would believe such force to be necessary. Whether the defendant used a reasonable, or excessive, amount of force is considered under element four. See § 3.4(c).

their overall purpose. Together, they reflect the doctrine of apparent, or reasonable, necessity.

One of the three fundamental principles of self-defense is necessity.[8] Strictly construed, necessity means *actual necessity*, which requires a person to be "right" about two different things. First, the person must actually be facing death or great bodily harm. Second, the person's use of force must actually be necessary to avoid death or great bodily harm.[9]

Since a requirement of actual necessity would be an unforgiving standard, North Carolina has long recognized that self-defense may be based on *apparent*, or *reasonable*, necessity.[10] This doctrine allows room for error about either component of necessity: the existence of the threat of harm or the need for force in response. For example, if it reasonably appears to a person that he or she is threatened with death or great bodily injury, whether such a threat actually exists is irrelevant.

The honest-and-reasonable-belief requirement, embodied in the first two elements of *Norris*, was intended to effectuate the apparent necessity doctrine. Under the first element, a person must actually, or *honestly*, believe in the need to defend himself or herself from harm; under the second element, the person's belief must be *reasonable*. On the one hand, the honest-and-reasonable-belief formulation avoids some of the problems that arose in the past. In several cases before *Norris*, for example, trial courts erroneously instructed the jury that the defendant's actions were justified only if actually, not just reasonably, necessary.[11] The *Norris* test avoids this pitfall by integrating the concept of reasonableness into the first two elements.

---

8. *See supra* § 2.1(b).

9. *See* 1 Wayne R. LaFave & Austin W. Scott, Jr., Substantive Criminal Law 649–50 (1986); 2 Paul H. Robinson, Criminal Law Defenses 4–5 (1984).

10. *See, e.g.*, State v. Castle, 133 N.C. 770, 777–78, 46 S.E. 1, 4 (1903) ("right of self-defense depends upon the use of such force as is necessary, or reasonably appears to be necessary"); State v. Barrett, 132 N.C. 1005, 1007–08, 43 S.E. 832, 833 (1903) (characterizing as the more "humane doctrine" that the defendant may act in self-defense if it reasonably appears to be necessary).

11. *See, e.g.*, State v. Lee, 258 N.C. 44, 48, 127 S.E.2d 774, 777 (1962) (trial court's instructions erroneously suggested that defendant's claim of self-defense had to rest upon actual necessity, not actual or apparent necessity); State v. Fowler, 250 N.C. 595, 596–97, 108 S.E.2d 892, 893–94 (1959) (to same effect); State v. Goode, 249 N.C. 632, 633–34, 107 S.E.2d 70, 71–72 (1959) (to same effect); State v. Anderson, 230 N.C. 54, 55, 51 S.E.2d 895, 896 (1949) (to same effect); State v. Ellerbe, 223 N.C. 770, 772–73, 28 S.E.2d 519, 520–21 (1944) (to same effect). A number of early court of appeals decisions also had difficulty applying the principle of reasonable neces-

On the other hand, the belief formulation has proved troublesome. What must a defendant believe to satisfy the honest-and-reasonable-belief requirement? How precise must that belief be? As discussed in the following sections, some cases have strictly interpreted the belief requirement of *Norris*, making it as potentially unforgiving as a requirement of actual necessity.[12]

## (b) Honest Belief

### *(1) What Makes a Belief "Honest"*

The first element of the *Norris* test focuses on the defendant's state of mind at the time of the encounter, requiring that the defendant *believe* in the need to defend himself or herself from harm. The element is thus subjective in nature. Determining whether a person actually, or *honestly,* held such a belief is like proving or disproving any other mental state. It may be shown by direct or circumstantial evidence.

---

sity, finding that the defendant's use of force had to be apparently but not reasonably necessary. *See, e.g.,* State v. Smith, 8 N.C. App. 77, 77–78, 173 S.E.2d 489, 489–90 (1970); State v. Hardee, 3 N.C. App. 426, 429, 165 S.E.2d 43, 45 (1969). As indicated in the text, however, reasonableness is an inherent part of the apparent necessity doctrine.

12. Theoretically, a defendant could bypass the honest-and-reasonable belief requirement, and the obstacles it may pose, by claiming that he or she acted out of actual necessity. Under such an approach, if a defendant actually needed to defend himself or herself, it would be inconsequential whether the defendant believed it necessary to do so. Commentators differ on whether self-defense always requires that a defendant entertain some belief in the need to defend himself or herself. *Compare* 2 Robinson, *supra* note 9, at 12–29 (arguing that justification defenses, such as self-defense and other defensive-force defenses, should not depend on whether person believed his or her conduct was justified) *with* Rollin M. Perkins & Ronald N. Boyce, Criminal Law 1114 (3d ed. 1982) (arguing that defendant should not benefit from self-defense if he or she was unaware of impending danger). At one time, the prevailing standard in North Carolina appeared to be that a defendant *could* defend himself or herself when actually necessary and, if not actually necessary, when apparently necessary. *See, e.g.,* State v. Marshall, 208 N.C. 127, 129, 179 S.E. 427, 428 (1935); State v. Johnson, 166 N.C. 392, 396–97, 81 S.E. 941, 943 (1914). Although those cases have not been expressly overruled, more recent decisions invariably require the defendant to satisfy the *Norris* test, including the honest-and-reasonable-belief requirement. Actual necessity may still play a part, however, in assessing whether the defendant has met the fourth element of the *Norris* test, the excessive force element. *See Norris,* 303 N.C. at 530, 279 S.E.2d at 572 (amount of force used by defendant is not excessive if such force is *or* reasonably appears to be necessary); *see generally* § 3.4 *infra* (discussing excessive force element).

For example, the courts have allowed the defendant to testify that he or she was fearful of the victim.[13] The courts also have allowed evidence about the defendant's prior experiences with the victim to explain why the defendant believed it necessary to defend himself or herself from the victim.[14] The circumstances of the encounter itself may be particularly relevant in assessing the defendant's state of mind. Thus, in one case, the court rejected the defendant's claim that he had an honest belief in impending danger where the evidence showed that the defendant shot through the back of a car as it was speeding away.[15] In another case the court inferred from the circumstances of the encounter that the defendant believed that he needed to defend himself even though the defendant did not testify.[16] The kinds of evidence bearing on a defendant's mental state are discussed in greater detail in Chapter 7.

The question of how to prove or disprove the defendant's state of mind is not what makes this element difficult to apply, however. The harder part is understanding exactly what the law requires a defendant to believe in. As phrased, the "honest belief" element of the *Norris* test actually requires two "beliefs" of the defendant, one concerning the existence of the threat of harm and the other concerning the need for force to avoid the threatened harm. Both are discussed separately in the next two sections. The concluding section on "honest belief" examines the effect of the supreme court's recent decision in *State v. Richardson*.[17] There, the court appears to have reaffirmed the first belief (concerning

---

13. *See, e.g.,* State v. Webster, 324 N.C. 385, 389–93, 378 S.E.2d 748, 751–54 (1989); State v. Reed, 324 N.C. 535, 537–38, 379 S.E.2d 828, 829–30 (1989).

14. *See, e.g.,* State v. Johnson, 270 N.C. 215, 219–220, 154 S.E.2d 48, 52 (1967) (finding "no better way to impart the knowledge of fear or apprehension on the part of the defendant" than by giving the jury the benefit of the defendant's prior experience with the victim).

15. State v. Ligon, 332 N.C. 224, 240–41, 420 S.E.2d 136, 145–46 (1992). *See also* State v. Boykin, 310 N.C. 118, 123–24, 310 S.E.2d 315, 318 (1984) (defendant returned to scene after fight had ended and shot decedent; insufficient evidence of "honest belief" to warrant instructions); State v. Griffin, 308 N.C. 303, 311, 302 S.E.2d 447, 453–54 (1983) (defendant took woman's purse, fifty-three-year-old man grabbed defendant's arm, and defendant shot him; insufficient evidence of "honest belief" to warrant instructions); State v. Bush, 307 N.C. 152, 159–60, 297 S.E.2d 563, 568–69 (1982) (sixty-five-year-old man pushed defendant, who was twenty years old, and defendant stabbed him; insufficient evidence of "honest belief" to warrant instructions).

16. State v. Deck, 285 N.C. 209, 211, 214–15, 203 S.E.2d 830, 832, 834 (1974) (victim came at defendant with ice pick, and during struggle defendant got control of ice pick and stabbed victim in chest; error not to instruct on self-defense).

17. 341 N.C. 585, 461 S.E.2d 724 (1995), *rev'g* 112 N.C. App. 252, 435 S.E.2d 84 (1993).

the existence of the threat of harm), but modified the second belief (concerning the need for defensive force).

### (2) Belief in the Threat of Harm

For the most part, the first belief required of a defendant is a straightforward one. The defendant must believe that he or she is in danger of death or great bodily injury.[18] On occasion, however, this requirement has led to some difficulty in interpretation.

**Multiple Threats of Harm.** One question is whether a defendant may rely on more than one defensive-force defense when he or she believes that more than one threat of harm exists. For example, may a defendant who shoots an attacker, believing that the attacker intends to injure the defendant and another person, rely on both self-defense and defense of others? Most cases recognize that a defendant is entitled to have the jury determine whether his or her use of force was justified under any applicable defensive-force defense.[19] As long as a defendant believes that he or she must defend against more than one type of harm, it is inconsequential whether one of the harms loomed larger than another in the defendant's mind. The reason is that a person's motive for acting is ordinarily not determinative of a person's liability under the criminal law.[20]

On occasion, the courts appear to have departed from these principles concerning the defendant's belief. For example, in one case, the evidence indicated that the defendant believed that he was threatened with death or great bodily injury *and* sexual assault. Finding that the defendant's paramount concern was to avoid bodily injury, the

---

18. Whether a person also must believe that the threat is *imminent* is considered in § 3.2(d) *infra*.

19. *See, e.g.*, State v. Jones, 299 N.C. 103, 107–08, 261 S.E.2d 1, 5–6 (1980) (supreme court holds that defendant could rely on both defense of habitation and defense of others and reverses court of appeals decision upholding denial of instructions on defense of habitation), *rev'g* 41 N.C. App. 465, 468–69, 255 S.E.2d 232, 235 (1979); State v. Miller, 267 N.C. 409, 411, 148 S.E.2d 279, 282 (1966) (error in instructing only on self-defense where evidence also supported defense of habitation). *See also* cases cited *infra* § 8.4(c) (instructions on multiple defensive-force defenses).

20. *See* 1 LaFave, *supra* note 9, at 322–23 ("[M]otive is not relevant once it is shown that the defendant was aware of facts which would give rise to a defense. Just as the defendant's intent to bring about certain consequences may be established without proof of any motive for it, so too as to a defense to liability."); 2 Robinson, *supra* note 9, at 17–18 (criticizing efforts to rank defendant's purposes in using defensive force).

court held that the defendant was not entitled to instructions on the right to defend against a sexual assault in addition to the usual instructions on self-defense.[21] Such a holding, by seeking to gauge the relative importance of a person's reasons for acting, appears to be against the weight of authority.

**Source of Harm.** Another issue is whether the defendant must believe that the *victim* was the person who posed the threat of harm. For example, may a person defending against an attack rely on self-defense if he or she unintentionally kills a third party? Traditional principles of *transferred intent* would allow the defendant's claim of self-defense in these circumstances even though he or she did not believe that the third party was the person posing harm. LaFave provides the following example of how transferred intent operates in cases of self-defense:

> If A aims at his attacker B in proper self-defense, but hits C instead, he is not generally guilty of murder or battery of C. Once again, he is only as guilty as to C as he would have been had his aim been accurate enough to have hit B.[22]

A may still be criminally liable if other facts are shown. Thus, if A *intentionally* shoots C to save himself or herself from B's attack, A may be guilty of murder; or, if A's use of force against B is so reckless as to endanger C, A may be guilty of involuntary manslaughter.[23] But A does not automatically lose the right of self-defense simply because A does not believe that C is the attacker.

For the most part North Carolina cases are in accord with this analysis.[24] On occasion, however, the courts have required a more precise

---

21. State v. Hunter, 305 N.C. 106, 113–15, 286 S.E.2d 535, 540–41 (1982). A person's right to defend against a sexual assault is discussed further in § 4.2 *infra*.

22. 1 LaFave, *supra* note 9, at 401–02. *See also* Ferdinand S. Tinio, Annotation, *Unintentional Killing of or Injury to Third Person during Attempted Self-Defense*, 55 A.L.R. 3d 620 (1974).

23. 1 LaFave, *supra* note 9, at 661 & n.74.

24. *See* State v. Wynn, 278 N.C. 513, 519, 180 S.E.2d 135, 139 (1971) (finding under doctrine of transferred intent that when defendant unintentionally kills third person, defendant is guilty or innocent as if fatal act had caused death of adversary); State v. Braxton, 265 N.C. 342, 343–44, 144 S.E.2d 5, 5–6 (1965) (evidence was sufficient to warrant instruction on self-defense; defendant testified that the victim sicced his dogs on him, that the defendant shot at one of the dogs who was attacking the defendant's son, and that the defendant unintentionally hit the victim); State v. Correll, 38 N.C. App. 451, 455–56, 248 S.E.2d 451, 454–55 (jury acquitted defendant of murder of motorcyclist, apparently on grounds of self-defense, but convicted defendant of involuntary manslaughter for unintentional shooting of rider; court finds that even if shooting of motorcyclist was justified, performance of

belief of the defendant. For example, in one case, the defendant claimed that a violent fight had broken out among several people in a bar; that he was fearful of the fighting going on around him and fired his gun toward the floor; and that he did not intend to hit the deceased or anyone else. The supreme court rejected the defendant's claim of self-defense on a number of grounds, but one is particularly noteworthy here. The court stated that the defendant was not entitled to an instruction on self-defense because he did not specifically fear that he would suffer death or great bodily injury *at the hands of the deceased*.[25] At least as a general statement of the law of self-defense in North Carolina, such a requirement about the source of harm appears too absolute.

### (3) Belief in the Need for Force

The second "belief" that has been required of a defendant—a belief in the need for force to avert the threatened harm—has proved more troublesome. In *Norris*, the court stated that, as a precondition to a self-defense claim, the defendant must have "believed it to be necessary to kill." Some cases have interpreted this language literally, requiring a belief in the need to *kill*. More recently, in *State v. Watson*, the supreme court said that such a belief is not essential—that in some circumstances it may be sufficient if the defendant believed in the need to use deadly force.[26] Then, in *State v. Richardson*, the court disavowed *Watson* and came up with a different approach.[27] *Richardson* appears to require that the defendant believe in the need to protect himself or

---

that act could have been so reckless as to constitute culpable negligence as to rider), *rev. denied*, 296 N.C. 107, 249 S.E.2d 805 (1978). *See also* State v. Musselwhite, 54 N.C. App. 68, 74 & n.4, 283 S.E.2d 149, 154 & n.4 (1981) (Becton, J., dissenting) (dissent argues that defendant who fired into occupied building could claim self-defense even though he did not identify person he was shooting at; "[w]hether a defendant who shoots into a home is culpably negligent is another question"), *aff'd per curiam*, 305 N.C. 295, 287 S.E.2d 897 (1982).

25. State v. Reid, 335 N.C. 647, 671–72, 440 S.E.2d 776, 789–90 (1994). *See also Musselwhite*, 54 N.C. App. 68, 283 S.E.2d 149 (majority of court of appeals upholds denial of self-defense instructions on charge of shooting into occupied dwelling; court finds, among other things, that defendant did not fire at anyone in particular to save himself from death or great bodily injury).

26. 338 N.C. 168, 449 S.E.2d 694 (1994), *cert. denied*, __ U.S. __, 115 S. Ct. 1708, 131 L. Ed. 2d 569 (1995).

27. 341 N.C. 585, 461 S.E.2d 724 (1995), *rev'g* 112 N.C. App. 252, 435 S.E.2d 84 (1993).

herself from harm, but eliminates any requirement that the defendant believe in the need to use a specific level of force. Because of the importance of this issue—and the potential for further changes in this area—the development of the law is reviewed at length below.

**Conflict in Case Law.** One line of cases after *Norris* held that the defendant could not claim that a killing was in self-defense unless he or she believed in the "need to kill." These cases found that the belief requirement of *Norris* was not satisfied by a belief in the need to use any lesser degree of force in self-defense.[28] *State v. Blankenship* is an example of such a decision.[29] There, the defendant's evidence showed that the victim lifted the defendant off the ground, pinned him against the wall, and began choking him. Having trouble breathing, the defendant took out his gun and tried to hit the victim with the barrel. The two men then began to struggle over the gun and it went off, killing the victim. The defendant claimed that at the time the gun went off, he had not decided whether it was necessary to shoot. The supreme court held that the defendant was not entitled to instructions on self-defense. According to the court, even if the evidence could be construed as showing that the defendant intended to shoot the victim, the evidence did not show that he intended to *shoot to kill*. Since the defendant did not believe in the need to kill, he failed the first element of the *Norris* test and could not rely on either perfect or imperfect self-defense.

Under this interpretation, a defendant who did not believe in the need to kill, but nevertheless caused the death of his or her assailant, would still be entitled to instructions on the defense of accident, a fully exculpatory defense. But the jury would not receive instructions on self-defense as a possible theory of acquittal. Also, a defendant limited to the defense of accident would not be entitled to have voluntary manslaughter submitted to the jury. Voluntary manslaughter is a per-

---

28. *See Reid*, 335 N.C. at 671–72, 440 S.E.2d at 789–90 (defendant claimed to have shot toward ground during fighting; court finds that since defendant did not have belief in need to kill, defendant was not entitled to instruction on self-defense); State v. Mize, 316 N.C. 48, 54, 340 S.E.2d 439, 443 (1986) (court states in dicta that defendant did not satisfy first element of *Norris* and was not entitled to instructions on self-defense because he did not aim shotgun to kill victim); State v. Daniels, 87 N.C. App. 287, 289–90, 360 S.E.2d 470, 471 (1987) (defendant testified that he was trying to ward off victim with knife but did not mean to stab him; since defendant did not have belief in need to kill, defendant was not entitled to nonsuit).

29. 320 N.C. 152, 154–55, 357 S.E.2d 357, 358–59 (1987), *rev'g* 82 N.C. App. 285, 287–88, 346 S.E.2d 171, 172–73 (1986).

missible verdict only under the defenses of imperfect self-defense or heat of passion.[30]

Many other cases, however, either implicitly or explicitly rejected a requirement of a belief in the need to kill. Several simply ignored the existence of any such requirement, allowing defendants to proceed on the ground of self-defense even though they disavowed any intention of killing the victim. In those cases, though the defendants claimed that they were only trying to stop their assailants, or wound them, or scare them off, they still were able to assert that the killing was in self-defense.[31] These cases have an intuitive appeal in that a person trying to stop an assailant would seem to be acting in self-defense as much as a person trying to kill an assailant. These cases also avoid the awkward result of denying the benefit of self-defense to those who try *not* to kill, thus suggesting that the law requires people to use the maximum force possible.

Some cases took a more indirect approach. They assumed that a defendant had to believe in the need to kill to claim self-defense. Then they finessed the requirement by combining the state's evidence, which showed that the defendant intended to kill the victim, with the defendant's evidence, which showed that the defendant was acting defensively. These cases found that the jury could credit some of each party's evidence and conclude that the defendant believed in the need to kill.[32] The rulings in these cases rest on two general principles of law:

---

30. *See* State v. Wilkerson, 295 N.C. 559, 583, 247 S.E.2d 905, 918–19 (1978). The defense of heat of passion has its own distinct requirements and is beyond the scope of this book.

31. *See* State v. McAvoy, 331 N.C. 583, 417 S.E.2d 489 (1992) (defendant testified that he was trying to stop victim); State v. Buck, 310 N.C. 602, 313 S.E.2d 550 (1984) (defendant testified that he was trying to defend against felonious assault but that fatal wound was not intentional); State v. Ray, 299 N.C. 151, 261 S.E.2d 789 (1980) (defendant testified that he shot at victim's feet in an effort to avoid killing him); State v. Potter, 295 N.C. 126, 143, 244 S.E.2d 397, 408 (1978) (in precursor to *Norris*, court states first requirement of self-defense in terms of defendant's belief in need to shoot, not kill, the victim); State v. Hughes, 82 N.C. App. 724, 348 S.E.2d 147 (1986) (defendant testified that he was scared for his life but that he did not intend to kill the victim).

32. *See* State v. Hayes, 88 N.C. App. 749, 751–52, 364 S.E.2d 712, 713 (1988) (drawing from evidence offered by defendant and by state in finding that defendant was entitled to instruction on self-defense in first-degree murder case); State v. McConnaughey, 66 N.C. App. 92, 96–97, 311 S.E.2d 26, 29–30 (1984) (drawing from state's evidence that defendant intended to kill in finding that defendant was entitled to instructions on self-defense in a second-degree murder case).

one, that defendants may rely on both their own evidence and the state's to support a defense;[33] and two, that defendants may rely on multiple, even conflicting, theories to justify or excuse their actions.[34]

**False Start in *Watson*.** In *State v. Watson*,[35] the supreme court attempted to resolve the above conflict in the case law. There, the defendant challenged the wording of the trial court's instructions on self-defense, which required that the defendant believe in the need to kill. The defendant argued that the instructions should have directed the jury to consider whether the defendant believed in the need for deadly force. The court appeared to accept this argument in large part. The court held that if there is evidence that the defendant intended to use deadly force but not to kill the victim—that the defendant intended to disable the victim, for example—it would be appropriate to instruct the jury in terms of the defendant's belief in the need for deadly force. When the evidence shows only that the defendant intended to kill, it would still be appropriate to instruct the jury in terms of a belief in the need to kill.

The approach taken in *Watson* left open a number of issues, however. Among other things, the decision did not address a lingering conflict over whether a defendant could claim self-defense if he or she intended to use *nondeadly* force to ward off a perceived attack and inadvertently killed the assailant in the process. Some North Carolina cases rejected claims of self-defense in these circumstances even though the evidence suggested that the defendants were trying to save themselves from death or great bodily injury. For example, in one case the evidence showed that the deceased (the defendant's live-in boyfriend) was hitting, kicking, and choking the defendant and had knocked her down into a corner of the kitchen; that the defendant grabbed a kitchen knife to protect herself; and that the deceased fell on the knife in trying to get at the defendant again. The court held that the defendant could rely on

---

33. *See, e.g.,* State v. Jones, 299 N.C. 103, 107, 261 S.E.2d 1, 5 (1980) (defendant could rely on own evidence or state's evidence or both to support defensive-force defense).

34. *See* State v. Todd, 264 N.C. 524, 530, 142 S.E.2d 154, 159 (1965) ("The defendant's plea of not guilty entitled him to present evidence that he acted in self-defense, that the shooting was accidental, or both. Election is not required. The defendant may rely on more than one defense."), *quoting* State v. Wagoner, 249 N.C. 637, 639, 107 S.E.2d 83, 85 (1959).

35. 338 N.C. 168, 449 S.E.2d 694 (1994), *cert. denied,* __ U.S. __, 115 S. Ct. 1708, 131 L. Ed. 2d 569 (1995).

the defense of accident, but not self-defense, because she did not intend to stab the deceased.[36]

Other cases, however, suggested that defendants simply must have believed it necessary to "use the force used" to save themselves from death or great bodily harm. Thus, in a case decided shortly before *Norris*, the supreme court determined that the defendant was not entitled to an instruction on self-defense because the record contained no evidence that "it was necessary or appeared to defendant to be necessary for him to kill *or use the force used* in order to save himself from death or great bodily harm."[37] In another case decided around the same time, the supreme court held that the trial court erred in not allowing the jury to consider whether "the defendant used *such force* as was necessary or *as appeared to him to be necessary* to save himself from death or great bodily injury."[38] This approach focused more on the actions taken by a defendant than on the resulting consequences, allowing a defendant to claim self-defense when he or she believed the actions necessary to avoid harm.

---

36. State v. Rawley, 237 N.C. 233, 234–37, 74 S.E.2d 620, 621–23 (1953). *See also* State v. Wallace, 309 N.C. 141, 147–48, 305 S.E.2d 548, 552–53 (1983) (gun went off as wife was trying to grab it from defendant); State v. Fleming, 296 N.C. 559, 563–64, 251 S.E.2d 430, 432–33 (1979) (defendant was trying to ward off knife attack by blocking deceased's blows and pushed knife into deceased; defendant not entitled to claim self-defense because he did not intend to cut assailant); State v. Ogburn, 60 N.C. App. 598, 599, 299 S.E.2d 454, 455 (defendant claimed that wife was trying to shoot him and as he pushed her hand away gun went off, killing her; defendant not entitled to claim self-defense because he did not intend to shoot wife), *rev. denied*, 308 N.C. 546, 304 S.E.2d 240 (1983); State v. Berry, 35 N.C. App. 128, 130–32, 240 S.E.2d 633, 635–36 (defendant claimed that he got gun to scare off person with knife and did not intend to shoot), *rev. denied*, 294 N.C. 737, 244 S.E.2d 155 (1978).

37. State v. Davis, 289 N.C. 500, 509, 223 S.E.2d 296, 302 (defendant killed law-enforcement officer in struggle over gun, but there was no evidence that the defendant did so to save himself from death or great bodily harm), *vacated on other grounds*, 429 U.S. 809, 97 S. Ct. 47, 50 L. Ed. 2d 69 (1976) (emphasis added).

38. State v. Deck, 285 N.C. 209, 215, 203 S.E.2d 830, 834 (1974) (emphasis added). *See also* State v. Hipp, 245 N.C. 205, 207–08, 95 S.E.2d 452, 454 (1956) (evidence raised inference of self-defense and required instructions to jury, notwithstanding defendant's "own declaration to others that the actual shooting was accidental"), *quoting* State v. Greer, 218 N.C. 660, 667, 12 S.E.2d 238, 241–42 (1940); State v. Adams, 2 N.C. App. 282, 287–89, 163 S.E.2d 1, 4–5 (1968) (defendant claimed that he was trying to shoot rifle in air to scare off father, who was threatening to kill defendant's mother and harm defendant; defendant was entitled to instructions on self-defense and defense of another so that jury could decide whether defendant

The court never considered how *Watson* applied to the above conflict. In *State v. Richardson*,[39] decided less than a year later, the court disavowed *Watson,* including the suggestion to trial courts that they should substitute "to use deadly force" for "to kill" in jury instructions on self-defense. The court developed a new approach to the problem of the defendant's belief.

### (4) The Richardson Approach

**Status of law before *Richardson*.** Before *Richardson,* three different formulations of the first *Norris* element existed:

1. The defendant had to believe it necessary *to kill* to prevent death or great bodily injury.
2. The defendant had to believe it necessary *to use deadly force* to prevent death or great bodily injury.
3. The defendant had to believe it necessary *to use the force used* to prevent death or great bodily injury.

All three formulations required two beliefs of the defendant: a belief that he or she was threatened with death or great bodily injury *and* a belief in the need for force in response. The second belief, however, represented by the italicized portions, differed in each formulation. The existence of three different phrasings created uncertainty in itself; in addition, each phrasing had its own drawbacks.

The first two formulations created two problems. First, each of the first two formulations could be construed as requiring the defendant to believe it necessary to use a particular level of force (killing in the first formulation, deadly force in the second). A defendant who did not entertain such a belief might fail the first *Norris* element even though he or she was trying to save himself or herself from death or great bodily injury. Second, both formulations made it difficult to distinguish the

---

had reasonable apprehension of death or great bodily injury to mother or himself when he killed father); State v. Hill, 744 P.2d 1228, 1236 (Kan. 1987) (critical issue is whether there is any evidence supporting defendant's statement that force she used was necessary to defend herself); PERKINS, *supra* note 12, at 1109, 1156 (stating that if a person uses nondeadly force in self-defense and death should unexpectedly result, the person's acts are still excusable); Milton Roberts, Annotation, *Accused's Right, in Homicide Case, to Have Jury Instructed as to Both Unintentional Shooting and Self-Defense,* 15 A.L.R. 4th 983 (1982) (comparing jurisdictions' treatment of issue).

39. 341 N.C. 585, 461 S.E.2d 724 (1995), *rev'g* 112 N.C. App. 252, 435 S.E.2d 84 (1993).

second element of the *Norris* test (the reasonable belief requirement) from the fourth element (the excessive force requirement). As long as the first element requires a defendant to believe in the need to use a particular level of force, the second element requires that a reasonable person believe that such force was necessary. The fourth element of *Norris* focuses on a similar issue. Whether the defendant's force was excessive certainly addresses the reasonableness of the force used by the defendant.[40]

The third formulation does not require a belief in a particular level of force, just a belief that the actions taken were necessary. As long as the defendant believes that his or her actions are necessary to avoid harm (and as long as that belief is reasonable under the second element of *Norris*), the defendant may rely on self-defense. The defendant would not lose the right of self-defense on the ground that the assailant suffered greater injuries than the defendant anticipated. Under the third formulation, however, it still remains difficult to distinguish the second *Norris* element from the fourth. The second element still requires that a reasonable person believe that the actions taken by the defendant were necessary. Yet, the fourth element also considers the reasonableness of the defendant's actions.

**Rephrasing of *Norris* Elements.** At first glance the supreme court's decision in *State v. Richardson* may not seem to make significant changes. The court ended up sustaining the trial court's instructions, which included language that the defendant had to believe in the "need to kill." But the court upheld the instructions because it concluded in essence that the jury would overlook the "need to kill" language, not because the language accurately reflected the requirements of self-defense (see "Impact on Instructions," below). At bottom, *Richardson* rephrases the first *Norris* element in a manner that represents a rejection of the three formulations set out above. *Richardson* essentially restates the first element as follows:

> The defendant must believe it necessary *to protect* himself or herself from death or great bodily injury.[41]

This revision appears to have two major effects.

---

40. For a further discussion of the difficulty of distinguishing the second and fourth elements of the *Norris* test, *see infra* § 3.4.

41. 341 N.C. at 593, 461 S.E.2d at 729. The text paraphrases the court's language: "[T]he focus in elements one and two is on the reasonableness of defendant's belief that he must protect himself from death or great bodily harm, not the force used by the defendant."

First, this formulation avoids the problems associated with requiring the defendant to believe in the need to kill or use deadly force. It continues to require two beliefs of the defendant: (1) a belief that he or she is threatened with death or great bodily injury and (2) a belief that he or she must protect himself or herself from that threat. But the second part of the formulation eliminates reference to any specific action by the defendant or any particular result of that action. Instead, it considers more generally whether the defendant believed in the need to take some action for self-protection.

Second, this formulation provides some basis for distinguishing the second element of the *Norris* test from the fourth element. The *Richardson* court recognized that the phrasing of the first *Norris* element (the honest belief requirement) affects the second element (the reasonable belief requirement). Since the first element no longer requires a belief in the need for a specific level of force, the second element no longer considers whether a reasonable person would have believed such force to have been necessary. Thus, in the words of the court, the force used by the defendant becomes "irrelevant" for purposes of determining the reasonableness of the defendant's belief under element two.[42] How much force a defendant uses remains critical, but under element four, the excessive force element. Under *Richardson,* that element addresses the "reasonableness of the defendant's choice of force" to protect himself or herself.[43]

The distinction drawn in *Richardson* finds some support in the basic principles of self-defense. The principle of necessity underlying the right of self-defense has two major components: a person must reasonably appear to be threatened with some harm and his or her use of force must be reasonably necessary to avoid the threatened harm. This second component of necessity can be broken down further: a person may use force only *when* and *to the extent* reasonably necessary to avoid harm. Although a person may need to take defensive action immediately

---

42. *Id.* at 590, 461 S.E.2d at 728 ("The instrumentality or method of force employed by defendant which ultimately results in the victim's death is irrelevant for purposes of determining the reasonableness of defendant's belief under element two.").

43. *Id.* at 592–93, 461 S.E.2d at 729 ("The fourth element of self-defense addresses the reasonableness of the defendant's choice of force used to protect himself from death or great bodily harm."). The fourth element of *Norris* avoids the troublesome belief formulation of elements one and two. It simply states that the defendant may not use more force than "was necessary or reasonably appeared to him to be necessary under the circumstances." For a further discussion of how *Richardson* affects the relationship between elements two and four, *see infra* § 3.4(c)(3).

to avoid harm, thus acting when necessary, he or she still may use only that amount of force reasonably necessary to avoid the harm.[44] Under *Richardson,* the requirement that a defendant reasonably believe in the need to take some action for self-protection corresponds roughly to the requirement that a defendant may act only *when* necessary. The requirement that a defendant not use excessive force approximates the requirement that a defendant may act only *to the extent* necessary.

This approach does not disturb other requirements of self-defense. Under the proportionality principle, for example, a person may use deadly force only to prevent some serious threat of harm.[45] That principle remains in effect under *Richardson* by virtue of the requirement that the defendant still must believe that he or she is threatened with death or great bodily injury. A defendant may not use deadly force to prevent mere bodily harm, offensive contact, or some other fairly minor injury. In addition, *Richardson* still requires that the defendant's belief be reasonable. An honest belief that a threat of death or great bodily harm exists is not enough; the belief also must be one that a reasonable person would have entertained.[46] Last, as required by other North Carolina cases, the threat of death or great bodily harm must be imminent or must reasonably appear to be so.[47]

Some uncertainty lingers because the court in *Richardson* described the first *Norris* element in two different ways. In some parts of the opinion, the court phrased the element in a manner that requires two beliefs of the defendant—a belief that he or she is threatened with death or great bodily injury *and* needs to protect himself or herself from that threat. In other parts of the opinion, the court appeared to require only one belief of the defendant—a belief that he or she is threatened with death or great bodily injury.[48] The practical difference between

---

44. *See* 2 Paul H. Robinson, Criminal Law Defenses 4–5 (1984). Robinson gives the following example to distinguish the two inquiries: "For instance, assume the [defendant] is a karate expert who can, with no risk of harm to himself, dislodge an attacker's weapon with a high kick. While the average person might be justified in shooting an armed attacker, this [defendant] may only use karate to disarm, since any more harmful force, such as shooting, is not *necessary* to protect himself." *Id.*

45. *See supra* § 2.2(b)(1).

46. For a further discussion of the reasonable belief requirement, *see infra* § 3.2(c).

47. For a further discussion of the imminence requirement, *see infra* § 3.2(d).

48. *See, e.g.,* 341 N.C. at 590, 461 S.E.2d at 728 ("The critical question for purposes of elements one and two of self-defense is whether defendant had a reasonable belief that he was in danger of great bodily harm or death.").

these two formulations may be minimal: Both have as their primary focus whether the defendant believed that he or she was in danger of being killed or suffering great bodily injury. At least in theory, however, the two formulations require different mental states. The court did not express a clear preference for one formulation over the other, and an argument can be made for either based on the language of the opinion. For purposes of this book, it is useful to settle on one formulation. Until the court provides further guidance, the "belief in the need to protect" phrasing seems preferable because it more closely resembles the two-belief structure of earlier formulations.

Another uncertainty arises because the court stated that self-defense involves an "admitted, intentional act."[49] By this statement, the court may have been attempting to distinguish between a purely accidental killing and one resulting from an act of self-defense. The meaning of the quoted language is unclear, however. First, it is unclear whether a person would literally have to "admit" to doing some act even when other evidence supports his or her claim of self-defense.[50] Second, it is unclear exactly what intent a person would have to entertain. The court may mean only that a person must entertain the intent inherent in believing that he or she must take some action for self-protection. Any additional "intent" requirement could reintroduce confusion about whether a person would have to believe in the need to use a specific level of force.[51]

**Impact on Instructions.** The impact of the changes made by *Richardson* on the trial of self-defense cases remains somewhat uncertain. In *Richardson* the trial court instructed the jury that it could find

---

49. *Id.* at 594, 461 S.E.2d at 730. In the same vein, the court quoted an earlier case, State v. Ray, 299 N.C. 151, 158, 261 S.E.2d 789, 794 (1980), which had characterized self-defense as a "plea of confession and avoidance."

50. *Compare supra* notes 33–34 (defendant may raise conflicting defenses and may rely on state's evidence, not just his or her own).

51. The North Carolina courts have imposed an admission requirement of sorts for the defense of entrapment because of the perceived uniqueness of that defense. Even there, however, the case law would only preclude a defendant from denying having taken the actions that constitute the charged offense, not from denying having acted with a particular intent. *See* State v. Neville, 302 N.C. 623, 625–26, 276 S.E.2d 373, 374–75 (1981) (discussing rule and exceptions); *see also* Mathews v. United States, 458 U.S. 58, 108 S.Ct. 883, 99 L.Ed.2d 54 (1988) (rejecting any admission requirement for entrapment defense in federal cases).

that the defendant acted in self-defense only if he believed it necessary *to kill*. The defendant argued that the instructions should have stated that the defendant need only have believed in the need *to use deadly force*. The court of appeals agreed with the defendant and ordered a new trial.[52] The supreme court, however, rejected the modification of the instructions. The supreme court's analysis of the instructions requires close reading.

Clearly, the supreme court disapproved of instructions phrasing the first two *Norris* elements in terms of whether the defendant believed in the need to use deadly force. The court specifically disavowed *Watson,* which had indicated that trial courts should use such instructions when the evidence supported them. The supreme court in *Richardson* noted that instructions requiring the defendant to have believed in the need to use deadly force could make elements one and two of *Norris* focus on the reasonableness of the force used by the defendant, an inquiry reserved for the fourth element.[53]

Is it still appropriate for trial courts to instruct the jury in terms of whether the defendant believed in the need to kill? *Richardson* sends mixed signals. On the one hand, the court found that the "belief in the need to kill" phrasing used by the trial court would not have misled the jury. According to the court, the instructions read as a whole adequately focused the jury on the essential inquiry under elements one and two of *Norris:* whether the defendant reasonably believed that he was in danger of death or great bodily injury. On the issue of the reasonableness of the defendant's force, the court found that the instructions properly directed the jury to consider that issue under element four, not elements one and two. In light of this part of the court's opinion, trial courts arguably may continue to phrase self-defense instructions in terms of the defendant's belief in the need to kill.[54]

---

52. 112 N.C. App. 252, 257–59, 435 S.E.2d 84, 86–88 (1993).

53. 341 N.C. at 596, 461 S.E.2d at 731 (proposed language "could potentially makes elements two and four involve similar considerations"). Cases using the *Watson* approach are presumably no longer good law. *See* State v. Burton, 119 N.C. App. 625, 642–43, 460 S.E.2d 181, 193–94 (1995) (since all evidence showed defendant intended to kill, defendant not entitled to self-defense instruction phrased in terms of defendant's belief in need to use deadly force).

54. The supreme court did not elaborate on why the "belief in the need to use deadly force" wording proposed by the defendant could have caused the jury to

On the other hand, the specific issue before the supreme court in *Richardson* was whether the trial court should have substituted "to use deadly force" for "to kill" in its self-defense instructions. Although the supreme court disapproved of the "deadly force" modification requested by the defendant, other changes would seem appropriate in light of the supreme court's reasoning. For example, after *Richardson* an instruction might read that the defendant must have believed in the need *to protect* himself or herself from death or great bodily injury and that such a belief must have been reasonable. Continuing to instruct the jury that the law

---

confuse elements two and four while the "belief in the need to kill" phrasing would not have had the same effect.

The court of appeals in *Richardson* raised several other concerns about the belief-in-the-need-to-kill requirement; however, because the supreme court found that the instructions would not have misled the jury, it rejected those concerns. Among other things, the court of appeals was troubled by the relationship between a requirement of a belief in the need to kill and the mental elements of second-degree murder. It found that such a requirement meant that a defendant claiming self-defense would have to act with the specific intent to kill. 112 N.C. App. at 257–59, 435 S.E.2d at 86–88. As a result, if a defendant admits to shooting the victim but not trying to kill, the evidence will be sufficient to show second-degree murder but insufficient to show self-defense. *See generally* State v. Reynolds, 307 N.C. 184, 191, 297 S.E.2d 532, 536 (1982) (jury may infer malice required for second-degree murder from intentional use of deadly weapon to inflict injury). If a defendant admits the intent to kill, he or she will have conceded the specific intent required for first-degree murder and possibly sacrificed the chance of mitigating first-degree murder to second-degree murder. *Cf.* 2 ROBINSON, *supra* note 9, at 17 (discussing difficulty of relating mental elements of offenses and mental elements of self-defense when law requires defendant to have acted for particular purpose in order to claim self-defense). Because the supreme court found that the jury would not have dwelt on the "belief in the need to kill" language in the trial court's instructions, it concluded that the jury would not have interpreted the instructions as requiring the defendant to entertain a specific intent to kill.

The court of appeals also was concerned that requiring a belief in the need to kill would affect the prosecution's burden of persuasion. *See generally* § 8.2(b) *infra* (prosecution has burden to prove beyond a reasonable doubt that defendant did not meet *Norris* elements). In the court of appeals' view, imposing such a requirement under the first element of *Norris* would render "impermissibly easier" the prosecution's burden to disprove the reasonableness of the defendant's belief under the second *Norris* element. 112 N.C. App. at 258, 435 S.E.2d at 87. In other words, the prosecution would have an easier time proving that it was unreasonable to kill the victim than that it was unreasonable to take some other action in self-defense. Again, the supreme court rejected this concern on the ground that the trial court's instructions would not have focused the jury on whether the defendant believed in the need to kill.

requires a defendant to have believed in the need to kill would seem problematic because *Richardson's* analysis of the *Norris* test clarifies that such a belief is not actually a requirement of self-defense.

*Richardson* affects more than just how trial courts should word instructions; it also affects the showing a defendant must make to obtain those instructions. In some cases, the courts have held that a defendant who does not produce evidence that he or she believed it necessary to kill is not entitled to instructions on self-defense.[55] After *Richardson*, a defendant would appear to be entitled to self-defense instructions regardless of whether he or she produced evidence of having such a belief.[56]

### (c) Reasonable Belief

#### (1) Relationship to Other Elements

Unlike the first element of *Norris*, which is subjective in nature, the second element has both subjective and objective components. The second element requires that the defendant's belief in the need to defend himself or herself be *reasonable*. A defendant's belief is considered reasonable if in light of the circumstances as they appeared to him or her at the time of the encounter (the subjective part) a person of ordinary firmness would have formed a like belief (the objective part).

Before analyzing the concept of *reasonableness* further, it is necessary to say another word on the meaning of *belief*. Whatever belief is required under the honest belief element of *Norris* (discussed in the preceding section), that belief must be one that a reasonable person would accept under the second element. The supreme court appears to have settled on the following construction of the first element: a person must believe it necessary to protect himself or herself from death or great bodily injury. Under the second element, therefore, that belief must be *reasonable* in all the circumstances.

---

55. *See supra* § 3.2(b)(3), "Conflict in Case Law."

56. This result creates additional tension with instructions stating that a defendant must have believed in the need to kill. Although a defendant would be entitled to self-defense instructions without producing evidence that he or she believed it necessary to kill, a jury might construe the instructions as allowing it to reject the defendant's self-defense claim on the ground that the defendant did not entertain such a belief. For a further discussion of the defendant's burden of production to obtain instructions, *see infra* § 8.2(c).

How the *beliefs* in elements one and two are phrased also affects the relationship between the second and fourth elements of *Norris*, the latter dealing with the concept of excessive force. Excessive force is discussed later in § 3.4.

## *(2) What Makes a Belief "Reasonable"*

Although most cases do not explicitly distinguish between the subjective and objective aspects of the second element of *Norris*, both are critical to an analysis of reasonableness. The court has frequently emphasized the subjective part of the analysis, requiring that the jury consider the facts as they appeared to the defendant at the time of the encounter. For example:

> [A] jury should, as far as is possible, be placed in defendant's situation and possess the same knowledge of danger and the same necessity for action, in order to decide if defendant acted under reasonable apprehension of danger to his person or his life.[57]

The cases also require that the defendant's belief be measured against an objective standard. Thus, the jury must consider whether, in the circumstances as they appeared to the defendant, a person of "ordinary firmness" would have formed a like belief. A person of "ordinary firmness" is not a perfect person, just a reasonable one in all the circumstances. As stated in one case, when a defendant is faced with a life-threatening situation, his or her actions should not be weighed in "gold scales."[58]

Is there any rote way to determine the circumstances that satisfy the standard of reasonableness? Some common factors have emerged from the cases:

- the relative size, age, and strength of the defendant and attacker,
- the fierceness or persistence of the assault on the defendant,

---

57. State v. Spaulding, 298 N.C. 149, 158, 257 S.E.2d 391, 396 (1979), *quoting* State v. Johnson, 270 N.C. 215, 219, 154 S.E.2d 48, 52 (1967). *See also* State v. Marsh, 293 N.C. 353, 355, 237 S.E.2d 745, 747 (1977) (reasonableness of belief "is to be determined by the jury from the facts and circumstances as they appeared to the accused at the time").

58. State v. Bullock, 91 N.C. 614, 616 (1884). *See also* Brown v. United States, 256 U.S. 335, 343, 41 S. Ct. 501, 502, 65 L. Ed. 961, 963 (1921) (Holmes, J.) ("Detached reflection cannot be demanded in the presence of an uplifted knife.").

- whether the attacker had or appeared to have a weapon, and
- the reputation of the attacker for danger and violence.[59]

But these factors are not preconditions to a finding of reasonableness. Nor do they exhaust the possible circumstances that may show a defendant's actions to be reasonable or unreasonable. Ultimately the question of reasonableness is a factual one, ordinarily for the jury to decide.[60] Several cases consider whether the trial court properly refused to instruct the jury on self-defense in light of the evidence of reasonableness.[61]

---

59. *See, e.g.,* State v. Clay, 297 N.C. 555, 563, 256 S.E.2d 176, 182 (1979) (reciting above factors); NORTH CAROLINA PATTERN JURY INSTRUCTIONS FOR CRIMINAL CASES 206.10 (North Carolina Conference of Superior Court Judges, Committee on Pattern Jury Instructions, Aug. 1994) (reciting above factors).

60. *See* State v. Jones, 299 N.C. 103, 111, 261 S.E.2d 1, 7 (1980) (reasonableness of defendant's belief is to be determined from facts and circumstances as they appeared to defendant at time of killing); State v. Holland, 193 N.C. 713, 718, 138 S.E. 8, 10–11 (1927) (it is for jury to determine reasonableness of grounds for defendant's belief in danger or necessity); State v. Stephens, 153 N.C. 604, 605, 69 S.E. 11, 12 (1910) (reasonableness of defendant's apprehension was for jury, not for court or defendant, to decide); State v. Hill, 141 N.C. 769, 771, 53 S.E. 311, 311 (1906) (right of self-defense is usually question for jury).

61. Cases holding the evidence *insufficient* to show reasonableness and to warrant an instruction on self-defense include: State v. Palmer, 334 N.C. 104, 431 S.E.2d 172 (1993) (defendant stabbed his mother as she was walking away and then shot her as she was crawling back and threatening to get him; insufficient evidence to warrant instruction); State v. Wilson, 304 N.C. 689, 285 S.E.2d 804 (1982) (defendant left scene of fight, returned with weapon, and shot victim in back; insufficient evidence to warrant instruction); State v. Bock, 288 N.C. 145, 217 S.E.2d 513 (1975) (defendant took knife from victim when she allegedly attacked him with it and then stabbed her fifty-five times; insufficient evidence to warrant instruction), *vacated on other grounds*, 428 U.S. 903, 96 S. Ct. 3208, 49 L. Ed. 2d 1209 (1976).

Cases holding the evidence *sufficient* to show reasonableness and warrant an instruction on self-defense include: State v. Spaulding, 298 N.C. 149, 257 S.E.2d 391 (1979) (victim had earlier threatened to get defendant and on day of homicide advanced on defendant with hand jammed in pocket; although victim turned out not to be armed, defendant's evidence was sufficient to show reasonableness and trial court erred in failing to instruct on self-defense); State v. Deck, 285 N.C. 209, 203 S.E.2d 830 (1974) (victim came at defendant with ice pick, and during struggle defendant got control of ice pick and stabbed victim in chest; error not to instruct on self-defense); State v. Hipp, 245 N.C. 205, 95 S.E.2d 452 (1956) (defendant's husband had beaten her repeatedly in past, and defendant killed her husband as he was beating her and threatening to kill her; error not to instruct on self-defense).

### (3) Problematic Circumstances

Generally speaking, the circumstances that bear on whether the defendant honestly believed in the need to defend himself or herself are relevant to whether the defendant's belief was reasonable. This conclusion follows from the principle that the jury must stand in the defendant's shoes when evaluating the reasonableness of his or her conduct. For example, the jury may consider the defendant's prior encounters with the victim, which tend to show that the defendant's apprehension concerning the victim was reasonable.[62] Similarly the jury may consider the advanced age or physical infirmity of the defendant, either of which would bear on the reasonableness of the defendant's apprehension.[63] The hypothetical person of "ordinary firmness" thus becomes a person of like experiences and characteristics as the defendant.

Evaluating the reasonableness of a defendant's state of mind can prove troublesome in some circumstances, however. For example, what if the defendant was intoxicated at the time he or she claims to have been attacked? Should the defendant's intoxication be considered in determining whether it was reasonable for the defendant to have believed it necessary to defend himself or herself? An older case in North Carolina begged the question, simply barring claims of voluntary intoxication and self-defense in the same case. In that case, the defendant claimed that he was experiencing an alcoholic blackout during the encounter and therefore lacked the capacity to form the specific intent to kill required for first-degree murder. The court held that, if the defendant was as intoxicated as claimed, he also would have been unable to form a subjective apprehension (that is, an *honest belief*) in the need to defend himself.[64] Even assuming this analysis is empirically sound, it no longer appears to be the law in North Carolina. More recent decisions indicate that the defenses of voluntary intoxication and self-defense are not mutually exclusive.[65]

---

62. *See, e.g.,* State v. Johnson, 270 N.C. 215, 219–20, 154 S.E.2d 48, 52 (1967) (finding "no better way to impart the knowledge of fear or apprehension on the part of defendant" than by giving the jury the benefit of defendant's prior experience with the victim).

63. *See, e.g.,* State v. Webster, 324 N.C. 385, 392–93, 378 S.E.2d 748, 753 (1989) (defendant testified that he was still sick and weak from hospital stay).

64. State v. Absher, 226 N.C. 656, 659–60, 40 S.E.2d 26, 28 (1946).

65. *See* State v. Edmonson, 283 N.C. 533, 539–40, 196 S.E.2d 505, 509 (1973) (finding no error in trial court's instructions to jury on both self-defense and voluntary intoxication); *see also* State v. Silvers, 323 N.C. 646, 658, 374 S.E.2d 858, 865–66

The problem remains of how to account for intoxication in assessing the *reasonableness* of a defendant's belief. On the one hand, a person of "ordinary firmness" presumably refers to a person whose perception is not distorted by alcohol or other drugs—"a reasonable *sober* man," in the words of LaFave.[66] It would seem to follow that a defendant's intoxication would not be a circumstance that would support reasonableness (although other evidence might still show that the defendant acted reasonably during the encounter). On the other hand, suppose the effect of the substance is to leave a defendant in a physically weaker condition, rendering him or her less able to defend against an attack? Or, suppose the defendant does not rely on the defense of voluntary intoxication at all, which requires a significant degree of impairment, but merely claims that he or she consumed a moderate amount of alcohol? What if a defendant's impairment resulted from the proper use of prescription medication, an act with no moral overtones? When cast in these more acceptable ways, a defendant's "intoxication" arguably would support the reasonableness of his or her belief in the need for defensive action.

### (d) Imminence of Harm

The last feature of the first two elements of the *Norris* test is the requirement of *imminence of harm. Norris* does not explicitly refer to imminence of harm as a requirement for killing in self-defense, but decisions both before and after *Norris* establish an imminence requirement in North Carolina.[67] The requirement modifies both the first and second elements of *Norris*. Under the first element, it must appear to the defendant and the defendant must believe it to be necessary to protect himself or herself from imminent death or great bodily injury. Under the second element, the defendant's belief must be reasonable.

---

(1989) (recognizing right to present voluntary intoxication and insanity in same case). As a practical matter, however, a defendant may have difficulty arguing both voluntary intoxication and self-defense in the same case. *See* State v. Neagle, 29 N.C. App. 308, 311–12, 224 S.E.2d 274, 275–76 (defendant testified that he was so intoxicated he had no memory of encounter; in absence of evidence from other witnesses indicating defendant acted in self-defense, instruction was properly denied), *rev. denied*, 290 N.C. 665, 228 S.E.2d 456 (1976).

66. 1 LaFave, *supra* note 9, at 558 (emphasis in original).

67. *See generally* Richard A. Rosen, *On Self-Defense, Imminence, and Women Who Kill Their Batterers*, 71 N.C. L. Rev. 371, 373 n.4 (1993) (discussing imminence requirement in North Carolina).

According to the supreme court, an *imminent* harm is one that poses an "immediate danger" or is "about to" happen.[68] If the defendant believes that the harm is to occur at some future time—or the defendant believes that the harm is imminent but a reasonable person would not have formed such a belief—the defendant cannot justify a killing as necessary in self-defense. Thus the imminence requirement introduces a sort of time limit into the analysis of necessity, one of the basic principles underlying the right to use defensive force.[69] In jurisdictions imposing an imminence requirement, defensive force is not considered reasonably necessary if the threat of harm does not reasonably appear to be imminent. Imminence requirements have come under greater scrutiny, however, because of cases involving battered persons (discussed further below and in § 4.5). It has been argued that such requirements may conflict with, rather than reinforce, the principle of necessity in some circumstances.

In most cases the concepts of imminence and necessity dovetail, with any difference being a matter of semantics. For example, suppose B threatens to kill A one week from now, and A responds by killing B immediately. A's actions could be said to be improper because the threat of harm was not imminent. A's actions also could be said to be improper under a necessity analysis because the use of defensive force is permissible only when reasonably necessary to avoid harm. By making a preemptive strike, A acted before it was reasonably necessary to do so.[70]

Many North Carolina decisions do not even mention the imminence requirement, presumably because the requirement so often overlaps with the analysis of necessity. Even in some of the cases that explicitly refer to the requirement of imminence, an analysis of necessity would likely have yielded the same result. For example, in one case, the defendant shot and killed the victim, with whom the defendant had been arguing. Although the victim was holding a stick during the argument, he made no move to attack the defendant. The court rejected the defendant's claim of self-defense, finding no evidence that an attack by the victim was imminent, but the court arguably could have rested its decision on the ground that the defendant resorted to force when not reasonably necessary to do so.[71]

---

68. State v. Norman, 324 N.C. 253, 261, 378 S.E.2d 8, 13 (1989).

69. *See supra* § 2.1(b) (discussing basic principles of defensive force).

70. *See* 2 ROBINSON, *supra* note 9, at 4–5 (person may use force only when necessary to avoid harm).

71. State v. Gappins, 320 N.C. 64, 73, 357 S.E.2d 654, 660 (1987). Application of

In some settings, however, the difference between imminence and necessity can be critical. Robinson provides the paradigm example of how the two concepts diverge. Take the previous example, in which B threatens to kill A in one week. Assume further, however, that B is holding A captive and that A's only chance to escape before the expiration of the week is to kill B. Taken literally, the imminence requirement would preclude A from acting until B was "standing over him with a knife."[72] Focusing instead on whether A reasonably needed to act at the time A did would yield a different, and in Robinson's opinion, fairer result. Under a necessity analysis, a court would have to consider, among other things, the effectiveness of alternative courses of action available to A and the likelihood that the kidnapper would inflict harm unless A acted first.[73]

The reported cases in North Carolina do not contain such a stark example, but cases involving battered persons illuminate the potential tension between the concepts of imminence and necessity. The question has arisen of whether the law of self-defense allows a battered person to kill his or her longtime batterer when the batterer is sleeping or otherwise not threatening imminent harm. In the one reported case in North Carolina directly addressing the question, *State v. Norman*,[74]

---

necessity principles would likely have led to the same result in other cases that referred to the concept of imminence. *See* State v. Mize, 316 N.C. 48, 53, 340 S.E.2d 439, 442 (1986) (victim had pursued defendant eight hours earlier; threat of harm not imminent); State v. Spaulding, 298 N.C. 149, 157, 257 S.E.2d 391, 396 (1979) (prisoner had hand jammed in pocket and was approaching defendant in menacing manner; threat of harm *was* imminent). *But compare* State v. McCray, 312 N.C. 519, 525, 531–32, 324 S.E.2d 606, 611, 614–15 (1985) (prisoner had threatened to kill defendant repeatedly, defendant obtained transfer to different part of prison, and defendant made preemptive strike after prisoner continued to seek out defendant; threat of harm not imminent) *with* 2 Robinson, *supra* note 9, at 56–57 n.36 (suggesting that in prison context, imminence requirement may conflict with principle of necessity because it may require prisoner to refrain from action until it is too late).

72. *See* 2 Robinson, *supra* note 9, at 78.

73. Robinson concludes that the imminence requirement should be eliminated entirely because the principle of necessity, standing alone, adequately regulates the use of defensive force. *Id.* at 76–77. The Model Penal Code retains a temporal limitation but modifies it to place the emphasis more directly on the question of necessity. Model Penal Code and Commentaries § 3.04(1) (American Law Institute 1985) ("use of force upon or toward another person is justifiable when the actor believes that such force is immediately necessary for the purpose of protecting himself against the use of unlawful force by such other person on the present occasion"). *See also* Rosen, *supra* note 67, at 377 n.11 (collecting suggested modifications of imminence requirement).

74. 324 N.C. 253, 378 S.E.2d 8 (1989).

the supreme court rejected the defendant's claim of self-defense. In so ruling, the court adhered to the requirement of imminence, stating that it reinforced the principle of necessity. The court's decision is discussed further in § 4.5, which deals with the subject of battered persons.

## § 3.3  The Aggressor Requirement

> *Defendant was not the aggressor in bringing on the affray, i.e., he did not aggressively and willingly enter into the fight without legal excuse or provocation.*
>
> —State v. Norris

### (a)  Purpose of the Aggressor Requirement

The third requirement for killing in self-defense, according to *Norris,* is that the defendant must not have been the aggressor in the conflict. When considered an aggressor, the defendant completely or partially forfeits the right to use defensive force even though the defendant may satisfy the other parts of the *Norris* test.[75] A defendant classified as an aggressor *with* murderous intent loses all right of self-defense; an aggressor *without* murderous intent loses the right of perfect, but not imperfect, self-defense.

The aggressor element reflects the law's concern for *fault,* one of the fundamental principles underlying the right of self-defense.[76] The issue of fault becomes important when a defendant claims to have acted from necessity, but the evidence indicates that the defendant may have created the necessity for action. In essence, a defendant's fault trumps his or her claim of necessity. For example, if a defendant provokes a conflict with another person and the other person responds with force, the defendant may find it necessary to use further force to protect himself or herself. But, because the defendant was at fault in provoking the encounter, he or she is considered the aggressor and loses the right of self-defense, either partially or completely.[77]

---

75. *See* State v. Norris, 303 N.C. 526, 530, 279 S.E.2d 570, 572–73 (1981). The four-part *Norris* test is discussed generally in §§ 2.2(c), 3.1 *supra.*

76. *See supra* § 2.1(b) (discussing basic principles of defensive force).

77. *See generally* Rosen, *supra* note 67, at 378–79.

In an effort to differentiate between degrees of fault, North Carolina recognizes two different types of aggressors—those with murderous intent and those without. This distinction is particularly important in homicide cases. An aggressor *with* murderous intent forfeits both the right of perfect and imperfect self-defense until he or she withdraws from the encounter in accordance with the rules applicable to aggressors with murderous intent. For example, if Mary shoots at John—and John shoots at Mary in self-defense—the law does not justify Mary's shooting back even to save herself from death or great bodily injury. The rationale for this result is twofold. First, if Mary kills John in the circumstances described above, the law would attribute the killing to Mary's original intent. As stated in an early North Carolina case, Mary's original purpose "communicates its character to [her] last act."[78] Second, if Mary attacks John with murderous intent, John ordinarily would be justified in using deadly force to defend himself. It would make little sense to allow Mary to use further force to defeat John's justifiable response.[79]

Suppose, however, that Mary only slaps John, and John still shoots at Mary in response. Although John is not acting in proper self-defense, North Carolina law would limit Mary's right to defend herself. She would be considered an aggressor *without* murderous intent and would forfeit the right of *perfect* self-defense until she withdrew from the encounter within the meaning of the rules applicable to aggressors without murderous intent. As a general rule, if she shoots and kills John before withdrawing, she could only claim *imperfect* self-defense and would remain liable for voluntary manslaughter. The rationale for this result is that, by slapping John, Mary has committed "a misdemeanor

---

78. State v. Hill, 20 N.C. 629, 632 (1839).

79. *See* 2 ROBINSON, *supra* note 9, at 31–32. In one set of circumstances, the defendant may act with *murderous intent* as defined in the law, yet not engage in conduct that would give the victim cause to use deadly force in response. Robinson refers to such a defendant as the "grand schemer." *Id.* at 39. An early case in North Carolina illustrates the problem. In State v. Martin, 24 N.C. 101, 115–17 (1841), there was evidence that the defendant cracked a whip at the victim with the intent of inducing the victim to draw his pistol so the defendant could kill him. Although the victim arguably was not justified in drawing his pistol on the defendant, the court held that the jury could find from this evidence that the defendant had no right of self-defense and was liable for murder. *Accord* State v. Sanders, 295 N.C. 361, 367, 245 S.E.2d 674, 679 (1978) (evidence would permit finding by jury that defendant goaded officer into his cell for purpose of provoking fight so that he could kill him; nonsuit properly denied).

involving a breach of the peace" and is therefore at least partially culpable for the ensuing conflict.[80]

Sections 3.3(c) and (d), below, discuss the two types of aggressors and how each regains the right of perfect self-defense. First, however, it is necessary to consider conduct that may seem "aggressive" in the lay sense of the term but does not necessarily make a person into an "aggressor" within the meaning of the law.

### (b) Defining "Aggressor"

As used in the law of self-defense, *aggressor* is a term of art. A person's conduct may be aggressive, provocative, even illegal as those terms are commonly understood, and still not make a person an *aggressor* within the meaning of the law. The North Carolina courts have not precisely set out what makes a person an aggressor, however. The questions below are intended to distill from North Carolina case law the essential characteristics of aggressors. [Whether a person's conduct would make him or her an aggressor *with* murderous intent, or *without*, is considered separately in §§ 3.3(c) and (d).] Ordinarily, a person may be considered an aggressor if his or her actions

- create the necessity for his or her subsequent use of force;
- occur in the current encounter;
- are taken without legal excuse or provocation; and
- are aggressive and willing.

---

80. State v. Crisp, 170 N.C. 785, 790, 87 S.E. 511, 513–14 (1916). Although many jurisdictions hold aggressors *without* murderous intent liable for voluntary manslaughter, commentators have been critical of the doctrine. They claim, first, that making aggressors without murderous intent liable for voluntary manslaughter overstates their culpability in the encounter. By definition, aggressors without murderous intent do not enter the encounter with the intent to kill or inflict serious bodily injury and therefore should not be held liable for an offense that requires such an intent. *See generally* MODEL PENAL CODE AND COMMENTARIES, *supra* note 73, § 3.02(2) (person should not be held liable for purposeful offense when his or her culpability inheres in recklessness or negligence). Commentators claim, second, that when a defendant acts without murderous intent—by committing a simple assault, for example—the other person ordinarily is not justified in responding with deadly force. Although the defendant should be held criminally responsible for the initial offense of assaulting the other person, he or she should not be held liable for his or her subsequent conduct in defending against the other person's unlawful actions. *See* 1 LaFave, *supra* note 9, at 658; PERKINS, *supra* note 12, at 1141–42; 2 ROBINSON, *supra* note 9, at 30–38; MODEL PENAL CODE AND COMMENTARIES, *supra* note 73, § 3.04(2)(b)(i) & cmt. 4(b).

## (1) Did the Defendant Create the Necessity for Force?

To be considered an aggressor, a defendant must have created the necessity for his or her use of force. In the typical case, the defendant unjustifiably takes some action against another person (such as striking the other person), which causes that person to use force in response, which then causes the defendant to believe it necessary to use further force. Even though the defendant's use of force may be necessary for self-protection during the final stage of the encounter, he or she is considered the aggressor and loses the right of self-defense, either partially or completely. Numerous cases fit this model.[81]

The above scenario concerns a defendant who unjustifiably initiates an encounter, but the same analysis can be applied to a defendant who unjustifiably prolongs an encounter. In some cases the *victim* initiates the conflict but then withdraws. The defendant then takes some action against the victim although no longer reasonably necessary to do so (the defendant unjustifiably "continues" the difficulty, some cases say), which causes the victim to respond with force, which then causes the defendant to use further force for self-protection. By unjustifiably prolonging the conflict, the defendant becomes the aggressor and loses the right of self-defense, either partially or completely.[82]

---

81. *See, e.g.,* State v. Potter, 295 N.C. 126, 144, 244 S.E.2d 397, 409 (1978) ("One who kills under a reasonable belief that it is necessary to do so to save himself from death or great bodily harm will not be entirely excused on the ground of self-defense if he is the aggressor."); State v. Watson, 287 N.C. 147, 156–57, 214 S.E.2d 85, 91 (1975) (if defendant provoked assault by deceased through use of abusive language and thereafter killed deceased, it would be for jury to determine whether language was calculated and intended to provoke fight, thereby making the defendant the aggressor); State v. Strater, 272 N.C. 276, 277–78, 158 S.E.2d 60, 62 (1967) (if the defendant was without fault in bringing on the difficulty, he had the right to defend himself when assaulted with a pistol); State v. Parker, 198 N.C. 629, 634, 152 S.E. 890, 893 (1930) (defendant struck wife, wife tried to cut defendant during ensuing combat, and defendant killed wife; court properly instructed jury on aggressor doctrine).

82. *See* State v. Cannon, 341 N.C. 79, 82–83, 459 S.E.2d 238, 240–41 (1995) (victim initiated argument but then withdrew; jury could find that defendant was aggressor based on his conduct thereafter); State v. Anderson, 230 N.C. 54, 56, 51 S.E.2d 895, 897 (1949) (defendant must not be at fault in provoking, engaging in, or continuing a difficulty). A defendant also could be considered an aggressor by engaging in an affray with the victim—that is, a fight in which the defendant and victim are mutually willing participants. In that circumstance, the defendant may find it necessary to use force for self-protection during the course of the fight; but, having created that

Whether a defendant "created the necessity for action" has been an issue in a number of cases concerning the trial court's instructions to the jury on self-defense. The court of appeals has held that when all the evidence shows that the victim initiated the conflict and that the defendant used force only in response, the trial court should *not* instruct the jury on the aggressor doctrine in instructing on self-defense. Under these cases, the jury may reject the defendant's claim of self-defense for other reasons, but it may not do so on the ground that the defendant was the aggressor.[83]

More often, the state's and defendant's evidence conflict. For example, the state's evidence may show that the defendant attacked and killed the victim without any provocation, and the defendant's evidence may show that the victim attacked the defendant and the defendant responded purely in self-defense. If the state's version of the facts and the defendant's version are viewed *separately*, the aggressor doctrine would seem inapplicable in either context. The state's version raises no issue of self-defense, and the defendant's version shows that the defendant acted only to prevent the victim's attack.[84]

---

necessity by willingly entering into the fight, the defendant loses the right of self-defense, either partially or completely. *See infra* § 3.3(d)(1) (discussing aggressors by mutual willingness to fight).

83. *See* State v. Temples, 74 N.C. App. 106, 109, 327 S.E.2d 266, 268 (when evidence showed only that victim attacked defendant and defendant responded with force, trial court erred in including aggressor doctrine in its instructions to jury on self-defense), *rev. denied*, 314 N.C. 121, 332 S.E.2d 489 (1985); State v. Tann, 57 N.C. App. 527, 530–31, 291 S.E.2d 824, 827 (1982) (to same effect); State v. Ward, 26 N.C. App. 159, 162–63, 215 S.E.2d 394, 396–97 (1975) (to same effect). *See also* State v. Washington, 234 N.C. 531, 535, 67 S.E.2d 498, 501 (1951) (error to instruct on duty of aggressor to retreat where evidence showed only that victim attacked defendant and defendant then responded with force). The courts also have held in general that the jury should not be instructed on a theory that is not supported by the evidence. *See, e.g.*, State v. Porter, 340 N.C. 320, 331, 457 S.E.2d 716, 721 (1995) ("Where jury instructions are given without supporting evidence, a new trial is required."); State v. Moore, 315 N.C. 738, 749, 340 S.E.2d 401, 408 (1986) ("It is generally prejudicial error for the trial judge to permit a jury to convict upon a theory not supported by the evidence.").

84. An older case, viewing the state's and defendants' evidence separately, concluded that an instruction on the aggressor doctrine was improper based in part on the reasons stated in the text. *See* State v. Miller, 223 N.C. 184, 25 S.E.2d 623 (1943) (state's evidence showed that defendants had concealed themselves, waylaid, and killed the victims, while defendants' evidence showed that victims had suddenly attacked defendants and defendants killed victims in self-defense; court finds that aggressor doctrine did not apply to either version of facts).

The courts have routinely upheld aggressor instructions in such cases, however. Although not clearly spelled out in the decisions, the explanation for this result appears to be that the state's and defendant's evidence may be construed *together*. Thus, considering both versions together, a jury could find from the evidence that the defendant induced any necessity for his or her use of force and therefore was the aggressor.[85]

### (2) Did the Defendant's Actions Occur in the Current Encounter?

As a general rule, the aggressor requirement must be applied separately for each encounter. Although a person may be the aggressor in one encounter, the slate is generally considered clean once that encounter is over.[86] In some cases this principle works to a defendant's benefit. The courts have found that where the earlier encounter had ended (in some instances the day before and in others just a few minutes earlier) and the defendant's adversary renewed the difficulty, the defendant should not have been considered the aggressor.[87]

Analyzing encounters separately may also work against a defendant. In a number of cases, the defendant claimed that he or she acted in response to the victim's previous behavior. Because the earlier encounter had ended—or at least a reasonable person would have concluded that the encounter had ended—the court found that the

---

85. *See, e.g.,* State v. Terry, 329 N.C. 191, 198–99, 404 S.E.2d 658, 662–63 (1991) (distinguishing *Miller, supra* note 84, court rejects argument that state's and defendants' evidence viewed separately did not support aggressor instruction; court finds aggressor instruction proper after review of both parties' evidence); State v. Bailey, 97 N.C. App. 472, 478, 389 S.E.2d 131, 134 (1990) (aggressor instruction proper); State v. Haight, 66 N.C. App. 104, 108, 310 S.E.2d 795, 798 (1984) (evidence sufficient to support conviction of voluntary manslaughter based on aggressor theory).

86. *See, e.g.,* State v. Jennings, 276 N.C. 157, 163, 171 S.E.2d 447, 451 (1970) ("Usually, whether the defendant is free from blame or fault will be determined by his conduct at the time and place of the killing.").

87. *Miller,* 223 N.C. 184, 25 S.E.2d 623 (defendants and victim had earlier engaged in fight but fight had ended and defendants went home before subsequent conflict arose); State v. Hill, 20 N.C. 629, 632–33 (1839) (defendant was not necessarily the aggressor on a "fresh quarrel"); State v. Moore, 111 N.C. App. 649, 653–56, 432 S.E.2d 887, 889–91 (1993) (defendant entered victim's house, shoved victim, and then left house, but as defendant was trying to leave, victim came out of house and attacked defendant with a hammer; jury could find that defendant was not aggressor in second altercation).

defendant was responsible for renewing the conflict and could be considered the aggressor.[88] Analyzing encounters separately may not work well, however, in cases involving battered persons who, having suffered physical abuse repeatedly in the past, may have initiated the latest encounter to avoid further abuse. Cases involving battered persons are considered further in § 4.5.

### (3) Did the Defendant Act without Legal Excuse or Provocation?

Proper application of the aggressor requirement also depends on determining whether the defendant lawfully entered into or engaged in the encounter. In early cases in North Carolina the trial court would instruct the jury that the defendant should be considered the aggressor if he or she "aggressively and willingly" entered the fight. As the supreme court recognized, however, a defendant who intentionally uses force against another person almost always does so aggressively and willingly. The supreme court therefore established that a defendant is properly considered the aggressor only if he or she aggressively, willfully, and *wrongfully* enters the fight.[89] The wording of the aggressor element in *Norris* reflects this principle, providing that a person is an aggressor only if he or she acts aggressively, willingly, and *without legal excuse or provocation.*

Any legal doctrine that would justify a defendant's taking of some action would be an appropriate basis for finding that the defendant was not the aggressor.[90] Typically the reported cases have involved situations in which the defendant was exercising his or her right to use

---

88. *See, e.g.,* State v. Hunter, 315 N.C. 371, 374, 338 S.E.2d 99, 102 (1986) (victim had assaulted defendant earlier but then moved to other part of bar); State v. Wynn, 278 N.C. 513, 519, 180 S.E.2d 135, 139 (1971) (victim had quit combat and run out of house).

89. *See* State v. Pollard, 168 N.C. 116, 119–20, 83 S.E. 167, 168–69 (1914).

90. The courts have not always been alert to this principle. *See, e.g.,* State v. Gappins, 320 N.C. 64, 71–73, 357 S.E.2d 654, 659–60 (1987) (defendant followed victim because defendant thought victim had taken something out of defendant's truck; court states that defendant was aggressor from start even though defendant arguably had right to retrieve property or detain victim); State v. Bennett, 67 N.C. App. 407, 408–09, 313 S.E.2d 277, 278–79 (court states that defendant was at fault in bringing on difficulty by attempting to slap at his sixteen-year-old daughter when daughter became verbally aggressive; defendant arguably had authority as parent to

defensive force. The courts have found that when a defendant reasonably believed it necessary to prevent some threat of harm, he or she did not become an aggressor simply by taking action to prevent that harm from occurring.[91] A person also is insulated from criminal liability when he or she justifiably enters an encounter based on a defensive-force defense allowing only nondeadly force but the encounter turns deadly. For example, if B tries to take A's property, A has the right to use nondeadly force to prevent the taking and therefore would not properly be considered the aggressor. If B then responds with deadly force, A would have the right to use deadly force to defend himself or herself.[92]

The reverse of the principle discussed here is that if a defendant's entry into an encounter is not justified or excused, he or she may be considered an aggressor (assuming the other requisites for being an aggressor are present). In a number of cases, the defendant claimed that he or she was defending against another's attack. Because the other person's actions were insufficient to warrant the defendant's use of force, the court held that the defendant could be considered the aggressor in the encounter.[93]

---

discipline daughter), *rev. denied*, 311 N.C. 764, 321 S.E.2d 147 (1984). Notwithstanding these cases, *Norris* designates a person as an aggressor only if he or she acts "without legal excuse or provocation." 303 N.C. at 530, 279 S.E.2d at 572–73. This language certainly seems broad enough to protect a person who acts pursuant to a justification defense. *See supra* § 2.1(a) (discussing justification defenses generally). Although not closely analyzed in the cases, the quoted language also may apply when a defendant's initial conduct is not protected by a justification defense but is otherwise excused or provoked.

91. *See, e.g.,* State v. Moore, 185 N.C. 637, 638–39, 116 S.E. 161, 161–62 (1923) (employee justifiably entered fight to defend his employer's property); State v. Pollard, 168 N.C. 116, 119–20, 83 S.E. 167, 168–69 (1914) (defendant justifiably entered fight to defend himself); State v. Spencer, 27 N.C. App. 301, 306–07, 219 S.E.2d 231, 234–35 (1975) (trial court erred in failing to explain that one is not an aggressor if he or she justifiably enters fight in defense of another).

92. *See* State v. Morgan, 25 N.C. 186, 193–94 (1842); Perkins, *supra* note 12, at 1154.

93. *See, e.g.,* State v. Mize, 316 N.C. 48, 53, 340 S.E.2d 439, 442 (1986) (although victim had earlier threatened to kill defendant, victim had taken no action at time defendant attacked); State v. McCray, 312 N.C. 519, 529–32, 324 S.E.2d 606, 613–15 (1985) (victim had earlier taunted and baited defendant but had taken no action at time defendant attacked).

## (4) Did the Defendant Enter the Conflict Aggressively and Willingly?

Last, the defendant must enter the conflict *aggressively* and *willingly* to be considered an aggressor. Most cases do not explicitly address the meaning of these terms. Rather, the terms have gained their meaning from cases considering whether the defendant was an aggressor *with* or *without* murderous intent. A defendant is considered an aggressor *with* murderous intent when he or she brings about the conflict with the intent to kill or inflict serious bodily injury. The cases hold that a defendant would be an aggressor *without* murderous intent by assaulting another with nondeadly force, by a mutual willingness to fight, or by language or conduct calculated and intended to bring about a fight. These ideas are explored in §§ 3.3(c) and (d) below. A few general observations can be made here, however, about when a person's conduct would be considered *aggressive* and *willing*.

First, the defendant's actions must be provocative. For example, the courts have held that the mere possession of a deadly weapon by the defendant, even if unlawful, does not make the defendant the aggressor. A person can be prepared to fight, the cases hold, and still not be the provocateur.[94]

Second, the defendant must engage in some voluntary, aggressive conduct. It is not sufficient that the defendant's actions may be incidentally provocative. For example, in one case the evidence showed that the defendant and the victim had a history of bad relations; that on the day in question, the defendant went to the victim's gas station; and

---

94. *See* State v. Spaulding, 298 N.C. 149, 155, 257 S.E.2d 391, 395 (1979); State v. Tann, 57 N.C. App. 527, 531, 291 S.E.2d 824, 827 (1982). *See also* State v. Erby, 56 N.C. App. 358, 359–61, 289 S.E.2d 86, 87–88 (1982) (defendant should have been permitted to explain why he had loaded gun). When coupled with some provocative conduct, however, a defendant's possession of a weapon may bolster a finding that the defendant was an aggressor. *See* State v. Watkins, 283 N.C. 504, 509–11, 196 S.E.2d 750, 754–55 (1973); State v. Brooks, 37 N.C. App. 206, 208–09, 245 S.E.2d 564, 565 (1978). *See also* State v. McAvoy, 331 N.C. 583, 593, 417 S.E.2d 489, 496 (1992) (defendant's illegal possession of weapon, which defendant used during incident in question, was proper subject of cross-examination by prosecution because it was "relevant to the manner in which he possessed the gun at the time of the killing"). The *victim's* possession of a weapon may be relevant as well to whether the *victim* was the aggressor. *See* State v. Moore, 339 N.C. 456, 466–68, 451 S.E.2d 232, 237–38 (1994) (evidence that victim had illegal weapon under mattress was not relevant in this case to whether victim was aggressor because weapon had no relationship to events leading to victim's death).

that, fearful of the defendant's intentions, the victim fired at the defendant and the defendant fired back. Concluding that the jury could find from this evidence that the defendant did not voluntarily and aggressively enter into an armed confrontation with the victim, the court held that the trial court erred in not submitting instructions to the jury on the right of the defendant to defend himself.[95]

In another case, the defendant had engaged in "immoral acts" with the victim's wife for a period of years, which eventually provoked the victim to attack the defendant. The trial court instructed the jury that the defendant's killing of the victim would be in proper self-defense only if the defendant had been free from fault in bringing about the conflict with the victim. The supreme court held that the trial court should have explained to the jury that the defendant's relations with the victim's wife, no matter how blameworthy, did not deprive him of the right to act in self-defense.[96]

### (c) Aggressors with Murderous Intent

An aggressor with murderous intent forfeits the right of both perfect and imperfect self-defense.[97] This section describes the meaning of *murderous intent* and the way a person who acts with such an intent regains the right of self-defense.

### (1) Meaning of "Murderous Intent"

The North Carolina Supreme Court has defined *murderous intent* as the "intent to take life or inflict serious bodily harm."[98] This intent

---

95. State v. Marsh, 293 N.C. 353, 355, 237 S.E.2d 745, 747 (1977); *see also* 2 ROBINSON, *supra* note 9, at 33 (person's choice of paint color for his or her house may be so upsetting as to provoke attack by neighbor, but that conduct would not deprive person of right of self-defense).

96. State v. Jennings, 276 N.C. 157, 162–63, 171 S.E.2d 447, 450–51 (1970). *See also* State v. Wilson, 16 N.C. App. 307, 310–11, 192 S.E.2d 72, 74–75 (1972) (trial court erred in not clarifying in instructions that defendant's homosexual act immediately prior to incident would not render him at fault and deprive him of right of self-defense); State v. Taylor, 15 N.C. App. 303, 307–09, 190 S.E.2d 254, 256–58 (1972) (defendant's adulterous relationship with deceased's estranged wife did not deprive defendant of right to act in self-defense).

97. *See supra* § 3.3(a).

98. State v. Mize, 316 N.C. 48, 52–53, 340 S.E.2d 439, 442 (1986); State v. Potter, 295 N.C. 126, 144 n.2, 244 S.E.2d 397, 409 n.2 (1978).

may be inferred when a defendant unjustifiably initiates an encounter with deadly force.[99] It also may be inferred from conduct short of the use of deadly force. In a few cases, the defendant had not yet used deadly force when the victim began to use force or otherwise resist. The court found that the defendant's actions and statements were sufficiently definite to show that he or she provoked the conflict with the intent of taking life or inflicting serious bodily injury.[100]

### (2)  Regaining the Right of Self-Defense

Few recent cases address how an aggressor with murderous intent regains the right of self-defense, but older cases appear to recognize two ways this can happen. First, an aggressor with murderous intent regains the right of self-defense once the encounter is concluded—that is, when both sides have broken off the fight.[101] As discussed earlier, each encounter must be analyzed separately.[102]

Second, the cases suggest that an aggressor with murderous intent regains the right of self-defense if he or she clearly withdraws from the encounter and thus removes any reasonable apprehension from the person assaulted. A defendant who demonstrates, by words or conduct, that he or she has terminated any "murderous" attack obviates the need for the other person to use defensive force; should the other person continue to use force, the defendant's right of self-defense is restored.[103]

---

99. See State v. Pearson, 288 N.C. 34, 39, 215 S.E.2d 598, 603 (1975) (treating murderous intent and deadly force as equivalent). The meaning of deadly force is discussed in § 2.2(b)(2) supra.

100. See State v. Baldwin, 330 N.C. 446, 464–65, 412 S.E.2d 31, 42 (1992) (defendant armed himself and hid in closet at victim's house for purpose of killing victim); State v. Wetmore, 298 N.C. 743, 750–51, 259 S.E.2d 870, 875–76 (1979) (defendant admitted that he went to father's bedroom for purpose of killing him); State v. Sanders, 295 N.C. 361, 367–69, 245 S.E.2d 674, 679–80 (1978) (evidence would permit finding by jury that defendant goaded officer into cell for purpose of provoking fight and killing officer); State v. Martin, 24 N.C. 101, 115–17 (1841) (defendant cracked whip at victim in attempt to goad victim into deadly exchange).

101. See State v. Miller, 223 N.C. 184, 187, 25 S.E.2d 623, 625 (1943) (the aggressor in one encounter is not "deprived forever thereafter" of the right to defend himself or herself); State v. Hill, 20 N.C. 629, 632–33 (1839) (if the defendant enters the first fight with malice, and then there is a second fight on a "fresh quarrel," it cannot be said that the second fight is moved by the old grudge unless it so appears from the circumstances of the affair).

102. See supra § 3.3(b)(2).

103. See State v. Medlin, 126 N.C. 1127, 1133, 36 S.E. 344, 346 (1900); PERKINS, supra note 12, at 1130 (aggressor with murderous intent must remove any "just appre-

If, however, the person first assaulted responds so fiercely and suddenly that the defendant does not have the opportunity to manifest an intent to withdraw, the defendant must abide by the consequences of his or her original aggression. The law does not permit an aggressor with murderous intent to act in self-defense even if his or her life is imperiled.[104] The withdrawal requirements here are more exacting than the withdrawal requirements applicable to aggressors *without* murderous intent (see § 3.3(d)(2), below).

### (d) Aggressors without Murderous Intent

An aggressor without murderous intent loses the right of perfect self-defense. If such a person kills without withdrawing—even if the killing is reasonably necessary to avoid death or great bodily injury—he or she may claim only imperfect self-defense.[105] This section describes the different types of aggressors without murderous intent and the ways they regain the right of perfect self-defense.

### *(1) Types of Aggressors without Murderous Intent*

The courts have identified three ways that a person may be an aggressor without murderous intent. They are

1. by assault or battery,
2. by mutual willingness to fight, and
3. by language or conduct calculated and intended to bring about a fight.

Each of these categories covers behavior that is a criminal offense in its own right or a close analog of a criminal offense.[106]

---

hension" from adversary); MODEL PENAL CODE AND COMMENTARIES, *supra* note 73, § 3.04 & cmt. 4(b) (if aggressor with murderous intent withdraws and other person continues fight, other person is considered responsible for renewing encounter).

104. *See* State v. Hensley, 94 N.C. 1021, 1035 (1886); State v. Brittain, 89 N.C. 481, 499–500 (1883); PERKINS, *supra* note 12, at 1129–30.

105. *See supra* § 3.3(a).

106. *See* State v. Crisp, 170 N.C. 785, 790–91, 87 S.E. 511, 513–14 (1916), *cited with approval in* State v. Potter, 295 N.C. 126, 144 n.2, 244 S.E.2d 397, 409 n.2 (1978). Conceivably, a person could be considered an aggressor without murderous intent for conduct that does not strictly fit within one of the listed categories if the person's conduct otherwise shows that he or she was an aggressor. *See supra* § 3.3(b) (discussing general features of aggressors). For example, in some instances, a trespasser could occupy the same status as an aggressor without murderous

The first two categories require some show of physical force, either actual or attempted. The offense of *assault* requires some overt act by the defendant, such as striking another person or attempting to strike another person.[107] The cases considering a person to be an aggressor by assault or battery impose a similar requirement.[108] "Mutual willingness to fight" refers to one form of the offense of *affray*. A defendant falls within this category of aggressor if he or she voluntarily engages in a fight without lawful excuse.[109]

An "aggressor by language or conduct calculated and intended to provoke a fight" is the most inexact of the types of aggressors without murderous intent. Although provoking a fight is also a form of affray, it does not necessarily involve a show of force by the defendant.[110] Apparently in an effort to circumscribe the scope of this category, the court has emphasized that the defendant's language or conduct must be both calculated *and* intended to provoke a fight.[111] The courts have not defined this principle further, however, applying it on a case-by-case basis to the defendant's behavior.[112]

---

intent. *See infra* § 3.5(b) (discussing relationship of aggressor and retreat principles when person is in a place where he or she does not have "a right to be").

107. *See generally* Thomas H. Thornburg, North Carolina Crimes: A Guidebook on the Elements of Crime 76 (4th ed. 1996) [hereinafter North Carolina Crimes].

108. *See, e.g.,* State v. Tyson, 242 N.C. 574, 575, 577, 89 S.E.2d 138, 139–40 (1955) (defendant drew hand back as if to strike woman who was accompanying deceased); State v. Demai, 227 N.C. 657, 664, 44 S.E.2d 218, 222–23 (1947) (defendant had high-powered rifle in his hand and asserted his intention of immediately killing deceased); State v. Hamilton, 77 N.C. App. 506, 513–14, 335 S.E.2d 506, 511 (1985) (defendant pulled out pistol while threatening to kill deceased), *rev. denied*, 315 N.C. 593, 341 S.E.2d 33 (1986).

109. State v. Ritter, 239 N.C. 89, 92–93, 79 S.E.2d 164, 165–66 (1953) (evidence sufficient to show that defendant willingly entered affray; nonsuit denied); State v. Crisp, 170 N.C. 785, 790–91, 87 S.E. 511, 514 (1916) (giving basic definition). At one time, one of the elements of an affray was that the fight occur in a public place. Even if this element is still required for the *offense* of affray, it is not required to show that a person was an aggressor by mutual willingness to fight. *Compare* North Carolina Crimes, *supra* note 107, at 311 (indicating that a fight in a public place is an element of this form of affray) *with Crisp*, 170 N.C. at 791, 87 S.E. at 514 (1916) (stating that a fight in a public place is not necessary to show a mutual willingness to fight for purposes of self-defense).

110. *See* North Carolina Crimes, *supra* note 107, at 311; *Crisp*, 170 N.C. at 791, 87 S.E. at 514.

111. *See* State v. Robinson, 213 N.C. 273, 280, 195 S.E. 824, 829 (1938); *accord* State v. Watson, 287 N.C. 147, 156, 214 S.E.2d 85, 91 (1975).

112. *See, e.g.,* State v. Terry, 329 N.C. 191, 194, 198–99, 404 S.E.2d 658, 659, 662–63 (1991) (defendant said, "Come on, you son of a bitch, if you get out [of the car]

## (2)  Regaining the Right of Perfect Self-Defense

At least on the surface, aggressors *without* murderous intent regain their rights to perfect self-defense in the same manner as aggressors *with* murderous intent. First, they regain the right of perfect self-defense once the encounter ends.[113] Second, they regain their rights by "withdrawing" from the conflict—that is, by quitting the combat and giving notice to the other side.[114]

Unlike aggressors with murderous intent, however, aggressors without murderous intent need not withdraw in a manner that removes all "reasonable apprehension" from their adversary. It is sufficient if they attempt to withdraw and signal this intent to their adversary.[115] Further, some North Carolina cases suggest that a defendant who acts

---

I'll shoot you"; evidence sufficient to support aggressor instruction); State v. Benton, 299 N.C. 16, 260 S.E.2d 917 (1980) (nonsuit denied; majority finds that words spoken by defendant were sufficient to show defendant was aggressor, and dissent finds words insufficient); State v. Spaulding, 298 N.C. 149, 155, 257 S.E.2d 391, 395 (1979) (defendant said he wanted no trouble and did not want to hurt victim; "this is not language tending to incite an affray"); State v. Porter, 238 N.C. 735, 735–37, 78 S.E.2d 910, 910–11 (1953) (defendant, while intoxicated, walked up on victim's porch, cursed repeatedly, and called the victim vile names in front of the victim's nine-year-old daughter; evidence was sufficient to show defendant was aggressor); State v. Rowe, 155 N.C. 436, 445–56, 71 S.E. 332, 335–36 (1911) (court finds that it was for jury to decide whether defendant's words, in light of past quarrels between parties, were calculated and intended to bring on fight); State v. Temples, 74 N.C. App. 106, 109, 327 S.E.2d 266, 268 (insufficient evidence that defendant used any abusive or provocative language), *rev. denied*, 314 N.C. 121, 332 S.E.2d 489 (1985).

113. *See supra* § 3.3(b)(2) (discussing principle that encounters must be analyzed separately), § 3.3(c)(2) (discussing right of aggressor *with* murderous intent to use defensive force once earlier encounter ends).

114. State v. Bost, 192 N.C. 1, 2–3, 133 S.E. 176, 176–77 (1926). *Accord* State v. Correll, 228 N.C. 28, 44 S.E.2d 334 (1947) (defendant was trying to leave and said that he was not angry and had meant no offense); State v. Fairley, 227 N.C. 134, 135–36, 41 S.E.2d 88, 89 (1947) (evidence showed that defendant was trying to quit combat and was endeavoring so to notify deceased; defendant was backing up and motioning with hand for deceased to go back also); State v. Ramey, 4 N.C. App. 469, 470–71, 166 S.E.2d 868, 869–70 (1969) (evidence showed that defendant went into home after arguing with deceased and got his gun and shot deceased only after he saw deceased coming toward defendant's home with gun and asked deceased "not to do it").

115. *See* State v. Winford, 279 N.C. 58, 67–69, 181 S.E.2d 423, 429–30 (1971) (withdrawal does not necessarily require physical withdrawal, but defendant must make attempt in good faith to withdraw and in some manner make his intention known to adversary).

without murderous intent need not even attempt to withdraw if the person assaulted resorts to deadly force so suddenly that the defendant cannot withdraw without risking death or great bodily injury.[116] For example, if Mary slaps John, and John responds so swiftly with deadly force that Mary cannot withdraw in safety, Mary may kill in perfect self-defense. Other North Carolina cases are to the contrary, however, indicating that aggressors without murderous intent must still attempt to withdraw even though they would risk death or great bodily injury by doing so.[117]

## § 3.4   The Excessive Force Requirement

> *Defendant did not use excessive force, i.e., did not use more force than was necessary or reasonably appeared to him to be necessary under the circumstances to protect himself from death or great bodily harm.*
>
>            —State v. Norris

### (a) Purpose of the Excessive Force Requirement

The above provision, prohibiting the use of excessive force, is the fourth and last element of the *Norris* test.[118] Unlike the aggressor element, which in some circumstances completely deprives a defendant of the right to act in self-defense, the excessive force element acts

---

116. *See* State v. Washington, 234 N.C. 531, 535, 67 S.E.2d 498, 501 (1951) (approving, in dicta, instruction to effect stated in text); State v. Kennedy, 91 N.C. 572, 578 (1884) (in course of discussing retreat, court suggests that person in mutual conflict—i.e., aggressor by mutual affray—may kill if adversary assails person so fiercely that person cannot yield without risking death or enormous bodily injury); State v. Ingold, 49 N.C. 217, 220–21 (1856) (if prisoner willingly entered fight and was "sorely pressed," killing would be excusable homicide and not manslaughter; court construes "sorely pressed" to mean being "put to wall" or being placed in situation where prisoner would have died or suffered great bodily harm). *See also* PERKINS, *supra* note 12, at 1128–29 & n.91 (agreeing with principle stated in text).

117. *See* State v. Winford, 279 N.C. 58, 67–69, 181 S.E.2d 423, 429–30 (1971); State v. Kennedy, 169 N.C. 326, 331–32, 85 S.E. 42, 44–45 (1915) (disapproving *Ingold, supra* note 116).

118. *See* State v. Norris, 303 N.C. 526, 530, 279 S.E.2d 570, 572–73 (1981). The *Norris* test is discussed in general in §§ 2.2(c), 3.1 *supra*.

only as a partial limitation in homicide cases. If the defendant uses excessive force, but meets the first two elements of the *Norris* test and is not an aggressor with murderous intent, he or she would be guilty of no more than voluntary manslaughter.

This doctrine is firmly established in North Carolina, appearing in numerous decisions before and after *Norris*. On the one hand, the courts have looked to the excessive force requirement as a basis for mitigating murder to manslaughter. Thus, in cases in which the defendant was convicted of murder, the appellate courts have found that the trial court erred in not instructing the jury that it could return a verdict of voluntary manslaughter if the defendant used excessive force but otherwise acted in proper self-defense.[119] On the other hand, the courts have relied on the excessive force requirement to justify imposing some criminal liability and denying complete acquittal. Thus, in cases in which the defendant was convicted of voluntary manslaughter, the appellate courts have refused to reverse the conviction in light of evidence that the defendant used excessive force.[120]

Despite its place in North Carolina jurisprudence, however, the excessive force element has been difficult to apply. The principal difficulty has been with distinguishing the requirement that the defendant's force *not be excessive*, or unreasonable, from the reasonable belief requirement embodied in the second element of *Norris*. Section 3.4(b), below, examines two different interpretations of the excessive force element that appear in North Carolina case law, each of which presents its own analytical difficulties. Section 3.4(c) discusses recent cases in which the court was asked to address the overlap in the second and fourth elements of the *Norris* test. The court now appears to take the position that the second element measures whether the defendant had a reasonable belief in the need to protect himself or herself from death or

---

119. *See, e.g.,* State v. Ferrell, 300 N.C. 157, 163–64, 265 S.E.2d 210, 214 (1980) (error not to instruct jury of possibility of mitigating murder to manslaughter based on theory that defendant used excessive force in self-defense); State v. Rummage, 280 N.C. 51, 58, 185 S.E.2d 221, 226 (1971) (to same effect); State v. McConnaughey, 66 N.C. App. 92, 95–98, 311 S.E.2d 26, 28–30 (1984) (to same effect).

120. *See, e.g.,* State v. Cooper, 273 N.C. 51, 57–58, 159 S.E.2d 309 (1968) (evidence sufficient for state to resist nonsuit and warrant defendant's conviction of voluntary manslaughter); State v. Moxley, 78 N.C. App. 551, 556, 338 S.E.2d 122, 125 (1985) (evidence sufficient for state to resist nonsuit and warrant conviction of voluntary manslaughter), *rev. denied,* 316 N.C. 384, 342 S.E.2d 904 (1986). *See also* State v. Marshall, 208 N.C. 127, 129–30, 179 S.E. 427, 428 (1935) (instructions properly explained that defendant would be guilty of manslaughter if he used excessive force).

great bodily injury. The fourth element considers whether the defendant used a reasonable amount of force to ward off the perceived harm.[121]

### (b) Types of Excessive Force

To understand the purpose of the excessive force element, it is useful to distinguish between *legally* excessive and *factually* excessive force. Force can be said to be *legally* excessive when

1. the defendant uses deadly force in the belief that such force is necessary to prevent a particular harm, such as the loss of property, but
2. the law does not permit the use of deadly force against that type of harm.

Force can be said to be *factually* excessive when

1. the defendant uses deadly force in the belief that such force is necessary to prevent a particular harm, and
2. the law allows the defendant to use deadly force to prevent the harm, but
3. the defendant's perception of the facts is unreasonable. [122]

### (1) "Legally" Excessive Force

Some North Carolina cases have used the term *excessive* to describe situations in which the defendant's use of force was *legally* excessive. For example, the North Carolina courts have held that deadly force is "excessive as a matter of law" to prevent mere bodily harm or offensive contact.[123] In other words, the law does not permit the use of deadly force to avert bodily harm or offensive contact. Similarly the use of deadly force to prevent the theft of property is legally excessive because such force exceeds the amount of force allowed under the law to defend property.[124]

---

121. *See* State v. Richardson, 341 N.C. 585, 461 S.E.2d 724 (1995), *rev'g* 112 N.C. App. 252, 435 S.E.2d 84 (1993), discussed further in § 3.4(c)(3) *infra*.

122. This distinction between legally excessive and factually excessive force is based largely on Robinson's analysis of the types of mistakes that a person may make in using defensive force. *See* 2 ROBINSON, *supra* note 9, at 408–09.

123. State v. Hunter, 315 N.C. 371, 373–74, 338 S.E.2d 99, 102 (1986); *accord* State v. Clay, 297 N.C. 555, 563, 256 S.E.2d 176, 182 (1979).

124. *See* State v. Lee, 258 N.C. 44, 46–47, 127 S.E.2d 774, 776 (1962) (person has

Despite the court's reference to the term *excessive* in the above circumstances, it does not appear that the court meant to use the term in the sense of the fourth element of *Norris*. The limitations on the use of deadly force are intended precisely for the purpose of preventing the taking of human life to avert comparatively minor harms. Robinson puts the matter succinctly in the following example:

> Where [a defendant] has no other option but deadly force to prevent the stealing of apples from his orchard, a jurisdiction that prohibits deadly force to protect property essentially requires him to sacrifice his apples out of regard for the thieves' lives.[125]

It therefore seems unlikely that the North Carolina courts would allow a person to claim an imperfect defensive-force defense, and thereby mitigate murder to manslaughter, when the person's force is legally excessive. Rather, having used deadly force when the applicable defense prohibits such force, the person would lose the protection of that defense entirely.[126]

### (2) "Factually" Excessive Force

The North Carolina courts have more often used the term *excessive* to describe situations in which the defendant's force was *factually* excessive. Numerous cases have described the force used by defendants

---

right to use force to prevent injury to or loss of personal property, but human life must not be endangered or great bodily harm inflicted); State v. Morgan, 25 N.C. 186, 193 (1842) (a person may not kill or cause great bodily injury to prevent a mere trespass; such force is justified only to save life or limb, prevent a great crime, or accomplish a necessary public duty).

125. *See* 2 Robinson, *supra* note 9, at 5. Limitations on the use of deadly force are discussed generally in § 2.2(b)(1) *supra*.

126. A person may be able to claim heat of passion in an appropriate case and still mitigate murder to manslaughter, but that topic is beyond the scope of this book.

Some jurisdictions recognize a mistake-of-law defense when the defendant uses *legally* excessive force. Such a defense allows a defendant to assert that he or she was operating under a reasonable but mistaken belief that the law authorized the use of deadly force to avert the particular harm. *See* 2 LaFave, *supra* note 9, at 273 & nn.11–12; 2 Robinson, *supra* note 9, at 414–18. Currently, North Carolina recognizes as a mitigating factor in sentencing that the defendant "reasonably believed that [his or her] conduct was legal." G.S. 15A-1340.16(e)(10).

as excessive when the defendants believed that they needed to kill to avoid death or serious bodily injury but either their perception of the threat of death or great bodily injury, or the amount of force used in response, were unreasonable.[127] Under this construction of excessive force, however, it was difficult to distinguish the fourth element of the *Norris* test from the second. The courts appeared to take the position that defendants failed the second element if either their belief in the threat of death or great bodily injury or their belief in the need for force in response was unreasonable.

This overlap in elements two and four made it difficult to determine when imperfect self-defense was an appropriate defense and voluntary manslaughter an appropriate verdict. The crux of the dilemma was that a jury could find the defendant's actions *unreasonable*, yet reach two different verdicts depending on whether it focused on the second or fourth element of *Norris*. If the jury found the defendant's actions unreasonable under the second element of *Norris*, it could reject the defendant's claim of perfect *and* imperfect self-defense and convict the defendant of first-degree murder. If the jury found the defendant's actions unreasonable under the fourth element only, it could allow the defendant's claim of imperfect self-defense and convict the defendant of voluntary manslaughter.

Similarly, a determination that the defendant's force was *reasonable* could lead to either acquittal or conviction of voluntary manslaughter. If a jury found the defendant's actions reasonable under the second *and* fourth elements of *Norris*, it could acquit the defendant. If it found the defendant's force reasonable under the second

---

127. *See, e.g.,* State v. Ferrell, 300 N.C. 157, 163–64, 265 S.E.2d 210, 214 (1980) (evidence indicated that deceased attacked defendant with box cutter; it was for jury to decide whether force used by defendant in response was unreasonable so as to reduce crime to voluntary manslaughter); State v. Ray, 299 N.C. 151, 158–59, 261 S.E.2d 789, 794 (1980) (evidence suggested that victim was retreating and no longer presented threat to defendant when defendant shot him; such evidence could support verdict of voluntary manslaughter on ground that force used was excessive); State v. Cooper, 273 N.C. 51, 58, 159 S.E.2d 305, 310 (1968) (it was for jury to decide whether defendant was guilty of voluntary manslaughter by using more force than was or "reasonably appeared necessary under the circumstances to protect himself from death or great bodily harm"); State v. Oden, 72 N.C. App. 360, 362–63, 324 S.E.2d 285, 287 (evidence was sufficient for jury to convict defendant of voluntary manslaughter where evidence indicated that defendant may have used more force than was reasonably necessary to protect himself from death or great bodily harm), *rev. denied,* 313 N.C. 609, 330 S.E.2d 614 (1985).

element and unreasonable under the fourth element, it could return a verdict of voluntary manslaughter.

In a series of recent cases before the supreme court, discussed below, defendants challenged the wording of the instructions given to the jury. They argued that the instructions did not adequately distinguish between the second and fourth elements of the *Norris* test and therefore did not adequately apprise the jury of when it should return a verdict of voluntary manslaughter based on imperfect self-defense.[128] In the first two cases, the court turned back the defendant's arguments. In a third case, *State v. Watson,* the court appeared to modify the *Norris* elements in part. Then, in *State v. Richardson,* the court disavowed *Watson* and came up with another solution to the problem of distinguishing elements two and four.

### (c) Proposals to Modify Imperfect Self-Defense

### *(1) "Honest but Unreasonable" Force*

The first case to reach the court on this issue was *State v. McAvoy.*[129] There the defendant urged the court to modify the rules of imperfect self-defense and require that instructions to the jury reflect those changes. The defendant argued that a person should be able to claim imperfect self-defense when his or her belief is *honest* within the meaning of the first element of *Norris,* but *unreasonable* within the meaning of the second element. The defendant argued that such an approach provided a rational basis for distinguishing between situations calling for a verdict of first-degree murder and those calling only for voluntary manslaughter. The defendant reasoned further that this approach properly reflected the difference in culpability between someone who kills without any belief in the need for defensive force and someone who kills out of an *honest but unreasonable* belief that his or her actions are necessary. In the latter situation, the defendant argued, the person has not acted with the malice required for murder and should be held liable only for voluntary manslaughter. Some jurisdictions have accepted

---

128. Typically, the overlap in the two elements has not affected trial courts' decisions about whether to submit instructions to the jury on imperfect self-defense. The case law suggests that when the evidence supports an instruction on perfect self-defense, trial courts ordinarily should submit instructions on both perfect and imperfect self-defense. *See infra* § 8.4(a).

129. 331 N.C. 583, 595–601, 417 S.E.2d 489, 497–501 (1992).

this position.[130] And at least some cases in North Carolina before *McAvoy* appeared to agree.[131]

The supreme court rejected the argument, however, adhering to those decisions holding that a defendant must meet the first two elements of the *Norris* test to be eligible for imperfect self-defense.[132] The court either distinguished or disapproved cases suggesting that an *honest but unreasonable* belief could reduce murder to manslaughter. The court did not, however, explain how to differentiate between *unreasonable force* within the meaning of the second element of *Norris* and *excessive force* within the meaning of the fourth.

The issue again came before the court in *State v. Potts*.[133] There the defendant argued that the instructions should have permitted the jury to return a verdict of voluntary manslaughter upon finding (1) that it was reasonable for the defendant to have used deadly force against the victim at the outset of the encounter, but (2) that the defendant continued to use deadly force after it was no longer reasonably necessary to do so. This approach, according to the defendant, provided at least some basis for distinguishing between the second and fourth elements of *Norris*. Some support for the defendant's argument can be found in earlier cases, in which the supreme court ruled in similar circumstances that the evidence was sufficient to warrant jury instructions on voluntary manslaughter based on an excessive-force theory.[134]

---

130. *See* 1 LaFave, *supra* note 9, at 663 & n.84 (referring to this approach as the "more humane view" and citing North Carolina as a state that seemed to take the same position); 2 *id.* at 271–72 (collecting cases from other jurisdictions); Douglas M. Jarrell, Recent Case, *Criminal Law—Imperfect Self-Defense—State v. McAvoy*, 71 N.C. L. Rev. 1954, 1960 n.52 (1993) (collecting cases from other jurisdictions).

131. *See, e.g.*, State v. Jones, 299 N.C. 103, 112, 261 S.E.2d 1, 8 (1980); State v. Woods, 278 N.C. 210, 217–18, 179 S.E.2d 358, 363 (1971); State v. Thomas, 184 N.C. 757, 761–62, 114 S.E. 834, 836–37 (1922); State v. Best, 79 N.C. App. 734, 737, 340 S.E.2d 524, 526–27 (1986); State v. Clark, 65 N.C. App. 286, 288, 308 S.E.2d 913, 915 (1983), *rev. denied*, 310 N.C. 627, 315 S.E.2d 693 (1984).

132. State v. Maynor, 331 N.C. 695, 698–700, 417 S.E.2d 453, 455–56 (1992), decided the same day as *McAvoy*, reached the same result.

133. 334 N.C. 575, 579–80, 433 S.E.2d 736, 738 (1993).

134. *See, e.g.*, State v. Tyson, 242 N.C. 574, 577–78, 89 S.E.2d 138, 140 (1955) (jury could find that defendant used excessive force by continuing to shoot the deceased as deceased was running away); State v. Robinson, 188 N.C. 784, 785–86, 125 S.E. 617, 618–19 (1924) (jury could have found that first shot by defendant, in response to shot by victim, was in self-defense and that subsequent shots were unnecessary and excessive; trial court therefore erred in failing to submit voluntary manslaughter as possible verdict); State v. Cox, 153 N.C. 638, 644–45, 69 S.E. 419, 422 (1910) (jury could find defendant used excessive force by continuing to fire

The court in *Potts* rejected the defendant's argument. The court found that once it was no longer reasonable for the defendant to believe that he was in danger, his continued use of deadly force was not protected by the doctrine of perfect or imperfect self-defense. Again, however, the court did not articulate the difference between unreasonable force and excessive force.

### (2) Distinguishing "Deadly Force" from "Force Resulting in Death"

In a third case, *State v. Watson,* the court addressed the issue again.[135] There the defendant focused on the "belief" formulation contained in the first two elements of the *Norris* test. The trial court instructed the jury that the defendant had to believe in the *need to kill* under the first element and that the defendant's belief had to be *reasonable* under the second element. The defendant argued that the instructions should have been phrased in terms of the *need for deadly force.* Under this approach, the first element would require only that the defendant actually, or honestly, believe in the need for some degree of deadly force, and the second element would turn on whether *that* belief was reasonable.[136]

This change, according to the defendant, would serve to distinguish the second and fourth elements of the *Norris* test. A jury could find that some degree of deadly force was reasonably necessary under the second element—for example, firing one shot at a nonvital part of the body—but that the amount of deadly force used was excessive under the fourth element—for example, firing four shots into the heart. The court appeared to accept this argument. It held that when there is evidence that the defendant intended to use deadly force but not to kill the victim, it would be appropriate to instruct the jury "in terms of the need for deadly force" under the first two elements of *Norris* and "in terms of whether the amount of deadly force used was excessive" under the fourth element of *Norris.*[137]

---

when not reasonably necessary); State v. Quick, 150 N.C. 820, 825, 64 S.E. 168, 170 (1909) (to same effect).

135. 338 N.C. 168, 449 S.E.2d 694 (1994), *cert. denied,* __ U.S. __, 115 S. Ct. 1708, 131 L. Ed. 2d 569 (1995).

136. The impact of this interpretation on the first two elements of the *Norris* test is discussed in §§ 3.2(b)(3) and (4) *supra.*

137. 338 N.C. at 182–83, 449 S.E.2d at 703.

The *Watson* approach left open a number of questions, however. One was how the jury should distinguish between deadly force intended to disable and deadly force designed to kill. The law defines "deadly force" as force "likely to kill or cause serious bodily harm."[138] If the circumstances warrant the use of force "likely to kill or cause serious bodily harm," it is not entirely clear when achieving one of those results—namely, the death of the attacker—would be excessive.[139] Also, what of defendants who believed in the need to use deadly force to kill, not just to disable? *Watson* did not address how to distinguish the second and fourth elements in such cases.

These issues became moot, however, with the next major self-defense decision issued by the supreme court, *State v. Richardson*.[140]

### (3) Refining Element One to Distinguish Elements Two and Four

In *Richardson*, the court again looked at the belief requirement contained in the first element of the *Norris* test. The court disavowed the approach it took in *Watson* and came up with a different interpretation. The *Richardson* approach resolves a number of questions about the meaning of the first element, although it raises others concerning the proper wording of jury instructions on that element [discussed at length above, in § 3.2(b)(4)]. The court's interpretation of the first element is relevant here because it affects how the second and fourth elements of the *Norris* test should be applied.

The *Richardson* court essentially rephrased the first *Norris* element as follows:

> The defendant must believe in the need to protect himself or herself from death or great bodily injury.[141]

---

138. *See supra* § 2.2(b)(2).

139. *Cf.* Brown v. United States, 256 U.S. 335, 343, 41 S. Ct. 501, 502, 65 L. Ed. 961, 963 (1921) (Holmes, J.) ("[I]n this court, at least, it is not a condition of immunity [based on self-defense] that one . . . should pause to consider whether a reasonable man might not think it possible to fly with safety, or to disable his assailant rather than to kill him.").

140. 341 N.C. 585, 461 S.E.2d 724 (1995), *rev'g* 112 N.C. App. 252, 435 S.E.2d 84 (1993).

141. 341 N.C. at 593, 461 S.E.2d at 729. The text paraphrases the court's language: "[T]he focus in elements one and two is on the reasonableness of defendant's belief that he must protect himself from death or great bodily harm, not the force used by the defendant."

This formulation essentially requires two beliefs of a defendant: that he or she (1) is faced with death or great bodily injury and (2) needs to protect himself or herself from that threat of harm. Previous formulations of the first element also required two beliefs of a defendant, but the second belief differed. Previously, a defendant had to believe in the need to use a specific level of force. The *Norris* decision itself could be read as requiring the defendant to have believed in the need "to kill" to avoid death or great bodily injury. In *Watson*, the parties wrangled over whether the defendant had to believe in the need "to kill" or just in the need "to use deadly force." In contrast, the *Richardson* formulation requires only that a defendant have believed in the need *to protect* himself or herself from death or great bodily injury. This places the emphasis on what the defendant perceived rather than on how he or she chose to respond.

The supreme court in *Richardson* recognized that the phrasing of the first *Norris* element affects the application of the second element. The second element essentially provides that the belief required under the first element must be reasonable. Under *Richardson*, the first element no longer requires a belief in the need for a specific level of force, so the second element no longer considers whether a reasonable person would have believed such force to be necessary. As the court stated:

> The instrumentality or method of force employed by defendant which ultimately results in the victim's death is irrelevant for purposes of determining the reasonableness of defendant's belief under element two.[142]

The amount of force used by the defendant remains critical, but under element four (the excessive force element) and not element two:

> The fourth element of self-defense addresses the reasonableness of the defendant's choice of force used to protect himself from death or great bodily harm.[143]

This approach provides some basis for distinguishing the second element of *Norris* from the fourth element. Element two now focuses primarily on the reasonableness of the defendant's belief that he or she was in danger of death or great bodily injury. Element four considers the reasonableness of the force that the defendant used to avoid the perceived threat. Thus, if A kills B based on an unreasonable belief that B poses a threat of death or great bodily injury, A fails element two

---

142. *Id.* at 590, 461 S.E.2d at 728.
143. *Id.* at 592–93, 461 S.E.2d at 729.

and loses all right of self-defense. If A's belief about the threat posed by B is reasonable, but A uses an unreasonable amount of force to avoid the threat, A satisfies element two but fails element four. Then, A may rely on imperfect, but not perfect, self-defense.

Although the object of the inquiries under elements two and four differ, both employ the same general standard of reasonableness. Under element two, the test of reasonableness is a combination of subjective and objective factors. The same is true under element four. A defendant's use of force would not be excessive if in the circumstances as they appeared to the defendant (the subjective part), a reasonable person would have considered it necessary to use the amount of force used by the defendant (the objective part). The same considerations that go into determining the reasonableness of a defendant's belief under element two—such as the fierceness of the attack on the defendant or the attacker's reputation for violence—also bear on the reasonableness of the defendant's use of force under element four.[144]

The biggest question left open in *Richardson* is how it affects instructions to the jury on self-defense. The decision primarily concerns the wording of instructions on the first element of the *Norris* test, not the second and fourth elements. It should be noted here, however, that the phrasing of the first element ultimately determines whether the jury will be able to distinguish between the second and fourth elements. In *Richardson,* the defendant argued that the trial court should have substituted "to use deadly force" for "to kill" in instructing the jury on the first *Norris* element. Clearly, the supreme court disapproved of the proposed modification. What is less clear is whether other modifications must be made. On the one hand, the supreme court in *Richardson* let stand the trial court's instructions, which phrased the first element in terms of a belief in the need to kill. On the other hand, the court in *Richardson* was asked only to consider the "deadly force" modification requested by the defendant. Although the supreme court held that trial courts need not use the proposed instructions, other modifications would still seem appropriate in light of the supreme court's reasoning. For example, after *Richardson,* instructions might read that the defendant must have believed in the need *to protect* himself or herself from death or great bodily injury (pursuant to element one), that such a

---

144. For a discussion of the reasonable belief requirement, *see supra* § 3.2(c); for a discussion of the types of evidence that may bear on reasonableness, *see infra* §§ 7.2 and 7.3.

belief must have been reasonable (pursuant to element two), and that the amount of force used by the defendant must not have been excessive (pursuant to element four).[145]


## § 3.5  The Duty to Retreat

### (a)  Is There a Duty to Retreat in North Carolina?

The four-part *Norris* test governs whether a person has the right to kill in self-defense.[146] This section considers whether North Carolina imposes a *duty to retreat* in addition to those requirements.

The duty to retreat is commonly understood to mean that a person must retreat, if he or she can do so in safety, before killing in self-defense. Only when a person's "back is at the wall," in the sense that further retreat would be unsafe, may a person kill in self-defense (assuming the other requirements for killing in self-defense are met). Since aggressors are already under an obligation to withdraw from the encounter, this duty primarily affects nonaggressors—those not at fault in bringing about the conflict. Consequently, in jurisdictions imposing a duty to retreat, both aggressors and nonaggressors must take some action to disengage from the encounter.[147]

*Does North Carolina require a person who was not the aggressor to retreat before killing in self-defense?* One line of cases says no. Several decisions provide that a person may kill or use a lesser degree of *deadly* force, without retreating, if the person was not the aggressor and the other elements of self-defense are satisfied. The courts also have held that a person who is not the aggressor may use *nondeadly* force without retreating if the other elements of self-defense are

---

145. The impact of *Richardson* on self-defense instructions is discussed further in § 3.2(b)(4) *supra*.

146. The *Norris* test is discussed generally in §§ 2.2(c), 3.1 *supra*.

147. *See* Perkins, *supra* note 12, at 1133; 1 LaFave, *supra* note 9, at 659–61. It is not clear how the doctrines of *withdrawal* and *retreat* differ in terms of the physical requirements imposed on a defendant, but it appears that the former imposes a greater obligation. For example, an aggressor with murderous intent must withdraw from the encounter even if unsafe to do so, while persons required to retreat must do so only when safe. The difference is not so clear, however, for aggressors without murderous intent since such persons may not need to withdraw when unsafe to do so. *See supra* §§ 3.3(c)(2), (d)(2) for a further discussion of withdrawal requirements applicable to aggressors.

satisfied. Taken together, these cases would appear to exhaust the circumstances in which a person might be required to retreat. This result is consistent with the view of the majority of jurisdictions. It appears that all jurisdictions allow a nonaggressor to use *nondeadly* force in self-defense without retreating and that a majority of jurisdictions allow a nonaggressor to use *deadly* force without retreating.[148]

A second line of cases suggests, however, that North Carolina follows the minority view: that, subject to certain exceptions, a person must retreat before using *deadly* force in self-defense. This position is suggested by cases involving self-defense within the home or business. In numerous instances the North Carolina courts have held that the trial court must instruct the jury that a defendant need not retreat before using deadly force when the encounter occurs within his or her home or business. Such rulings imply that a person *does* have a duty to retreat in conflicts *outside* the home or business, a proposition contradicted by the first line of cases.[149]

Before reviewing how these two lines of cases developed and whether they can be reconciled (see § 3.5(c), below), it is useful to consider the themes common to both.

### (b) Common Themes

Whichever line of cases on retreat is controlling, both have one main restriction—namely, that a person is entitled to stand his or her ground only if he or she is not at fault in the encounter.[150] The circumstances that would render a person at fault, requiring the person to retreat, appear to be the same as the circumstances that would make a person an aggressor under the third element of the *Norris* test, requir-

---

148. 1 LaFave, *supra* note 9, at 659–60.

149. Based on this second line of cases, some writers have assumed that North Carolina law requires a person to retreat except in specified circumstances, such as when the conflict occurs within the home or business. *See, e.g.,* Rachel V. Lee, Note, *Criminal Law—A Further Erosion of the Retreat Rule in North Carolina,* 12 Wake Forest L. Rev. 1093 (1976). They so concluded, however, without considering the effect of decisions holding that a nonaggressor does not have a duty to retreat before using deadly *or* nondeadly force.

150. *See, e.g.,* State v. Pearson, 288 N.C. 34, 39–40, 215 S.E.2d 598, 603 (1975) (defendant need not retreat within home or business if without fault); State v. Washington, 234 N.C. 531, 534–35, 67 S.E.2d 498, 500 (1951) (defendant need not retreat in face of murderous assault if without fault).

ing the person to withdraw.[151] This approach ensures that a person who is the aggressor in an encounter cannot avoid his or her obligation to withdraw by claiming that he or she did not have to retreat.

This limitation may have more theoretical than practical significance, however. When the evidence is in conflict over whether the defendant was the aggressor, the jury must ultimately decide the defendant's status. Consequently, the trial court must still instruct the jury that the defendant, if not the aggressor, was not obligated to retreat.[152]

Some cases also suggest that a person is under an obligation to retreat if the person is in a place where he or she does not have a "right to be."[153] This language, however, is merely a corollary of the principle that a person must be free from fault in the encounter. For example, suppose the defendant is trespassing on another's property and refuses to leave when requested by the owner. The owner would have the right to use reasonable, nondeadly force to evict the defendant; and the defendant, having aggressively and willingly entered into the conflict

---

151. *See generally* PERKINS, *supra* note 12, at 1132–33. The aggressor element of *Norris* is discussed in § 3.3 *supra*.

152. *See* State v. Lilley, 318 N.C. 390, 392–94, 348 S.E.2d 788, 790–91 (1986), *aff'g* 78 N.C. App. 100, 105–07, 337 S.E.2d 89, 93 (1985) (court of appeals and supreme court both find that trial court erred in failing to give no-duty-to-retreat instruction; however, because reasonable juror could have found that defendant was aggressor, failure to give instruction was not plain error); State v. Hearn, 88 N.C. App. 103, 106, 365 S.E.2d 206, 208 (1988) (where evidence is in conflict over whether defendant was aggressor, trial court must give no-duty-to-retreat instruction). *But cf.* State v. Watson, 338 N.C. 168, 186, 449 S.E.2d 694, 705 (1994) (court does not question trial court's decision that evidence supported instructions to jury on perfect self-defense, which suggests that evidence was in conflict over whether defendant was aggressor; yet, court finds that trial court did not err in failing to give no-duty-to-retreat instruction because evidence showed that defendant *was* aggressor), *cert. denied*, __ U.S. __, 115 S. Ct. 1708, 131 L. Ed. 2d 569 (1995); State v. Bennett, 67 N.C. App. 407, 409, 313 S.E.2d 277, 279 (to same effect), *rev. denied*, 311 N.C. 764, 321 S.E.2d 147 (1984).

153. *See* State v. Absher, 220 N.C. 126, 130–31, 16 S.E.2d 656, 659 (1941) (defendant was not necessarily trespasser, and trial court erred in not instructing on right of person to act in self-defense when person is in place where he or she has right to be); State v. Musselwhite, 54 N.C. App. 68, 75, 283 S.E.2d 149, 153 (1981) (Becton, J., dissenting) (noting "right to be" language), *aff'd per curiam*, 305 N.C. 295, 287 S.E.2d 897 (1982). *See also* PERKINS, *supra* note 12, at 1132–33 (person should be recognized as "without fault" in encounter where, among other things, person was where he had a lawful "right to be").

without legal excuse or provocation, would be considered the aggressor and would have an obligation to withdraw.[154]

A few recent cases may place an additional qualification on the right to stand one's ground—namely, that the defendant must actually have been attacked by the victim.[155] This requirement is difficult to reconcile, however, with other principles of defensive force. The question in defensive-force cases is not whether the defendant was *actually* faced with harm, but whether the defendant *reasonably believed* that the assailant posed some threat of harm. This principle is reflected in the first two elements of the *Norris* test.[156] If a court finds sufficient evidence to warrant instructions on self-defense, it necessarily has found sufficient evidence that the defendant's belief was reasonable within the meaning of *Norris*. It seems inconsistent to say that a person who reasonably perceives a threat of death or great bodily injury nevertheless has an obligation to retreat unless the evidence also shows an actual attack.[157]

---

154. The example in the text is consistent with general aggressor principles. *See supra* § 3.3(b). A person who merely goes on another's property without prior authorization is not necessarily an aggressor (or even a trespasser), although technically not in a place where he or she has a "right to be." *Cf.* NORTH CAROLINA CRIMES, *supra* note 107, at 287, 290 (interpreting elements of first- and second-degree trespass as requiring some notification to defendant that entering or remaining on premises is forbidden).

155. *See* State v. McAvoy, 331 N.C. 583, 594–95, 417 S.E.2d 489, 496–97 (1992) (majority of the supreme court finds that there was sufficient evidence to support instructions on self-defense based on theory that defendant reasonably apprehended threat of death or great bodily injury, but majority also rules that there was no evidence of an assault on the defendant and therefore no basis for instructing the jury that the defendant was not required to retreat within his place of work); State v. Williams, 100 N.C. App. 567, 572, 397 S.E.2d 364, 367 (1990) (to same effect), *rev. denied*, 328 N.C. 576, 403 S.E.2d 520 (1991).

156. *See supra* § 3.2(a) (discussing concept of reasonable, or apparent, necessity).

157. *See McAvoy*, 331 N.C. at 602, 417 S.E.2d at 501 (Mitchell, J., dissenting) (describing as "incredible" majority's determination that defendant was not entitled to a no-duty-to-retreat instruction in light of evidence showing that defendant had reasonable belief in need to defend himself); State v. Ellerbe, 223 N.C. 770, 772–73, 28 S.E.2d 519, 520–21 (1944) (trial court instructed jury that defendant had no duty to retreat if assault was actually made on him with felonious purpose; supreme court finds error because trial court failed to indicate that defendant should get benefit of this principle if he had *reasonable ground to believe* assault was made on him with felonious purpose); State v. Riley, 56 N.C. App. 461, 463, 289 S.E.2d 41, 42 (1982) (since there was ample evidence from which jury might have determined that the defendant acted in self-defense, it was error to fail to give no-duty-to-retreat instruction).

### (c) Conflicting Lines of Cases

#### (1) Line 1: Felonious and Nonfelonious Assaults

One line of cases supports the view that North Carolina does not impose any duty to retreat on a nonaggressor. To understand this line of cases, a review of the historical development of the law is necessary.

Modern self-defense law focuses on the *harm* reasonably posed to a defendant. The essential inquiry is whether the defendant reasonably believes that he or she is facing death or great bodily injury, or bodily harm or offensive physical contact, or some other harm.[158] Early self-defense law in North Carolina, however, was more closely tied to the common-law privilege of crime prevention, which was concerned with the character of the *offense* committed by the assailant. For example, in early cases applying the crime prevention privilege, North Carolina allowed a person to kill to prevent a felony, but not to prevent a misdemeanor.[159]

This distinction between felonies and misdemeanors carried over to the courts' treatment of the duty to retreat. The courts applied one rule for "felonious assaults." Beginning in 1876 the North Carolina Supreme Court held that a person who reasonably believes that he or she is faced with a "felonious assault" (also referred to in the cases as an "assault with murderous intent") may kill without retreating.[160] Isolated decisions can be found around the turn of the twentieth century, holding that a person had a duty to retreat before killing to prevent a felonious assault (decisions which drew vigorous dissents that the majority had misinterpreted prior case law).[161] After that time, however, the courts rejected any requirement of retreat against felonious assaults.[162]

---

158. *See supra* § 2.2(a) (discussing different harms triggering right to use defensive force).

159. *See* State v. Roane, 13 N.C. 58, 62 (1828); State v. Rutherford, 8 N.C. 457, 458–60 (1821). The privilege of crime prevention survives in modified form and is discussed in § 5.1 *infra*.

160. *See* State v. Dixon, 75 N.C. 275, 279–80 (1876).

161. *See* State v. Lilliston, 141 N.C. 857, 54 S.E. 427 (1906); State v. Gentry, 125 N.C. 733, 34 S.E. 706 (1899).

162. *See* State v. Watson, 338 N.C. 168, 186, 449 S.E.2d 694, 705 (1994), *cert. denied*, __ U.S. __, 115 S. Ct. 1708, 131 L. Ed. 2d 569 (1995); State v Guss, 254 N.C. 349, 351, 118 S.E.2d 906, 907 (1961); State v. Washington, 234 N.C. 531, 534–35, 67 S.E.2d 498, 500 (1951); State v. Ellerbe, 223 N.C. 770, 775, 28 S.E.2d 519, 522 (1944); State v. Godwin, 211 N.C. 419, 422, 190 S.E. 761, 763 (1937); State v. Ray, 166 N.C. 420, 430–31, 81 S.E. 1087, 1090 (1914); State v. Nixon, 117 N.C. App. 141, 150–51, 450 S.E.2d

The courts took a dual approach to "nonfelonious assaults," differentiating between simple assaults and assaults with a deadly weapon. For simple assaults, a person always could use *nondeadly* force without retreating. For nonfelonious assaults with a deadly weapon, the person assaulted could kill or use a lesser degree of *deadly* force to avoid death or great bodily injury. Before resorting to deadly force, however, the person assaulted had to retreat "to the wall."[163]

The following language, found throughout many of the older cases, signified the court's dual approach to nonfelonious assaults: "[A person] may not stand his ground and kill his adversary if there is any way of escape open to him, though he is allowed to repel force by force and give blow for blow."[164] This language meant that a person could use nondeadly force without retreating. The person also could use deadly force to defend against a nonfelonious assault with a deadly weapon, but if there were "any way of escape open," the person first had to retreat.

The courts recognized an exception to this retreat requirement when the conflict occurred within a person's home or business. The courts held that if a person were assaulted in his or her home or business, the person did not have to retreat "regardless of the character of the assault"—that is, regardless whether the assault was felonious or nonfelonious.[165] This exception did not give persons assaulted within

---

562, 567–68 (1994); State v. O'Neal, 67 N.C. App. 65, 67, 312 S.E.2d 493, 494, *modified on other grounds*, 311 N.C. 747, 321 S.E.2d 154 (1984). A few decisions suggested in dicta that a duty to retreat might exist, but none actually required retreat in the case under review. *See, e.g.,* State v. Satterwhite, 238 N.C. 674, 675, 78 S.E.2d 603, 604 (1953) (court bolsters conclusion that defendant was entitled to self-defense instruction by finding that defendant had "no way to get out"); State v. Sally, 233 N.C. 225, 226–27, 63 S.E.2d 151, 154 (1951) (court assumes that instruction providing that defendant had duty to retreat was correct as general statement of law, but finds instruction erroneous because defendant was in own home and place of business).

163. *See* State v. Blevins, 138 N.C. 668, 670–71, 50 S.E. 763, 764 (1905) (person need not retreat before using deadly force against assault made with "felonious purpose," but "[i]t is otherwise in ordinary assaults, *even with deadly weapons*"; in latter situation, person must retreat as far as consistent with safety) (emphasis added). *Accord* State v. Lucas, 164 N.C. 471, 473–74, 79 S.E. 674, 675 (1913) (quoting *Blevins* with approval); State v. Dove, 156 N.C. 653, 658, 72 S.E. 792, 794 (1911) (to same effect); *see also* State v. Glenn, 198 N.C. 79, 81, 150 S.E. 663, 664 (1929) (trial court gave instruction in accord with *Blevins*; supreme court found error, however, because defendant's back was already to the wall).

164. *See, e.g.,* State v. Bryant, 213 N.C. 752, 756, 197 S.E. 530, 532 (1938), *quoting* State v. Hough, 138 N.C. 663, 667, 50 S.E. 709, 711 (1905).

165. State v. Walker, 236 N.C. 742, 744, 73 S.E.2d 868, 870 (1953); State v. Pennell, 231 N.C. 651, 654, 58 S.E.2d 341, 342–43 (1950). *See also* State v. Harman, 78 N.C. 515, 519 (1877) (defendant, being in his own house, was not obliged to flee).

their home or business unlimited license to kill; they still could use deadly force only to avoid death or great bodily injury. The exception represented a departure, however, from the requirement that a person had to retreat before using deadly force against a potentially deadly assault classified under the law as nonfelonious.

Thus the courts recognized three categories on retreat and one exception: (1) a person could use deadly force, without retreating, against a felonious assault; (2) a person could use nondeadly force, without retreating, against a simple assault; and (3) a person could use deadly force against a nonfelonious assault with a deadly weapon, if he or she first retreated, except that a person had no duty to retreat if the conflict occurred inside the person's home or business.

The court's approach seems curious today, with the focus of self-defense law on the harm perceived by the defendant and not on the offense committed by the assailant. Because of this shift in focus, the one set of circumstances in which a defendant potentially had a duty to retreat (that is, when faced with a nonfelonious assault with a deadly weapon) has lost its significance. The courts still speak of "felonious assaults," stating that a person who reasonably apprehends such an assault may use deadly force without retreating. In the context of defensive-force cases, however, the term *felonious assault* has become a synonym for conduct sufficient to raise a reasonable apprehension of death or great bodily injury or some other threat of harm sufficient to warrant the use of deadly force in response.[166] It therefore follows from this first line of cases that a person may use deadly *or* nondeadly force, without retreating, as long as he or she is not the aggressor and meets the other requirements for the particular defensive-force defense asserted.[167]

### (2) Line 2: Home or Business

The above line of cases would appear to make it irrelevant whether a conflict occurs within or away from a person's home or business: in either circumstance a nonaggressor would not have a duty to

---

166. *See supra* § 2.2(b)(1) (discussing circumstances in which person may use deadly force).

167. *See* State v. Musselwhite, 54 N.C. App. 68, 75, 283 S.E.2d 149, 153 (1981) (Becton, J., dissenting) (in course of decision on another issue, dissent reviews history of North Carolina law and concludes that the common-law duty to retreat has been "supplanted" in this state by the doctrine that a person who is not the aggressor "may stand his ground, meet force with force, and if need be, kill his assailant"), *aff'd per curiam*, 305 N.C. 295, 287 S.E.2d 897 (1982).

retreat. Yet the North Carolina courts have continued to emphasize that defendants do not have a duty to retreat before using deadly force in their home or business, implying that they *do* have a duty to retreat elsewhere. The court's continued reliance on this principle is explainable in part as an effort to enhance the protections accorded to those places, especially the home.

The idea that "one's home is one's castle" has real meaning in the law.[168] For example, the criminal law recognizes a separate defense of habitation (discussed later in § 5.4). However, defense of habitation applies only to situations involving certain unlawful entries into the home; it does not cover all conflicts within the home. Perhaps in response to this limitation, the courts have considered a number of different ways to enhance the legal protections of persons drawn into physical conflicts inside their homes but unable to rely on defense of habitation.

Some cases have stated that when the encounter occurs inside a person's home, the person is entitled "to increase his force, so as not only to resist, but also to overcome the assault and secure himself from all harm."[169] The problem with this rule is that it provides no real additional protection to persons assaulted inside the home. Any person acting in proper self-defense has the right to secure himself or herself from all harm, regardless of the location of the conflict.[170]

A few cases also have suggested that a person may use deadly force to defend against mere bodily harm or offensive physical contact

---

168. *See* State v. Stevenson, 81 N.C. App. 409, 412, 344 S.E.2d 334, 335 (1986) ("The 'castle doctrine' is derived from the principle that one's home is one's castle and is based on the theory that if a person is bound to become a fugitive from her own home, there would be no refuge for her anywhere in the world.").

169. State v. Benge, 272 N.C. 261, 263, 158 S.E.2d 70, 72 (1967), *quoting* State v. Johnson, 261 N.C. 727, 729–30, 136 S.E.2d 84, 86 (1967); *accord* State v. Morgan, 315 N.C. 626, 642, 340 S.E.2d 84, 94 (1986). *See also* State v. Brown, 117 N.C. App. 239, 240–42, 450 S.E.2d 538, 540–41 (1994) (error not to give requested no-duty-to-retreat instruction, which contained language quoted in text), *rev. denied*, 340 N.C. 115, 456 S.E.2d 320 (1995); *but see* State v. Mixion, 110 N.C. App. 138, 148–49, 429 S.E.2d 363, 369 (defendant not entitled, in addition to standard no-duty-to-retreat instruction, to instruction that he had right to "increase his force" inside his home), *rev. denied*, 334 N.C. 437, 433 S.E.2d 183 (1993).

170. *See* State v. Washington, 234 N.C. 531, 534–35, 67 S.E.2d 498, 500 (1951) (in defending person, habitation, or property, defendant may pursue adversary "until he has secured himself from all danger").

when the encounter occurs inside the person's home.[171] This doctrine has not taken hold, however. The law today is that a person is limited to nondeadly force to prevent mere bodily harm or offensive contact, regardless of the location of the conflict.[172]

The North Carolina courts have always returned to the no-retreat doctrine as a way of emphasizing the rights of persons assaulted inside the home. The courts have applied the same no-retreat rule to persons assaulted within their place of business. To give force to this doctrine, the courts have held that defendants are entitled to instructions to the jury to the effect that they do not have a duty to retreat in encounters within the home or business. In all other respects, a person defending himself or herself inside the home or business must abide by "the usual rules" of self-defense.[173]

As a result of this policy, the courts have developed a large body of law on what constitutes the home or business, which occupants are entitled to no-duty-to-retreat instructions, and related questions. (These issues are addressed separately in § 4.4, covering self-defense within the home or business.) Ultimately, however, this approach and the rulings it has generated have meaning only if a person engaged in a conflict *outside* the home or business has a duty to retreat. If such a duty does not exist, the supposed protections extended to persons within the home or business would be no greater than those enjoyed by any other person using defensive force.

---

171. *See* State v. Francis, 252 N.C. 57, 58–59, 112 S.E.2d 756, 757–58 (1960); State v. Frizzelle, 243 N.C. 49, 50–51, 89 S.E.2d 725, 726–27 (1955). *See also* State v. Kelly, 24 N.C. App. 670, 672–73, 211 S.E.2d 854, 856 (1975) (error in failing to instruct on defendant's right to evict trespasser where defendant shot victim after victim refused to leave defendant's home and started to grab defendant).

172. *See* State v. Pearson, 288 N.C. 34, 41–43, 215 S.E.2d 598, 604–05 (1975) (holding that *Francis, supra* note 171, was limited to facts of case). *See also* State v. King, 49 N.C. App. 499, 503–05, 272 S.E.2d 26, 29–30 (1980) (disapproving *Kelly, supra* note 171), *rev. denied*, 302 N.C. 220, 276 S.E.2d 917 (1981).

173. State v. McCombs, 297 N.C 151, 157, 253 S.E.2d 906, 910 (1979) (holding that "the usual rules" of self-defense apply inside the home, except that there is no duty to retreat). New G.S. 14-51.1 reiterates the common-law rule that a lawful occupant within a home or other residence need not retreat. The statute also appears to expand the rights of occupants defending against intruders who have gained entry into the home or residence. Although in a literal sense the statute covers confrontations that occur inside the home, it is better viewed as a modification of the specialized rules on defense of habitation. *See infra* § 5.4(a) (discussing defense of habitation).

### (3) Irreconcilable Differences?

Both lines of cases discussed above continue to flourish, but it does not appear that they can be reconciled. As indicated by the first line of cases, there no longer appears to be any difference between the retreat rules in cases involving the home or business and the retreat rules in other cases. In other words, North Carolina no longer appears to recognize a duty to retreat. The second line of cases, by emphasizing that a person does not have a duty to retreat inside the home or business, implies that a duty to retreat exists elsewhere; but the case law does not bear out this proposition.

One could argue, as a way of maintaining some distinction in the retreat rules, that a person who is not an aggressor does not have a duty to retreat anywhere, but is only entitled to a no-duty-to-retreat instruction for conflicts inside the home or business. Although this approach would preserve the policy of protecting the home or business, it would be problematic analytically. If the law does not require a nonaggressor to retreat, then he or she would appear to be entitled to instructions reflecting the state of the law. The appellate courts have held generally that trial courts must give the substance of instructions requested by a defendant when they accurately reflect the law.[174] And recent appellate decisions indicate that defendants faced with a felonious assault or an assault with deadly force are entitled to no-duty-to-retreat instructions.[175]

The foregoing analysis means that persons using defensive force inside the home or business stand on the same legal footing as persons defending themselves elsewhere. Thus, if the courts wish to maintain their commitment to providing greater protection to the home or business, they will need to develop a mechanism other than the retreat doctrine to accomplish this purpose.[176]

---

174. *See, e.g.,* State v. Rose, 323 N.C. 455, 458, 373 S.E.2d 426, 428 (1988); State v. Corn, 307 N.C. 79, 86, 296 S.E.2d 261, 266 (1982).

175. *See* State v. Watson, 338 N.C. 168, 186, 449 S.E.2d 694, 705 (1994), *cert. denied,* __ U.S. __, 115 S. Ct. 1708, 131 L. Ed. 2d 569 (1995); State v. Nixon, 117 N.C. App. 141, 150–51, 450 S.E.2d 562, 567–68 (1994). One purpose of such an instruction would be to dispel any preconceptions a jury might have about the law on retreat. *See* PERKINS, *supra* note 12, at 1127–28 n.84.

176. New G.S. 14-51.1 expands the circumstances in which a person may rely on defense of habitation when defending against an intruder. Even with the addition of this statute, however, defense of habitation does not cover many of the conflicts that may arise within the home or business. *Compare infra* § 4.4 (self-defense within home or business) *with* § 5.4 (defense of habitation).

# 4 Variations on Self-Defense

# 4 Variations on Self-Defense

&#x2767;&#x2767;&#x2767;   This chapter considers variations on defense of oneself—situations that either do not involve killing in self-defense or are sufficiently distinctive to warrant separate treatment. Many of the principles of defensive-force defenses discussed elsewhere in this book apply here and so will not be repeated in each section.[1]

## § 4.1  Using Deadly Force

In most respects the rules that apply when a person uses deadly force but does not kill are the same as the rules governing a person's right to kill in self-defense. The same harm must be, or reasonably appear to be, threatened: a person may neither kill nor use some lesser degree of deadly force unless the person has a reasonable belief that he or she is faced with death or great bodily injury.[2] Also, the principles

---

1. The reader should refer to the following sections for principles of general application. As discussed in § 2.2 *supra*, each defensive-force defense is subject to a three-step analysis. Each permits a person to use force to prevent a particular threat of *harm* [§ 2.2(a)]; each either allows or disallows the use of *deadly* force to prevent that harm from occurring [§ 2.2(b)]; and each is regulated in large part by the rules embodied in State v. Norris, 303 N.C. 526, 279 S.E.2d 570 (1981) [§ 2.2(c)]. Sections 3.1 through 3.4 *supra* contain a detailed analysis of the *Norris* test, which itself contains four parts: the *honest belief* requirement; the *reasonable belief* requirement; the *aggressor* requirement; and the *excessive force* requirement. Section 4.1 *infra* discusses the potential differences in the application of the *Norris* test in homicide and nonhomicide cases.

2. *See, e.g.*, State v. Marsh, 293 N.C. 353, 354, 237 S.E.2d 745, 747 (1977) (defendant has right to use deadly force in self-defense when such force is or reasonably appears to be necessary to save defendant from death or great bodily injury); State v. Anderson, 230 N.C. 54, 55, 51 S.E.2d 895, 897 (1949) (person who inflicts wounds on another with intent to kill is absolved from criminal liability on ground of self-defense only if person is in actual or apparent danger of death or great

embodied in the *Norris* test generally apply when a defendant either kills in self-defense or uses a lesser degree of deadly force.[3] Although the courts have not always referred to the *Norris* test explicitly when a defendant has been charged with assault rather than homicide, many of the same principles are evident.[4]

---

bodily harm); State v. McGinnis, 70 N.C. App. 421, 425, 320 S.E.2d 297, 301 (1984) (court upholds denial of self-defense instruction upon finding no real or apparent threat of death or great bodily harm).

3. The *Norris* test is discussed generally in § 2.2(c) *supra*.

4. Several cases address whether the defendant's actions were reasonably necessary. For cases finding the evidence *insufficient* to support an instruction on self-defense, *see, e.g.*, State v. Wills, 110 N.C. App. 206, 212, 429 S.E.2d 376, 379 (victim had punched defendant two days earlier and threatened to assault defendant earlier in the day; evidence insufficient to show that it was reasonably necessary for defendant to shoot victim), *rev. denied*, 334 N.C. 438, 433 S.E.2d 184 (1993); State v. Lovell, 93 N.C. App. 726, 728–29, 379 S.E.2d 101, 103 (1989) (defendant believed that victim had taken contract out on his life, and defendant sought out victim and stabbed him; no reasonable necessity). For cases finding the evidence *sufficient* to support an instruction, *see, e.g.*, State v. Satterwhite, 238 N.C. 674, 675–76, 78 S.E.2d 603, 604–05 (1953) (victim was advancing on defendant with open knife when defendant shot him; trial court erred in failing to instruct on self-defense); State v. Dorsey, 39 N.C. App. 480, 250 S.E.2d 327 (1979) (victim brandished pistol, threatened to kill defendant, and fired first shot; error in failing to instruct on self-defense); State v. Shelton, 25 N.C. App. 207, 210, 212 S.E.2d 545, 547–48 (1975) (during fight, defendant saw pistol fall to floor, picked it up, saw victim reach for shiny object from belt, and reacted by firing pistol at victim; evidence of reasonable apprehension sufficient to warrant jury instructions).

There also are several cases addressing the aggressor doctrine. For cases finding the evidence *insufficient* to support an instruction on self-defense, *see, e.g.*, State v. Hunter, 315 N.C. 371, 374, 338 S.E.2d 99, 102 (1986) (victim assaulted defendant, who left and later returned with knife; defendant was aggressor in second conflict); State v. McKinnon, 54 N.C. App. 475, 476, 478, 283 S.E.2d 555, 556–58 (1981) (defendant swung at victim with knife, victim threw rock at defendant's foot, and defendant stabbed victim; defendant was aggressor and did not satisfy withdrawal requirements). For cases finding the evidence *sufficient* to support an instruction, *see, e.g.*, *Marsh*, 293 N.C. at 354–55, 237 S.E.2d at 747 (although defendant and victim had history of bad relations, evidence indicated that defendant only walked up to victim's gas station on day in question; evidence was sufficient for jury to find that defendant was not aggressor and trial court erred in failing to instruct on self-defense); State v. Moore, 111 N.C. App. 649, 653–56, 432 S.E.2d 887, 889–91 (1993) (defendant entered victim's house, shoved victim, and then left house, but as defendant was trying to leave, victim came out of house and attacked defendant with a hammer; jury could find that defendant was not aggressor in second altercation and trial court erred in failing to instruct on self-defense).

The principal legal difference between killing in self-defense and using a lesser degree of deadly force is that no North Carolina cases have recognized the doctrine of imperfect self-defense in the latter context. When the charge is a felonious assault (such as assault with a deadly weapon with intent to kill), a defendant may not claim imperfect self-defense to reduce the charged offense to a lesser degree. If the defendant uses excessive force or is the aggressor, with or without murderous intent, he or she completely loses the right of self-defense.[5] It may still be important, however, to determine whether the defendant was an aggressor with or without murderous intent because the withdrawal rules differ for the two types of aggressors. The initial aggressor in an encounter may still claim self-defense in an assault case if he or she withdrew from the encounter within the meaning of the law (just as a defendant charged with homicide may still rely on perfect self-defense if he or she was the aggressor and withdrew). When a defendant is an aggressor *without* murderous intent, the withdrawal requirements are not as stringent.[6]

At one time particular elements of the *Norris* test may have applied somewhat differently in homicide and nonhomicide cases. For example, in some homicide cases the courts required a defendant to believe in the "need to kill" under the first element of the *Norris* test.[7] Was such a belief required in a felony assault case as well? Decisions

---

5. *See, e.g.,* State v. Hall, 89 N.C. App. 491, 493–94, 366 S.E.2d 527, 528 (1988) (self-defense is defense when defendant meets all of elements); State v. Brewer, 89 N.C. App. 431, 434–35, 366 S.E.2d 580, 582–83 (to same effect), *rev. denied,* 322 N.C. 482, 370 S.E.2d 229 (1988). Some have questioned why a person who uses deadly force and kills is entitled to the mitigating effect of imperfect self-defense but a person who causes a lesser harm does not obtain a similar benefit. *See* 2 Paul H. Robinson, Criminal Law Defenses 35 (1984). One possible reason for the difference is that the courts have considered imperfect self-defense to be a device that "displaces" the element of malice, which is required only for murder. *See supra* § 3.1. This explanation is not entirely satisfactory, however, since the malice required for murder is similar to the elements of various felonious assaults. For example, "intent to kill" is an element of assault with a deadly weapon with intent to kill. Since such an intent would be a sufficient basis to infer malice if the assault resulted in death, it is not clear why imperfect self-defense would not "displace" that intent when the charge is assault. *Cf.* Faulkner v. State, 458 A.2d 81, 82–83 (Md. Ct. Spec. App. 1983) (recognizing that imperfect self-defense is applicable to assault with intent to murder), *aff'd,* 483 A.2d 759, 770–71 (Md. 1984).

6. *Compare* § 3.3(c)(2) *supra* (discussing withdrawal requirements for aggressors *with* murderous intent) *with* § 3.3(d)(2) (discussing withdrawal requirements for aggressors *without* murderous intent).

7. *See supra* § 3.2(b)(3).

varied,[8] but such a requirement seemed out of place in that context. The issue may be moot because the supreme court now appears to take the position that a person does *not* have to believe in the need to kill to rely on self-defense against a homicide charge. To satisfy the first *Norris* element, the person must believe only that it is necessary to protect himself or herself from death or great bodily injury. Such an approach would be workable in nonhomicide cases as well.[9]

## § 4.2  Against Sexual Assault

Early cases suggest that North Carolina has always recognized that a person could use deadly force to prevent a sexual assault.[10] Only recently, however, have the courts explicitly addressed the right. In *State v. Molko*, a 1981 case, the court of appeals attempted to fit the use of de-

---

8. *Compare* State v. Kinney, 92 N.C. App. 671, 675–76, 375 S.E.2d 692, 695 (1989) (stating in one place that person may use deadly force in self-defense if it reasonably appears necessary and stating in another place that person must have reasonable belief in need to kill) *with Hall*, 89 N.C. App. at 493–94, 366 S.E.2d at 528 (defendant must have believed in need for deadly force, not in need to kill). *See also* North Carolina Pattern Jury Instructions for Criminal Cases 308.45 at 1 (North Carolina Conference of Superior Court Judges, Committee on Pattern Jury Instructions, Sept. 1986) [hereinafter N.C.P.I.—Crim.] (providing essentially that defendant must have believed in necessity for action taken, not in need to kill).

9. *See* State v. Richardson, 341 N.C. 585, 461 S.E.2d 724 (1995), discussed in §§ 3.2(b)(4) and 3.4(c)(3) *supra*. Another concept typically associated with killing in self-defense is the requirement of *imminence of harm*. As indicated in § 3.2(d) *supra*, the threat of death or great bodily injury must be *imminent*, or at least must reasonably appear to be so, before a person may kill in self-defense. *See* State v. Norman, 324 N.C. 253, 260–61, 378 S.E.2d 8, 13 (1989) (justifying imminence requirement in homicide cases because "the killing of another human being is the most extreme recourse" allowed under the law). The cases seem to impose a similar imminence requirement when a person uses a lesser degree of deadly force, but they do not give the matter close attention. *See, e.g.*, State v. Lovell, 93 N.C. App. 726, 729, 379 S.E.2d 101, 103 (1989) (stating without discussion that defendant must have been in actual or apparent danger of imminent death or great bodily harm before he or she may use deadly force); State v. Kidd, 60 N.C. App. 140, 142, 298 S.E.2d 406, 408 (1982) (to same effect), *rev. denied*, 307 N.C. 700, 301 S.E.2d 393 (1983). The cases do not appear to address whether the threat of harm must be imminent before a person may use *nondeadly* force in self-defense.

10. *See* State v. Neville, 51 N.C. 424, 432–33 (1859) (suggesting that woman could kill to avoid being "violated"); *see also* State v. Bryant, 65 N.C. 327, 328–29 (1871) (suggesting that person has right to kill to prevent escape of rapist).

fensive force against sexual assault into the traditional requirements of self-defense. The court ruled that "a person put in fear of a homosexual assault is put in fear of great bodily harm."[11] Apparently concerned that a sexual assault would not always meet the traditional definition of *great bodily harm*, the supreme court in *State v. Hunter* recognized a separate right to defend against sexual assault. The court held that both males and females have the right to use deadly force to repel a sexual assault.[12]

In recognizing this defense, *Hunter* relied on the pattern jury instructions, which already included a separate instruction for self-defense to sexual assault. At the time of *Hunter*, the pattern instruction defined *sexual assault* as a rape, attempted rape, any forcible crime against nature, or attempted forcible crime against nature. The current pattern instruction has been expanded to include any sex offense or attempted sex offense.[13]

*Hunter* also appears to have recognized the general applicability of the *Norris* test to self-defense against sexual assault.[14] There may be some difficulty, however, in applying the aggressor element of *Norris* to such cases. A person is considered an aggressor only when he or she brings about or provokes a conflict.[15] When a person commits a simple assault on another and is sexually assaulted in return—for example, Mary slaps John and John sexually assaults Mary—it is more difficult to argue that the first person caused the ensuing conflict and therefore is limited in the right to use defensive force.[16]

---

11. 50 N.C. App. 551, 552, 274 S.E.2d 271, 272 (1981).

12. 305 N.C. 106, 113–15, 286 S.E.2d 535, 540–41 (1982).

13. *Compare* N.C.P.I.—Crim., *supra* note 8, at 308.70 n.1 (Dec. 1986) (current instruction) *with Hunter*, 305 N.C. at 114 n.*, 286 S.E.2d at 540 n.* (quoting note 1 of then-existing instruction).

14. 305 N.C. at 114 n.*, 286 S.E.2d at 540 n.* (quoting then-existing pattern instruction). Although *Hunter* did not directly address the issue, a defendant would seem to be able to rely on both perfect *and* imperfect self-defense against sexual assault in an appropriate case. The *Norris* test and the availability of perfect and imperfect defensive-force defenses are discussed in general in § 2.2(c) *supra*; the four parts of the *Norris* test are analyzed in detail in §§ 3.1 through 3.4 *supra*; and the potential differences in the application of the *Norris* test in homicide and nonhomicide cases are discussed in § 4.1 *supra*.

15. *See generally* § 3.3(b) *supra* (discussing general features of aggressors).

16. The current pattern instruction no longer contains the aggressor element as a standard part of the instruction. Instead, it provides in a footnote that the trial

## § 4.3  Using Nondeadly Force

Although not typically regarded as a separate defense, the right to use nondeadly force to defend against a nondeadly assault has the earmarks of one. It covers a particular threat of harm: namely, the threat of bodily harm or offensive physical contact. And, the courts have found that when the evidence supports the defendant's right to defend against both death or great bodily injury *and* bodily harm or offensive physical contact, it is error not to instruct on both doctrines.[17] Although the *Norris* elements have not been explicitly applied in the context of nondeadly force in self-defense, similar concepts are apparent in the case law.[18]

Some older cases state that a person facing a nonfelonious assault may not "stand his ground and kill his adversary, if there is any way of escape open to him, though he is allowed to repel force by force and give blow for blow."[19] This language, however, is a remnant of an earlier interpretation of the duty to retreat and no longer has any real significance.[20]

---

court should instruct on the defendant being the aggressor when appropriate. *See* N.C.P.I.—Crim., *supra* note 8, at 308.70 n.2 (Dec. 1986).

17. *See, e.g.*, State v. Fletcher, 268 N.C. 140, 141–42, 150 S.E.2d 54, 55–56 (1966) (trial court erred in instructing jury that defendant could claim self-defense only if threatened with death or great bodily injury; jury should also have been instructed that defendant could use such force as was actually or reasonably necessary to protect against bodily injury or offensive physical contact); State v. Anderson, 230 N.C. 54, 55–56, 51 S.E.2d 895, 897 (1949) (to same effect); State v. Beaver, 14 N.C. App. 459, 462–63, 188 S.E.2d 576, 579 (1972) (trial court erred in not instructing on right to defend against bodily harm or offensive physical contact where victim came toward defendant with a tree limb and defendant threw rock at victim).

18. *See, e.g.*, *Fletcher*, 268 N.C. at 141–42, 150 S.E.2d at 55–56 (applying concepts of reasonable necessity and fault; error not to instruct on right to use nondeadly force in self-defense); State v. Jones, 77 N.C. 520, 521–22 (1877) (noting that jury should consider whether force was in excess of what was necessary in self-defense); State v. Grant, 57 N.C. App. 589, 591–92, 291 S.E.2d 913, 915 (woman slapped man, and man slapped her back; insufficient evidence that defendant's slapping of woman was reasonably necessary to prevent further harm), *rev. denied*, 306 N.C. 560, 294 S.E.2d 225 (1982). The *Norris* test is discussed in general in § 2.2(c) *supra*; the four parts of the test are analyzed in detail in §§ 3.1 through 3.4 *supra*; and the potential differences in the application of the test in homicide and nonhomicide cases are discussed in § 4.1 *supra*.

19. State v. Anderson, 230 N.C. 54, 56, 51 S.E.2d 895, 897 (1949), *quoting* State v. Dixon, 75 N.C. 275, 279 (1876).

20. *See supra* § 3.5(c)(1) (discussing evolution of North Carolina's approach to retreat).

Regardless of the original purpose of the quoted language, the law today is clear that a defendant may not use *deadly* force to prevent mere bodily harm or offensive physical contact. The defendant does not gain the right to use deadly force simply by retreating from the encounter.[21] The authorities are equally clear that a person may use *nondeadly* force, without retreating, to prevent bodily harm or offensive contact.[22]

## § 4.4  Within Home or Business

### (a) In General

The law of defensive force recognizes the special status of the home through two separate doctrines. One is defense of habitation (discussed later in § 5.4), which applies when a person defends against certain unlawful entries into the home. The other is self-defense within the home or business, the subject of this section, which applies to a greater range of conflicts that may occur inside a person's home or business.

The courts have often said that the distinguishing feature of self-defense within the home or business is that one who is free from fault in the encounter has no obligation to retreat. In an appropriate case defendants are entitled to instructions to the jury that they are under no obligation to retreat within their home or business. In all other respects the rules of self-defense are the same.[23]

It is unclear whether this no-retreat doctrine provides any additional protection to persons drawn into conflicts within their home or business. One line of cases (discussed earlier in § 3.5) suggests that North Carolina does not impose any duty to retreat on a person who is not the aggressor in the encounter. If those cases are controlling, then it would be inconsequential whether a person is defending against an assault

---

21. *See* State v. Hunter, 315 N.C. 371, 373–74, 338 S.E.2d 99, 101–02 (1986) (deadly force not permitted to protect against mere bodily harm or offensive physical contact); State v. Clay, 297 N.C. 555, 562–63, 256 S.E.2d 176, 182 (1979) (to same effect); State v. Scott, 26 N.C. 409, 414–16 (1844) (defendant could not claim killing was in self-defense when he was aware that deceased only wanted fight without weapons).

22. *See supra* § 3.5(c)(1).

23. *See, e.g.,* State v. McCombs, 297 N.C 151, 157, 253 S.E.2d 906, 910 (1979) (holding that "the usual rules" of self-defense apply inside the home, except that the occupant does not have a duty to retreat).

inside, or away from, the home or business. This section, however, accepts at face value the courts' pronouncements on self-defense within the home or business and examines the conditions under which a person is entitled to a no-duty-to-retreat instruction.

Before considering these conditions, a few words should be said here about new G.S. 14-51.1, which became effective October 1, 1994.[24] That statute reiterates the rule that a lawful occupant within a home or other residence need not retreat. It modifies the law by allowing a lawful occupant to use deadly force against an intruder who is *attempting to enter*, or who has already *gained entry into*, the home or residence (previously, a lawful occupant could use deadly force against the former *only*). In a literal sense, this part of the statute deals with "encounters that take place within the home," or self-defense within the home. But the statute is better viewed as a modification of the rules on defense of habitation because its principal focus is on certain unlawful intrusions into the habitation. The doctrine discussed below covers many other conflicts that may occur within a home or business, including conflicts between a dwelling's residents and invited guests and conflicts between a business's employees and its patrons.

### (b) Meaning of "Home" and "Business"

The cases dealing with retreat within the home or business raise two principal questions: What premises are covered by self-defense within the home or business? And what persons have a sufficient interest in the premises to obtain a no-duty-to-retreat instruction?

On the first question, the cases unquestionably include a defendant's home and place of work.[25] The cases also include the curtilage of the defendant's home.[26] Some jurisdictions include any property owned or occupied by the defendant, not just the defendant's home or

---

24. 1994 N.C. Sess. Laws, Regular Sess., ch. 673.

25. *See, e.g.*, State v. Morgan, 315 N.C. 626, 641–42, 340 S.E.2d 84, 94 (1986); State v. Benge, 272 N.C. 261, 263–64, 158 S.E.2d 70, 72 (1967); State v. Strater, 272 N.C. 276, 277–78, 158 S.E.2d 60, 61–62 (1967).

26. *See* State v. Frizzelle, 243 N.C. 49, 51, 89 S.E.2d 725, 726 (1955) (curtilage includes at least yard around dwelling as well as barns, cribs, and other outbuildings); State v. Browning, 28 N.C. App. 376, 378–79, 221 S.E.2d 375, 377 (1976) (to same effect). Some court of appeals decisions take a strict view of what constitutes the home, holding that a person is not entitled to a no-duty-to-retreat instruction if the conflict occurs beyond the defendant's immediate property line. *See* State v. Lee, 42

business.[27] It is not clear whether the North Carolina courts agree with this position, although several cases state generally that a person is under no duty to retreat when attacked in "his own dwelling, home, place of business, *or on his own premises.*"[28]

On the question of who has a sufficient interest in the premises to obtain a no-duty-to-retreat instruction, the cases do not require that a person have an ownership interest in the property. In a decision involving the home, the court of appeals held that the person need not have a proprietary or leasehold interest in the dwelling as long as the person is at least a temporary resident.[29] Some jurisdictions have gone further, holding that a guest in another's dwelling does not have an obligation to retreat even if the guest is present just for a social visit and has no intent to take up residence.[30] New G.S. 14.51.1 provides that a "lawful occupant" does not have a duty to retreat within the home or other residence, but it is not entirely clear what the legislature meant by "occupant." In cases involving the workplace, the person need not be the owner of the business; it is sufficient that the person be employed there.[31]

Another problem is whether a defendant may claim the benefit of the no-retreat rule when the assailant is a co-occupant or co-worker. The court of appeals has held that an occupant of a dwelling is not required to retreat in defending against an assault from another occupant.[32] Although this issue apparently has not arisen in cases involving

---

N.C. App. 77, 78–79, 255 S.E.2d 602, 603 (1979) (home does not include alley adjoining home); *see also* State v. Smith, 39 N.C. App. 11, 14–15, 249 S.E.2d 466, 468–69 (1978) (home does not include courtyard of defendant's apartment complex), *rev. denied*, 297 N.C. 179, 254 S.E.2d 37 (1979).

27. *See* ROLLIN M. PERKINS & RONALD N. BOYCE, CRIMINAL LAW 1135–36 (3d ed. 1982).

28. State v. Pearson, 288 N.C. 34, 40, 215 S.E.2d 598, 603 (1975) (emphasis added). *Accord* State v. Johnson, 261 N.C. 727, 729–30, 136 S.E.2d 84, 86 (1964) (no duty to retreat on own "premises"); State v. Walker, 236 N.C. 742, 744, 73 S.E.2d 868, 870 (1953) (to same effect). The supreme court has ruled, however, that a prisoner may not claim that an entire prison is his or her home. *See* State v. McCray, 312 N.C. 519, 532–33, 324 S.E.2d 606, 615–16 (1985).

29. State v. Stevenson, 81 N.C. App. 409, 412–15, 344 S.E.2d 334, 335–37 (1986).

30. *See* State v. Osborne, 21 S.E.2d 178, 182 (S.C. 1942); Kelley v. State, 145 So. 816, 819 (Ala. 1933). *Cf. infra* § 5.4(b)(2) n.62 (citing authorities that guest may have right to defend habitation).

31. *See, e.g.*, State v. Strater, 272 N.C. 276, 277–78, 158 S.E.2d 60, 61–62 (1967); State v. Thornton, 211 N.C. 413, 418, 190 S.E. 758, 760–61 (1937).

32. *See* State v. Hearn, 89 N.C. App. 103, 105–06, 365 S.E.2d 206, 208 (1988); State v. Browning, 28 N.C. App. 376, 379–80, 221 S.E.2d 375, 377–78 (1976).

the workplace, the same reasoning would seem to apply to conflicts between co-workers.

### (c) Other Conditions for Obtaining No-Duty-to-Retreat Instruction

Another qualification on the no-duty-to-retreat rule is that the defendant must be free from fault in the encounter. A person generally is considered at fault when he or she is an aggressor within the meaning of the third element of *Norris*. This qualification may not be that significant as a practical matter, however. When the evidence is in conflict over whether the defendant was the aggressor, the trial court must still instruct the jury that the defendant, if not the aggressor, had no obligation to retreat.[33]

Some cases suggest an additional condition on obtaining a no-duty-to-retreat instruction: namely, that the defendant must actually have been attacked by the victim. This condition is difficult to reconcile, however, with other principles of self-defense. Under the first two elements of the *Norris* test, a defendant need only have a *reasonable* belief that the assailant will cause some harm. If a court finds sufficient evidence to warrant instructions on self-defense, it necessarily has found sufficient evidence of those two elements. It seems inconsistent to say that a defendant who reasonably perceives a threat of harm nevertheless has an obligation to retreat unless the evidence also shows an actual attack.[34]

## § 4.5 By Battered Persons

The law does not recognize a "battered-person defense" per se. Being a battered person does not by itself justify or excuse conduct. Nevertheless, prior abuse may play a critical role in establishing a recognized criminal-law defense such as self-defense.[35] Cases involving battered

---

33. *See supra* § 3.5(b).

34. *Id.*

35. A history of battering also may play a part in other defenses, such as diminished capacity and insanity. *See generally* State v. Clark, 324 N.C. 146, 158, 163–64, 377 S.E.2d 54, 61, 64–65 (1989) (finding on facts of case that evidence of defendant's mental state, which included evidence of battered woman syndrome, did not warrant instruction on diminished capacity).

persons also tend to challenge traditional thinking about self-defense.[36] This section begins by discussing some conventional applications of the rules of self-defense in cases involving battered persons, then considers the appropriateness of expert testimony on battered woman syndrome, and closes with the difficult questions raised by the North Carolina Supreme Court's decision in *State v. Norman*,[37] which involved a battered woman who killed her longtime abuser at a time when he was not posing an immediate threat of harm.

## (a) In General

A *battered person* can be defined generally as a person who has been the victim of repeated physical or psychological abuse by a husband, boyfriend, parent, or other close figure.[38] A victim of abuse does not need to meet this or any other definition, however, for past abuse to be relevant to a claim of self-defense. A number of self-defense cases have involved persons who might today be considered battered persons, but who were not identified as such. Their personal histories were nevertheless a central part of their defense and properly so.[39]

---

36. Among other things, it has been suggested that the "reasonable person" standard is applied in a manner that fails to account for the characteristics and perceptions of battered women and children; that battered persons are expected to "retreat" (by leaving their homes, for example) even though the law may not impose a duty to retreat; and that traditional interpretations of the imminence and aggressor doctrines, discussed in § 4.5(c) *infra*, are inappropriate in cases involving longstanding abuse by one person against another. *See generally* ANGELA BROWNE, WHEN BATTERED WOMEN KILL 172–74 (1987); LENORE E. WALKER, THE BATTERED WOMAN SYNDROME 142–43 (1984); LENORE E. WALKER, THE BATTERED WOMAN 220–21 (1979).

37. 324 N.C. 253, 378 S.E.2d 8 (1989).

38. *See* WALKER, THE BATTERED WOMAN, *supra* note 36, at xv (woman may be considered battered woman if battering cycle has occurred at least twice).

39. *See, e.g.*, State v. Hipp, 245 N.C. 205, 95 S.E.2d 452 (1956) (evidence of prior abuse supported that defendant acted out of reasonable necessity; error in failing to instruct on self-defense); State v. Greer, 218 N.C. 660, 12 S.E.2d 238 (1940) (to same effect); State v. Temples, 74 N.C. App. 106, 327 S.E.2d 266 (evidence showed deceased had abused defendant previously and initiated fatal encounter; error to instruct jury that it could find defendant was the aggressor), *rev. denied*, 314 N.C. 121, 332 S.E.2d 489 (1985); State v. Clark, 65 N.C. App. 286, 308 S.E.2d 913 (1983) (defendant charged with second-degree murder was convicted of voluntary manslaughter in killing of abusive husband, although court was unwilling to say as matter of law that force used was not excessive and that defendant was entitled to nonsuit), *rev. denied*, 310 N.C. 627, 315 S.E.2d 693 (1984).

The significance of prior abuse lies primarily in the first two elements of the *Norris* test, which in essence require that the defendant honestly and reasonably believe in the need to defend himself or herself from some harm.[40] A defendant's previous encounters with a batterer are almost always relevant to both elements. For example, a wife who has been beaten in the past by her husband may be more alert than the average person to when her husband is on the brink of violence. The wife's prior experiences thus tend to show why she *honestly* feared an attack on a particular occasion and believed in the need to protect herself. The prior experiences also tend to show the *reasonableness* of the wife's belief because a person of "ordinary firmness," possessed of the knowledge of the husband's tendencies, could have formed a similar belief.[41]

### (b) Battered Woman Syndrome

The admissibility of expert testimony about *battered woman syndrome*, although somewhat less certain than the admissibility of other evidence concerning abuse, still involves relatively routine principles of law. Battered woman syndrome has received more attention from courts and commentators, but similar concepts may apply to battered children and other persons.[42]

Battered woman syndrome does not refer solely to a woman's mental state. It is "a term used both to describe *patterns of violence* typically experienced by battered women and the *psychological impact* this violence has on the women."[43] Although at one time the courts were

---

40. The *Norris* test is discussed generally in § 2.2(c) *supra*; the four parts of the test are analyzed in detail in §§ 3.1 through 3.4 *supra*; and the potential differences in the application of the test in homicide and nonhomicide cases are discussed in § 4.1 *supra*.

41. Past incidents of abuse also may be relevant to whether the defendant's force was excessive within the meaning of the fourth *Norris* element, as that inquiry also deals with the reasonableness of the defendant's perceptions and actions. *See supra* § 3.4(c)(3) (discussing meaning of excessive force element). Methods of proving past abuse are discussed further in § 7.2 *infra*, which considers the admissibility of opinion and reputation testimony about the victim's violent nature and evidence of prior acts of violence and threats of harm by the victim.

42. *See generally* Kurt M. Bumby, *Psycholegal Considerations in Abuse-Motivated Parricides: Children Who Kill Their Abusive Parents*, 22 JOURNAL OF PSYCHIATRY & LAW 51 (1994); Annotation, *Admissibility of Evidence of Battered Child Syndrome on Issue of Self-Defense*, 22 A.L.R. 5th 787 (1994).

43. BROWNE, *supra* note 36, at 177 (emphasis added). Lenore Walker describes the *pattern of violence* as a three-stage cycle: (1) the tension building phase, which con-

divided on whether to admit expert testimony about battered woman syndrome, a majority of jurisdictions now permit it.[44] North Carolina has not directly addressed the question,[45] but expert testimony on battered woman syndrome would appear to be admissible under accepted evidentiary principles. Generally speaking, expert testimony is admissible in North Carolina if it assists the trier of fact in understanding the evidence or determining a fact in issue.[46] Expert testimony about battered woman syndrome would appear to satisfy this standard. Among other things, such testimony may help the jury understand the dangers posed to a battered woman and her reasons for remaining in the home despite those dangers.[47]

---

sists of minor battering incidents; (2) the acute battering phase, which is characterized by an explosion of violence; and (3) the contrite, loving phase, in which the batterer convinces the woman that the abuse will not be repeated. WALKER, THE BATTERED WOMAN, *supra* note 36, at 55–70. Walker relies primarily on the theory of learned helplessness to explain the *psychological impact* that battering has on women. That theory posits that when animals or humans are subjected to random and unavoidable negative stimuli, they learn that they cannot affect what is happening to them. Eventually, they cease making any effort to avoid the negative stimuli even when the means to do so are available. *Id.* at 45–51. Other theories, such as post-traumatic stress disorder, also may help explain the psychological impact of battering. *See generally* Bumby, *supra* note 42, at 55–64 (1994) (discussing theories of post-traumatic stress disorder, information processing of trauma, traumatic bonding, and battered person syndromes).

44. See Kerry A. Shad, Note, State v. Norman: *Self-Defense Unavailable to Battered Women Who Kill Passive Abusers*, 68 N.C. L. REV. 1159, 1165 n.44 (1990) (collecting cases dealing with expert testimony on battered woman syndrome and finding that majority of jurisdictions allow such testimony); James O. Pearson, Jr., Annotation, *Admissibility of Expert or Opinion Testimony on Battered Wife or Battered Woman Syndrome*, 18 A.L.R. 4th 1153 (1982).

45. In *State v. Norman*, the trial court allowed testimony on battered woman syndrome. 324 N.C. at 258, 378 S.E.2d at 11–12; *see also* State v. Clark, 324 N.C. 146, 158, 377 S.E.2d 54, 61 (1989) (trial court allowed testimony on battered woman syndrome in case involving diminished capacity). Although it does not appear that the appellate courts in North Carolina have directly considered the admissibility of such testimony, they have noted that battered woman syndrome has gained sufficient acceptance to be a clinically recognized syndrome. *See* State v. Torres, 330 N.C. 517, 520–21, 412 S.E.2d 20, 22 (1992).

46. *See* Rule 702, North Carolina Rules of Evidence.

47. *See* 2 ROBINSON, *supra* note 5, at 71 n.4 and authorities cited. In some instances, evidence of battered woman syndrome also may support the defenses of diminished capacity or insanity, both of which depend on some showing that the defendant was mentally impaired. Battered woman syndrome should not be equated with mental impairment, however. *See* BROWNE, *supra* note 36, at 176 (battered woman's behavior may be entirely reasonable in light of dangers posed to her). The subject of expert testimony in self-defense cases is discussed further in § 7.3(b) *infra*.

### (c) The *Norman* Decision

When a battered person is faced with an ongoing attack, he or she has the right to kill in accordance with the traditional rules of self-defense. The problem in some cases, however, is that a battered person may kill his or her abuser at a time when the abuser is not immediately threatening harm.[48] *State v. Norman* presented such a case.[49]

The evidence in *Norman* showed that the defendant's husband had repeatedly beaten her over a period of years. The defendant testified that she had left home on several occasions, but her husband had always found her, brought her home, and beaten her. In the days leading up to the incident in question, the husband's violence and threats to harm the defendant escalated. Among other things, the husband kicked her in the head, put out cigarettes on her body, threatened to cut off her breasts, and threatened to cut her throat if she called the authorities. On the day of the shooting, the husband continued to abuse the defendant and threaten to kill her. The defendant went to the department of social services to inquire about welfare benefits, but her husband followed her there, interrupted the interview, and forced her to return home. On the night of the shooting, the husband went to the bedroom to lie down and made the defendant lie on the floor next to the bed, calling her a bitch and a dog. After her husband had fallen asleep the defendant went next door to her mother's house, where she found her husband's gun in her mother's pocketbook, returned to her own home, and shot her husband three times while he slept, killing him. Two experts who examined the defendant after the shooting testified that her actions fit the profile of battered woman syndrome.

The trial court refused to submit any instruction on self-defense, and the defendant was convicted of voluntary manslaughter.[50] The court of appeals held that the defendant was entitled to an instruction on perfect self-defense and remanded the case for a new trial.[51] In a six-to-one

---

48. See Richard A. Rosen, *On Self-Defense, Imminence, and Women Who Kill Their Batterers*, 71 N.C. L. Rev. 371, 399–404 (1993) (reviewing studies on how frequently battered persons kill their abusers in such situations).

49. 324 N.C. 253, 378 S.E.2d 8 (1989), *rev'g* 89 N.C. App. 384, 366 S.E.2d 586 (1988).

50. Presumably, the jury based its decision on a heat-of-passion theory, although it is unclear from the opinions in the case how the jury arrived at that result.

51. The court of appeals held that the defendant was not entitled to an instruction on imperfect self-defense, 89 N.C. App. at 391, 366 S.E.2d at 590, but it is not clear why the court reached this result. *Compare infra* § 8.4(a) (suggesting that an

opinion, the supreme court reversed the court of appeals, agreeing with the trial court that the defendant was not entitled to any instruction on self-defense.

The principal ground for the supreme court's ruling was that the evidence was insufficient to show that at the time of the killing the defendant reasonably believed that she was confronted by a threat of *imminent* death or great bodily harm. According to the court, *imminent* means "immediate" or "about to" happen.[52] This requirement, the court reasoned, ensures that the law will allow one person to take another's life only when reasonably necessary to avoid death or great bodily injury. The court concluded that since the defendant's husband was sleeping at the time she shot him, no reasonable person would have apprehended a threat of *imminent* harm.

As recognized in the majority opinion, however, some courts and commentators have been troubled by the imminence requirement.[53] They reason that the requirement permits a battered woman to use force when she is least able to do so—namely, when her batterer is in the midst of attacking her—and thus effectively deprives her of the right of self-defense.[54] Courts and commentators also argue that a killing may be reasonably necessary in self-defense even if the threat of harm is not imminent. They advocate eliminating or modifying the imminence requirement and placing the focus more directly on whether the person's actions were or were not reasonably necessary to avoid harm.[55]

A second issue raised but not resolved in *Norman* concerns the aggressor doctrine. The law generally views encounters separately for purposes of the aggressor doctrine. The person who initiates an encounter is usually considered the aggressor, even if that person was the victim

---

instruction on imperfect self-defense ordinarily should be submitted to the jury when there is sufficient evidence to support an instruction on perfect self-defense).

52. 324 N.C. at 261, 378 S.E.2d at 13.

53. *Id.* at 263–64, 378 S.E.2d at 14–15 (citing authorities).

54. As stated by one court, "To require the battered person to await a blatant, deadly assault before she can act in defense of herself would not only ignore unpleasant reality, but would amount to sentencing her to 'murder by installment.'" State v. Gallegos, 719 P.2d 1268, 1271 (N.M. Ct. App. 1986). The court of appeals in *Norman*, 89 N.C. App. at 392–94, 366 S.E.2d at 591–92, as well as the dissent in the supreme court, 324 N.C. at 269–70, 378 S.E.2d at 18, were of a similar view.

55. *See, e.g.*, Model Penal Code and Commentaries § 3.04(1) (American Law Institute 1985) (cited with approval by dissenting opinion in *Norman*); 2 Robinson, *supra* note 5, at 76, 78 (discussed in § 3.2(d) *supra*); Rosen, *supra* note 48, at 377 n.11 (1993) (collecting proposals on modification of imminence requirement). For a further discussion of the imminence requirement in North Carolina, *see* § 3.2(d) *supra*.

in earlier encounters.[56] The court of appeals found that this approach should not be applied to the facts in *Norman*, finding that the husband had provoked the fatal encounter by his continuing aggression against the defendant.[57] The majority in *Norman* did not address the issue, however, basing its ruling on imminence grounds.

---

56. *See supra* § 3.3(b)(2) (discussing aggressors and separate encounters).

57. 89 N.C. App. at 393, 366 S.E.2d at 591. The dissent in the supreme court took a similar position. 324 N.C. at 274–75, 378 S.E.2d at 20–21.

# 5   Other Defensive-Force Defenses

# 5    Other Defensive-Force Defenses

◖◖◖ North Carolina recognizes several defensive-force defenses that do not necessarily involve defense of oneself. Many of the principles applicable to self-defense discussed earlier in this book apply here and so will not be repeated.[1]

## § 5.1 Crime Prevention

The privilege to prevent crime and the right to use defensive force are technically separate doctrines, but they are closely related. Like defensive-force defenses, the crime prevention privilege belongs to the group of defenses regarded as justifications; and, like most defensive-force defenses, the crime prevention privilege is fully exculpatory in effect.[2] Although most cases today look to the rules of defensive force in deciding whether a person's conduct is justified, the crime prevention privilege remains a part of North Carolina law and in an appropriate case may supplement an individual's rights. The privilege has two basic tenets:

> 1. A person may use force to *prevent* the commission of a crime; and

---

1. The reader should refer to the following sections for principles of general application. As discussed in § 2.2 *supra*, each defensive-force defense is subject to a three-step analysis. Each permits a person to use force to prevent a particular threat of *harm* [§ 2.2(a)]; each either allows or disallows the use of *deadly* force to prevent that harm from occurring [§ 2.2(b)]; and each is regulated in large part by the rules embodied in State v. Norris, 303 N.C. 526, 279 S.E.2d 570 (1981) [§ 2.2(c)]. Sections 3.1 through 3.4 *supra* contain a detailed analysis of the *Norris* test, which itself contains four parts: the *honest belief* requirement; the *reasonable belief* requirement; the *aggressor* requirement; and the *excessive force* requirement. Section 4.1 *supra* discusses the potential differences in the application of the *Norris* test in homicide and nonhomicide cases.

2. *See generally* ROLLIN M. PERKINS & RONALD N. BOYCE, CRIMINAL LAW 1108–12 (3d ed. 1982).

    2. A person may use force to *detain* someone who has committed a crime.

Each of these rights is addressed separately below.

### (a) Preventing Felonies and Misdemeanors

### *(1) In General*

The first aspect of the crime prevention privilege—the right to prevent the commission of crime—is often associated with cases in which one person comes to the aid of another. The courts have said that the privilege allows a person to use force to prevent a felonious assault against another. Such decisions remain significant because defensive-force defenses may not account for all of the circumstances in which a person may need to protect another. In essence, the crime prevention privilege fills in gaps in the law.[3]

The crime prevention privilege is not confined, however, to cases involving protection of another or to cases involving felonious assaults. Historically, the privilege allowed a person to use deadly force to prevent "dangerous" felonies and to use nondeadly force to prevent "nondangerous" felonies and certain misdemeanors. Although these rights have become largely redundant with the development of the different defensive-force defenses, they remain significant in cases in which defensive-force defenses do not adequately address the need to use force.[4]

### *(2) Dangerous Felonies*

Some older North Carolina cases appear to have allowed the use of deadly force to prevent the commission of *any* felony.[5] The better view, however, is that the crime prevention privilege permits the use of

---

3. *See infra* § 5.2 (discussing differing rationales for right to defend another person).

4. Perkins argues that when the right to prevent crime and the right to use defensive force overlap, both are available to the person benefited. Perkins, *supra* note 2, at 1108. Although this proposition may be theoretically correct, it seems unlikely that the courts today would give effect to both doctrines when redundant.

5. *See* State v. Harris, 46 N.C. 190, 193–94 (1853) (person may kill if there is reasonable ground to believe there is design to commit a felony); State v. Rutherford,

deadly force only to prevent "dangerous" felonies—that is, offenses involving great personal harm or an unreasonable risk of great personal harm.[6] This right remains significant because certain felonies, such as kidnapping, arson, and armed robbery, are clearly "dangerous"; yet, they may not threaten death or great bodily injury, a prerequisite for using deadly force under the rules of self-defense.[7] For a person to claim the protection of this privilege, a dangerous felony would not actually have to be committed. It should be sufficient, as in cases of self-defense, if the person reasonably believes that a dangerous felony is intended or in progress.[8]

### (3) Nondangerous Felonies and Certain Misdemeanors

At common law, a person had the right to use nondeadly force when it reasonably appeared necessary to prevent a misdemeanor amounting to a "breach of the peace," such as an assault and battery.[9] It appears that North Carolina has extended this right to persons seeking to prevent other offenses. G.S. 15A-404 allows a person to use nondeadly force to detain an offender for the following offenses: a felony, a breach of the peace, a crime involving physical injury to another person, and a crime involving theft or destruction of property. As North Carolina permits a person to use nondeadly force to detain an offender for these

---

8 N.C. 457, 458–59 (1821) (person may kill based on well-grounded belief that felony is about to be committed).

6. *See* PERKINS, *supra* note 2, at 1109–10 (defining "dangerous" felony); State v. Scott, 142 N.C. 582, 584, 55 S.E. 69, 70 (1906) (person may kill to prevent "great crime"), *quoting* State v. Morgan, 25 N.C. 186, 193 (1842); State v. Roane, 13 N.C. 58, 62 (1828) (person may kill to prevent "forcible felony").

7. *See generally* § 2.2(b) *supra* (discussing propriety of deadly force). Rape and other sexual assaults also constitute "dangerous" felonies, but the right to prevent such acts is now recognized under the rules of self-defense. *See supra* § 4.2.

8. *See, e.g.*, State v. Robinson, 213 N.C. 273, 282, 195 S.E. 824, 830 (1938) (if defendant had well-grounded belief that a felonious assault was about to be committed on another, "he had the right and it was his duty as a private citizen to interfere to prevent the supposed crime"); State v. Nash, 88 N.C. 618, 620 (1883) (reasonable belief that felony is in act of being committed will excuse killing though no felony was in fact intended); Robert L. Farb, *Defending Yourself and Your Property*, POPULAR GOVERNMENT, Summer 1987, at 1, 3 & n.13 (privilege applies when person has reasonable but mistaken belief that felonious assault is being committed upon innocent victim); PERKINS, *supra* note 2, at 1111.

9. PERKINS, *supra* note 2, at 1109.

offenses, it would seem that a person would be entitled to use at least the same amount of force to prevent those offenses from being committed.[10]

### (b) Detaining Offenders

G.S. 15A-404 grants a person the right to use force to detain an offender until a law-enforcement officer arrives. The right to *detain* offenders supplants the common-law right to *arrest* once granted private citizens in North Carolina. This change did not really have any practical effect on the physical actions that a private person may take; it was intended more to clarify that private persons do not have law-enforcement powers.[11]

The right to detain does differ from the right to use defensive force. Defensive-force defenses allow a person to use force only when reasonably necessary to prevent a harm (such as bodily injury) from occurring. The right to detain, in contrast, allows a person to use force after the offense has been committed and the immediate harm inflicted.[12]

Under G.S. 15A-404 a person has the right to use force to detain an offender when the person has probable cause to believe that one of the following offenses has been committed in his or her presence:

1. a felony;
2. a breach of the peace;
3. a crime involving physical injury to another person; or
4. a crime involving theft or destruction of property.

The statute's reference to "probable cause" means that a person's belief that such an offense has occurred must be judged by the standard of reasonableness. The statute also provides that a person may use "reasonable" force in light of the offense involved and the circumstances of the detention.

May a person ever use *deadly* force to detain an offender? In *State v. Wall*, the supreme court held that a person ordinarily may not use deadly force to detain someone who has committed a *misdemeanor*.[13] In *Wall*, the defendant was charged with felony murder based

---

10. *Id.* at 1108–09 (statutes authorizing arrest or detention may be construed as enlarging the common-law right to prevent crime). When the offense is a "dangerous" felony, as described in the previous section, a person may use deadly, not just nondeadly, force to prevent the offense from occurring.

11. *See* Official Commentary to G.S. 15A-404.

12. *See generally* 2 PAUL H. ROBINSON, CRIMINAL LAW DEFENSES 113–15 (1984).

13. 304 N.C. 609, 615–16, 286 S.E.2d 68, 72–73 (1982).

on shooting into an occupied vehicle. A teenager had taken beer from the defendant's store without paying for it (a misdemeanor larceny). As the teenager started to drive out of the parking lot, the defendant shot at the vehicle, killing the driver.[14]

The court ruled that the defendant's conduct was not justified, reasoning that a private person's right to use deadly force to detain an offender under G.S. 15A-404 is no greater than the right of a law-enforcement officer to use deadly force under G.S. 15A-401(d)(2). Under the latter statute, a law-enforcement officer may not use deadly force to apprehend a person except in special circumstances, such as when the person presents an imminent threat of death or serious physical injury to others unless apprehended without delay. The court's reasoning may also apply to detaining someone who has committed a *felony*. If so, a private person may use deadly force to detain a felon only when the circumstances would justify a law-enforcement officer in using deadly force.[15]

*Wall* also held that the detention statute did not protect the defendant's actions because his purpose was not to detain. The court based this conclusion on two findings: (1) the defendant testified that he was not trying to *stop* the person who had taken the beer but rather was trying to get the person to *return* the beer; (2) since the person was already leaving the parking lot, the person was no longer within the defendant's *control* and therefore no longer subject to being detained.[16]

---

14. Three members of the court dissented in the case. The dissenters argued that the evidence did not show that the defendant intended to shoot *into* the vehicle. *Id.* at 622–24, 286 S.E.2d at 76–77. They did not, however, question the general rule announced by the majority on when a person may use deadly force to detain an offender.

15. Earlier cases allowed a person greater latitude in using deadly force to detain a felon. Some held that a person could use deadly force to prevent the escape of someone who had committed a serious felony, such as murder or rape. *See* State v. Bryant, 65 N.C. 327, 328–29 (1871). Others appeared to allow a person to use deadly force to apprehend anyone who had committed a felony. *See* State v. Roane, 13 N.C. 58, 62 (1828) (person may kill during arrest of felon if person makes known that his or her object is to arrest and killing is necessary to make arrest); State v. Rutherford, 8 N.C. 457, 458–59 (1821) (to extenuate homicide in pursuit of individual who has committed felony, felony must actually have been committed and killing must be necessary to prevent felon from escaping).

16. *Wall*, 304 N.C. at 615–16, 286 S.E.2d at 72. The distinctions drawn by the court in this part of the opinion are somewhat difficult to grasp, however. It would seem difficult to distinguish between trying to *stop* a person from leaving and trying to get a person to *return* once the person has started to leave. *Cf. supra* § 3.2(b)(2), "Multiple Threats of Harm" (defendant's motive for acting ordinarily

The only other reported decision interpreting G.S. 15A-404, *State v. Ataei-Kachuei*,[17] involved circumstances similar to those in *Wall*, but the court of appeals found the defendant's actions to be protected under the detention statute. As in *Wall*, the defendant in *Ataei-Kachuei* was charged with felony murder based on shooting into an occupied vehicle. This defendant also shot and killed the victim as the victim was driving away. The court of appeals, however, made two findings to distinguish the case before it from *Wall*. First, the court found sufficient evidence that the defendant was shooting into the air in an effort to scare the victim and was not shooting at the vehicle. Since such conduct may not constitute *deadly* force, the defendant in *Ataei-Kachuei* arguably did not violate the general proscription on the use of deadly force to detain.[18] Second, the court found that the defendant's purpose was to *stop* the offender from leaving and that the offender, although trying to drive away, was still only a few feet from the defendant at the time of the shooting and therefore still within the defendant's *control*.

## § 5.2 Defense of Another

North Carolina recognizes *defense of others* as a defensive-force defense. Because of the potential limitations of that defense, however, a defendant also may rely on the crime prevention privilege to justify aiding another person. In an appropriate case, a defendant is entitled to have the jury instructed on both defense of others and the crime prevention privilege.[19] Each is discussed in turn below.

---

immaterial in determining right to use defensive force). It also would seem difficult to determine when a defendant loses *control* of an offender, especially in cases in which the defendant is in fresh pursuit of the person. *Cf. infra* § 5.3(a) (under most restrictive view of defense of property, a person may retake property if he or she does so during fresh pursuit of wrongdoer).

17. 68 N.C. App. 209, 212–14, 314 S.E.2d 751, 753–54, *rev. denied*, 311 N.C. 763, 321 S.E.2d 146 (1984).

18. *See supra* § 2.2(b)(2) (firing of warning shots may not constitute deadly force). Since the defendant in *Ataei-Kachuei* was trying to detain someone who had committed a felony, not a misdemeanor, the decision could be construed as authorizing the use of deadly force to detain a felon. To the extent *Ataei-Kachuei* so implies, however, it is questionable authority in light of *Wall*.

19. *See, e.g.*, State v. Robinson, 213 N.C. 273, 281–82, 195 S.E. 824, 829–30 (1938).

## (a) Defending Others

### (1) In General

In most respects, defense of others tracks the general principles applicable to defense of oneself. As in cases of self-defense, the seriousness of the harm that is or reasonably appears to be threatened determines the degree of force that may be used in response. For example, the threat of death or great bodily injury to another person triggers a defendant's right to use deadly force to protect that person. The threat of bodily harm, however, triggers only the right to use nondeadly force on behalf of that person.[20]

Cases involving defense of others also follow the principles embodied in the *Norris* test.[21] For example, the defendant must honestly and reasonably believe it necessary to protect another person from harm.[22] In homicide cases, if the defendant meets all of the *Norris* elements, he or she may rely on *perfect* defense of others; if the defendant meets the first two elements of *Norris*, but is an aggressor without murderous intent or uses excessive force, he or she may claim *imperfect* defense of others.[23]

20. *See, e.g.*, State v. Church, 229 N.C. 718, 721, 51 S.E.2d 345, 347 (1949) (defendant has right to defend another against threat of death or great bodily harm and other harms); State v. Anderson, 222 N.C. 148, 150, 22 S.E.2d 271, 273 (1942) (right to defend another is coextensive with right of other person to defend himself or herself).

21. The *Norris* test is discussed in general in § 2.2(c) *supra*; the four parts of the test are analyzed in detail in §§ 3.1 through 3.4 *supra*; and the potential differences in the application of the test in homicide and nonhomicide cases are discussed in § 4.1 *supra*.

22. *See, e.g.*, State v. McKoy, 332 N.C. 639, 643–44, 422 S.E.2d 713, 716 (1992) (evidence insufficient to show defendant reasonably needed to defend another); State v. Oxendine, 300 N.C. 720, 724–25, 268 S.E.2d 212, 215 (1980) (to same effect); State v. Shepherd, 220 N.C. 377, 380, 17 S.E.2d 469, 470–71 (1941) (defendant renewed difficulty and so could not claim that he reasonably needed to defend another). *Compare, e.g.*, State v. Jones, 299 N.C. 103, 108, 261 S.E.2d 1, 5 (1980) (evidence sufficient to show defendant reasonably needed to defend another); State v. Hodges, 255 N.C. 566, 568–69, 122 S.E.2d 197, 198–99 (1961) (to same effect).

23. *See* State v. Perry, 338 N.C. 457, 465–67, 450 S.E.2d 471, 476–77 (1994); *McKoy*, 332 N.C. at 643–44, 422 S.E.2d at 716; *Jones*, 299 N.C. at 111–12, 261 S.E.2d at 7–8.

Defense of others involves three potential problems, however. May a person rely on defense of others to come to the aid of a stranger? May a person rely on the defense if the person aided turns out to have been the aggressor in the encounter? And is there a duty to retreat in cases involving defense of others?

### (2) Defense of Strangers

Defense of others allows the use of force to prevent any *harm* covered by the rules of self-defense. At one time, however, it was not clear whether a person could intervene on behalf of any *person*. According to Perkins, defense of others originally represented an expansion of the right to defend property. A man could defend not only his inanimate possessions, but also his wife, his children, and his servants.[24] Although not so explicitly paternalistic, some North Carolina decisions reflect the common-law roots of the defense, as the courts appear to have insisted on some special relationship between the person giving aid and the person aided. Thus, family members could defend other family members, employers could defend employees, and hosts could defend guests.[25]

Although these cases have not been overruled, it seems unlikely that today's courts would follow the restrictions embodied in them. The apparently universal opinion of commentators is that such restrictions are outdated and that one person has the right to defend another person, even if the two are "strangers."[26] A recent supreme

---

24. PERKINS, *supra* note 2, at 1144–45.

25. *See, e.g.*, State v. Hornbuckle, 265 N.C. 312, 314–15, 144 S.E.2d 12, 13–14 (1965) (evidence sufficient to require instruction when defendant came to aid of passenger in defendant's car); State v. Davis, 222 N.C. 178, 179, 22 S.E.2d 274, 274 (1942) (error not to instruct on right to defend wife from assault); State v. Maney, 194 N.C. 34, 35–36, 138 S.E. 441, 442 (1927) (recognizing right to defend wife, parent, child, and servant); State v. Moses, 17 N.C. App. 115, 116, 193 S.E.2d 288, 289 (1972) ("[p]ersons in a family relation, and persons in the relation of master and servant, have the reciprocal right to come to the aid and defense of the person in that relation").

26. *See, e.g.*, Farb, *supra* note 8, at 1, 3; PERKINS, *supra* note 2, at 1144–45; 1 WAYNE R. LAFAVE & AUSTIN W. SCOTT, JR., SUBSTANTIVE CRIMINAL LAW 664 (1986). A relatively recent case before the court of appeals illustrates the artificiality of the common-law rules. In State v. Gilliland, 66 N.C. App. 372, 311 S.E.2d 40 (1984), the defendant struck Wanda, Ronnie came to Wanda's aid, and the defendant cut Ronnie. The defendant was charged with assaulting Ronnie with a deadly weapon and defended on the ground that Ronnie had unlawfully intervened on Wanda's behalf. According to the defendant, although Ronnie and Wanda had gone through a marriage ceremony,

court decision supports this view, assuming (without expressly deciding) that the defendant could rely on defense of others even though the defendant had no special relationship with the person to be defended.[27]

### (3) Defense of Aggressors

A person relying on defense of others must meet the principles embodied in the *Norris* test. Among other things, a person coming to another's defense must not be the aggressor in the encounter. But is defense of others available if the person *to be defended* is an aggressor? For example, suppose A strikes B, and B uses nondeadly force in lawful self-defense. C happens upon the scene, reasonably believes that B is unlawfully attacking A, and uses nondeadly force in A's defense. General language in some North Carolina cases suggests that C's conduct may not be justified under defense of others. The rationale is that C's right to defend A is coextensive with A's right to act in self-defense. Since A is the aggressor and does not have the right to defend against B's lawful use of force, C is not privileged to intervene.[28]

This doctrine has been criticized, however. Several commentators have argued that if a person reasonably believes that another is being unlawfully attacked, he or she should have the right to intervene and should not be held criminally liable even though the person aided turns out to have been the aggressor in the encounter.[29] Language from a recent supreme court decision suggests a fairly simple solution to the problem of the "unknowing" defendant. In the course of discussing an-

---

Wanda was not divorced from her first husband at the time of the marriage; therefore, Ronnie and Wanda were not legally married, and Ronnie could not justify his intervention under defense of others. The court of appeals rejected the defendant's argument, finding that Ronnie had the right to intervene to protect Wanda.

27. *McKoy*, 332 N.C. at 643–44, 422 S.E.2d at 715–16 (upholding denial of instruction on defense of others on ground that evidence was insufficient to show that defendant reasonably needed to protect other person).

28. *See* State v. McLawhorn, 270 N.C. 622, 629, 155 S.E.2d 198, 203–04 (1967); State v. Ritter, 239 N.C. 89, 93, 79 S.E.2d 164, 166 (1953); State v. Greer, 162 N.C. 640, 648–52, 78 S.E. 310, 312–14 (1913); State v. Cox, 153 N.C. 638, 645, 69 S.E. 419, 422 (1910); State v. Johnson, 75 N.C. 174, 175–76 (1876). It is unclear from the cited cases whether any of the defendants presented evidence that they were unaware that the person to be defended was the aggressor. As a result, despite the general language contained in those cases, it does not appear that the court directly addressed whether a person could rely on defense of others in the example described in the text.

29. *See, e.g.*, Farb, *supra* note 8, at 1, 3 & n.9; PERKINS, *supra* note 2, at 1146–47; 1 LAFAVE, *supra* note 26, at 665–66.

other issue the court stated that "the right to kill in defense of another cannot exceed such other's right to kill in his own defense *as that other's right reasonably appeared to defendant*."[30] Thus a defendant who is not the aggressor and otherwise meets the requirements of the *Norris* test may go to the defense of another person as long as the defendant reasonably believes that the person to be defended has the right to defend himself or herself.

### *(4) Retreat*

Whether North Carolina imposes any requirement of retreat in cases involving defense of oneself remains open to debate. One line of self-defense cases suggests that a person need not retreat as long as he or she meets the requirements for using defensive force; another line of self-defense cases holds that a person need not retreat inside the home or business, implying that a person has a duty to retreat elsewhere.[31] Cases involving defense of others shed no further light on this conflict, merely following the general rules stated for self-defense.[32] Assuming that North Carolina imposes a duty to retreat in some situations, could it be applied to cases involving defense of others? It would seem difficult to do so. Ordinarily, it would make little sense to inquire whether a person defending another could have retreated in safety when he or she could have avoided danger all along by not intervening in the first place.[33]

### (b) Preventing Crime against Others

The crime prevention privilege, discussed in § 5.1, above, is more straightforward than the right to defend others. The privilege pro-

---

30. State v. Terry, 337 N.C. 615, 623, 447 S.E.2d 720, 724 (1994) (emphasis added).

31. *See supra* § 3.5.

32. *See* State v. Anderson, 222 N.C. 148, 151, 22 S.E.2d 271, 273 (1942) (no retreat required in own home); State v. Dills, 196 N.C. 457, 460, 146 S.E. 1, 2–3 (1929) (no retreat required against felonious assault).

33. *See* 1 LaFave, *supra* note 26, at 667. The Model Penal Code advocates a modified duty to retreat in cases involving defense of others, but the Code's formulation introduces a degree of complexity that no reasonable person could fathom in the heat of conflict. For example, under the Code, the defendant must try to cause the person attacked to retreat if the defendant determines that the person has an obligation to retreat and the person could retreat in complete safety. Model Penal Code and Commentaries § 3.05(2) (American Law Institute 1985).

tects a defendant who acts to prevent a crime against another person, even when the person aided is a stranger. Also, as long as the defendant *reasonably* believes that the other person is the innocent victim of a crime—whether that person is, in fact, innocent in the encounter—the defendant may intervene under the privilege to prevent crime.[34]

In applying the privilege, however, the courts have introduced an additional uncertainty. They have said that the privilege applies only when the defendant reasonably believes that the assault on the other person is *felonious*.[35] Like the restrictions applicable to defense of others, this restriction may have developed more by accident than design and may no longer apply.[36]

## § 5.3 Defense of Property

The supreme court has said that "[a]s an incident to the indubitable right to acquire and own property, . . . a person . . . has the legal right to defend and protect it."[37] This right extends to both personal and real property, although the rules differ slightly depending on the type of property defended.

### (a) Defending Personal Property

A person has the right to defend personal property against any threatened loss, damage, or other encroachment.[38] Although the cases do not explicitly employ the four-part Norris test, similar principles apply.[39]

---

34. *See, e.g.*, State v. Robinson, 213 N.C. 273, 282, 195 S.E. 824, 830 (1938) (if defendant had well-grounded belief that a felonious assault was about to be committed on another, "he had the right and it was his duty as a private citizen to interfere to prevent the supposed crime"); State v. Graves, 18 N.C. App. 177, 181, 196 S.E.2d 582, 584 (1973) (to same effect). *See also* Farb, *supra* note 8, at 1, 3 & n.13.

35. *See, e.g.*, State v. Fields, 268 N.C. 456, 458, 150 S.E.2d 852, 854 (1966).

36. *See, e.g.*, Perkins, *supra* note 2, at 1145 (indicating that restriction has largely been eliminated).

37. State v. Lee, 258 N.C. 44, 46–47, 127 S.E.2d 774, 776 (1962).

38. *See* 2 Robinson, *supra* note 12, at 107 (defense of property applies to any trespass, attack, entry, crime involving danger to premises, unlawful carrying away, criminal mischief, burglary, tortious interference, or any other unjustified encroachment).

39. *See Lee*, 258 N.C. at 46–47, 127 S.E.2d at 776 (force used to retake property must be reasonably necessary to accomplish purpose); State v. Scott, 142 N.C. 582, 583–84, 55 S.E. 69, 70 (1906) (to same effect). The *Norris* test is discussed in general

The law never permits deadly force, however, to protect mere property.[40]

The main wrinkle in defense of property is whether a person may use force to recapture property once it has been taken. The common law allowed a person to use nondeadly force to recapture property if the recapture took place "at once or upon fresh pursuit."[41] The Model Penal Code would permit retaking *at any time* if the actor believes that the other person has no claim of right to possession of the property.[42] The issue has arisen infrequently in North Carolina. An older case held that a person may use "so much force as is reasonably necessary to protect his property or retake it, when it has wrongfully been taken by another or is withheld without authority."[43] It is unclear, however, whether the court intended to allow a person to retake his or her property at any time or only on fresh pursuit.

## (b) Defending Real Property and Evicting Trespassers

A person's right to defend real property is likewise triggered by any threatened harm to or encroachment on the property. A person may use reasonable force both to prevent damage to real property[44] and to remove trespassers from the property.[45]

---

in § 2.2(c) *supra*; the four parts of the test are analyzed in detail in §§ 3.1 through 3.4 *supra*; and the potential differences in the application of the test in homicide and nonhomicide cases are discussed in § 4.1 *supra*.

40. *Lee*, 258 N.C. at 46–47, 127 S.E.2d at 776; *Scott*, 142 N.C. at 583–84, 55 S.E. at 70. The right to defend property could be relevant, however, in an encounter in which the defendant initially uses nondeadly force and the other person responds with deadly force. Having justifiably entered the encounter to defend property, the defendant would have the right to use deadly force to defend himself or herself when the encounter turned deadly. *See supra* § 3.3(b)(3) (discussing general aggressor principles).

41. Perkins, *supra* note 2, at 1157.

42. Model Penal Code and Commentaries, *supra* note 33, § 3.06(1)(b)(ii). *See also* 1 LaFave, *supra* note 26, at 672–73 (comparing common-law view with Model Penal Code).

43. *Scott*, 142 N.C. at 583–84, 55 S.E. at 70 (finding that defendant had right to retake mules but that force used was excessive).

44. *See* State v. McCombs, 297 N.C. 151, 157, 253 S.E.2d 906, 911 (1979); State v. Austin, 123 N.C. 749, 751, 31 S.E. 731, 732 (1898) (right to use force to prevent person from taking cotton crop).

45. *See* State v. Goodson, 235 N.C. 177, 178–79, 69 S.E.2d 242, 243 (1952); State v. Spruill, 225 N.C. 356, 357–58, 34 S.E.2d 142, 143 (1945).

The right to defend real property and evict trespassers must be distinguished from the right to defend one's habitation (discussed below in § 5.4). Defense of habitation allows the use of *deadly* force in specialized circumstances—namely, to defend against an intruder into a person's home who intends to commit a felony or cause death or great bodily harm. The right to defend real property and evict trespassers is narrower in the sense that it allows the use of *nondeadly* force only.[46] It is broader, however, in the sense that a person may use force to defend any real property, not just the habitation, and to prevent relatively minor encroachments such as trespassing.[47]

The wrinkle in defense of real property is the doctrine of *molliter manus*, which applies to the eviction of trespassers. As interpreted by the North Carolina courts, this doctrine requires that a person first ask the trespasser to leave. If the trespasser refuses to leave, the person then may lay hands gently upon the trespasser to remove him or her. If the trespasser still does not leave, the actor then may employ additional nondeadly force to expel the trespasser.[48] Whether today's courts would hold a person criminally liable for not strictly following this formula is unclear. Even older cases recognize, however, that the doctrine of *molliter manus* does not apply if it would be dangerous for the person to ask the trespasser to leave or if harm would be done to the property before such a request could be made.[49]

---

46. *See* State v. McDonald, 49 N.C. 19, 21–23 (1856) (killing prohibited to avert trespass); State v. Morgan, 25 N.C. 186, 193 (1842) (to same effect); State v. Myers, 49 N.C. App. 197, 199–200, 270 S.E.2d 574, 575 (1980) (defendant who used deadly force to evict mere trespasser was not entitled to instruction on right to evict trespasser).

47. *See McCombs*, 297 N.C. at 157–58, 253 S.E.2d at 911 (recognizing right to defend against invasions of real property other than in circumstances giving rise to defense of habitation); *see also* Perkins, *supra* note 2, at 1150–51 (person may use nondeadly force to defend real property in circumstances when defense of habitation not applicable).

48. *See McCombs*, 297 N.C. 151, 157, 253 S.E.2d 906, 911 (1979); State v. Pettiford, 239 N.C. 301, 303, 79 S.E.2d 517, 518 (1954); State v. Crook, 133 N.C. 672, 675, 45 S.E. 564, 565–66 (1903); State v. Leggett, 104 N.C. 784, 785–86, 10 S.E. 464, 465 (1889).

49. *See* State v. Taylor, 82 N.C. 554, 555 (1880) (doctrine of *molliter manus* does not apply when trespasser is armed); State v. Davis, 80 N.C. 351, 352 (1879) (to same effect). *See also* 2 Robinson, *supra* note 12, at 107–08 (request not required where it would be useless or dangerous or where harm would result to property).

## § 5.4 Defense of Habitation

### (a) In General

The right to defend one's home, or habitation, is a separate doctrine from the right to defend property or oneself. The *harm* that the defense allows a person to prevent is a specialized one, derived from both case and statutory law. The case law provides that a person may rely on the defense when he or she is acting to prevent a forcible entry into the habitation by someone who intends to commit a felony or cause death or great bodily injury. In those circumstances, a person may use deadly force assuming he or she satisfies the requirements of the *Norris* test.[50] New G.S. 14-51.1 expands the right to defend one's home. It allows the use of deadly force to "terminate" an entry by an intruder who has already entered the habitation and who intends to commit a felony or cause death or great bodily injury.

Apart from the involved nature of the *harm* covered by defense of habitation, which is explored in the next section, the defense operates much like other defensive-force defenses. It is sufficient if the defendant *reasonably believes* that another is forcibly entering (or has entered) the habitation with the intent to commit a felony or cause death or great bodily injury.[51] Also, at one time the supreme court appeared to allow *imperfect* defense of habitation in homicide cases, a result that would seem to follow from the *Norris* test. In strongly worded dicta in a recent case, however, the court refused to recognize the theory of *imperfect* defense of habitation.[52]

---

50. *McCombs*, 297 N.C. at 156–57, 253 S.E.2d at 911; State v. Miller, 267 N.C. 409, 411, 148 S.E.2d 279, 281 (1966). The *Norris* test is discussed in general in § 2.2(c) *supra*; the four parts of the test are analyzed in detail in §§ 3.1 through 3.4 *supra*; and the potential differences in the application of the test in homicide and nonhomicide cases are discussed in § 4.1 *supra*.

51. *See* State v. Jones, 299 N.C. 103, 111–12, 261 S.E.2d 1, 7–8 (1980) (defendant's belief in need to defend habitation judged by standard of reasonableness); State v. Gray, 162 N.C. 608, 612–13, 77 S.E. 833, 834–35 (1913) (if defendant reasonably believed the danger existed, he had right to act).

52. *Compare Jones*, 299 N.C. at 112, 261 S.E.2d at 8 (court appeared to recognize imperfect defense of habitation in holding that if defendant uses excessive force in defending home the offense is voluntary manslaughter) *with* State v. Lyons, 340 N.C. 646, 664–66, 459 S.E.2d 770, 780–81 (1995) (after finding that defendant's argument did not warrant any instruction on defense of habitation, court states that it takes "opportunity to reject the theory of imperfect defense of habitation"; defendant

## (b) Specialized Requirements

### (1) Entry

Traditionally, a defendant claiming defense of habitation had to be acting to *prevent* entry. Once the intruder had gained entry, the rules governing self-defense within the home controlled.[53] Thus a person could kill to prevent entry by an intruder who intended to commit a felony in the habitation, but could not kill an intruder who had the same intent and who had already gained entry. The rationale given for this distinction was that the occupants of a dwelling had less ability to determine an intruder's intentions while the intruder was outside trying to get in.[54]

New G.S. 14-51.1 does away with this distinction. In addition to codifying the common-law right to defend habitation, it allows a lawful occupant within a home or other residence to use deadly force to "terminate an unlawful entry" in specified circumstances. Thus a lawful occupant may use any degree of force, including deadly force, against an intruder who has already gained entry into the habitation if the occupant reasonably believes that the intruder intends to commit a felony or cause death or great bodily injury and that such force is necessary to remove the intruder.

Under both the common law and G.S. 14-51.1, there still must be at least the appearance of entry or attempted entry. Defense of habitation does not apply if an assailant is outside a dwelling and the occupants do not have reasonable grounds to believe that the assailant is attempting to enter.[55] But if an assailant has entered a person's dwelling,

---

conceded that court had not previously recognized theory). *See also* State v. Roberson, 90 N.C. App. 219, 223, 368 S.E.2d 3, 6, *rev. denied*, 322 N.C. 484, 370 S.E.2d 237 (1988) (overlooking *Jones*, court of appeals states that North Carolina had not yet recognized imperfect defense of habitation). The supreme court's apparent decision to narrow defense of habitation contrasts with the General Assembly's resolve, discussed in the next section, to expand the defense.

53. *See* State v. Avery, 302 N.C. 517, 527, 276 S.E.2d 699, 705–06 (1981); *McCombs*, 297 N.C. at 157, 253 S.E.2d at 911; State v. Martin, 52 N.C. App. 326, 330–31, 278 S.E.2d 315, 318 (evidence indicated that shooting occurred either inside or outside trailer, but even when taken together evidence did not indicate that defendant believed that victim was attempting to enter), *rev. denied*, 303 N.C. 317, 281 S.E.2d 390 (1981).

54. *See McCombs*, 297 N.C. at 157, 253 S.E.2d at 911.

55. *See generally* State v. Reynolds, 212 N.C. 37, 38, 192 S.E. 871, 871–72 (1937)

has been ejected, and attempts to reenter, the person may rely on defense of habitation in resisting the attempt to reenter.[56]

What if an assailant does not physically attempt to enter but appears to be mounting some sort of attack on the home or its occupants, such as firing into the home? The cases suggest that such conduct would satisfy the entry requirement, the rationale being that defense of habitation applies to any invasion of the habitation that meets the other conditions of the defense.[57]

The cases also state generally that the entry must be *forcible*, but the meaning of the term is not entirely clear. An assailant's use of physical force in attempting entry—such as breaking down a door—would certainly satisfy the term.[58] It also seems appropriate to allow defense of habitation when the assailant does not use physical force in attempting entry, but it reasonably appears that the assailant is attempting to enter (or has entered) the habitation *unlawfully* with the intent to commit a felony or cause death or serious bodily injury.[59]

---

(jury could find from evidence that victim was unarmed and standing fifteen feet away from defendant's house when defendant shot him; nonsuit properly denied).

56. *See* State v. Marshall, 105 N.C. App. 518, 523–24, 414 S.E.2d 95, 98–99 (trial court erred in failing to instruct on defense of habitation), *rev. denied*, 332 N.C. 150, 419 S.E.2d 576 (1992).

57. *See* State v. Nash, 88 N.C. 618, 620–22 (1883) (defendant reasonably believed trespassers were firing into his home); State v. Edwards, 28 N.C. App. 196, 197–98, 220 S.E.2d 158, 159–60 (1975) (trial court erred in denying instructions on defense of habitation where assailant fired into defendant's house from outside); PERKINS, *supra* note 2, at 1150 (rationale for defense of habitation is to allow person to defend home and occupants from unlawful intrusion or attack).

58. *See* State v. Jones, 299 N.C. 103, 108, 261 S.E.2d 1, 5–6 (1980) (error not to instruct on defense of habitation; deceased beat on door, tore lock off screen door, tore screen, and broke several panes of glass, which put occupants of house in fear of deceased); State v. Miller, 267 N.C. 409, 410–11, 148 S.E.2d 279, 280–81 (1966) (error not to instruct on defense of habitation; deceased was "half drunk," tore screen out of door, and threatened to tear place up).

59. *See* State v. Hedgepeth, 46 N.C. App. 569, 572–73, 265 S.E.2d 413, 416 (1980) (trial court erred in not instructing on defense of habitation where deceased refused to leave defendant's yard after being asked to do so, returned to porch of house, threatened to kill defendant, and stuck head around threshold of door as if he were going to enter); *cf.* THOMAS H. THORNBURG, NORTH CAROLINA CRIMES: A GUIDEBOOK ON THE ELEMENTS OF CRIME 204, 210 (4th ed. 1996) [hereinafter NORTH CAROLINA CRIMES] ("breaking" requirement for burglary satisfied by making of some opening in habitation even though no destructive force is used; either "breaking" or "entry" without consent sufficient for felonious breaking or entering).

## (2) Habitation

The attack must be on the *habitation*. The cases on defense of habitation have not focused on the meaning of that term, however, and cases involving self-defense within the home or business may not always provide an appropriate definition. For example, the courts may be unwilling to hold that defense of habitation allows a person to use deadly force to prevent a person from entering the curtilage of the home, although in cases of self-defense within the home, the curtilage is considered part of the home.[60] A closer question is whether defense of habitation applies to a person's business. Although the North Carolina courts have not faced this question, some jurisdictions protect a person's business under defense of habitation.[61] Another issue is whether the person claiming defense of habitation must be the owner of the property. According to new G.S. 14.51.1, any "lawful occupant" has the right to defend the habitation. This statute reaffirms the common-law rule that the right to defend habitation does not depend on ownership.[62]

---

60. *See supra* § 4.4(b).

61. *See* Perkins, *supra* note 2, at 1151.

62. *See Miller*, 267 N.C. at 411, 148 S.E.2d at 281 (any "lawful occupant" may defend habitation); Perkins, *supra* note 2, at 1151–52 (tenant, servant, or guest has right to defend habitation); 2 Robinson, *supra* note 12, at 89–91 (person has right to defend property of another). *See also* State v. Avery, 302 N.C. 517, 527, 276 S.E.2d 699, 705–06 (1981) (court assumed without deciding that a person who was not a resident of the dwelling could defend against unlawful entry by law-enforcement officer).

Perkins states that an occupant may not rely on defense of habitation against a co-occupant, but it is not clear why he adopts such a position for defense of habitation and not for defense of other property that may be subject to joint ownership or use. Perkins, *supra* note 2, at 1151–52. The court of appeals has likewise held that defense of habitation is unavailable in a case involving co-occupants. In State v. Teel, 65 N.C. App. 423, 423–24, 310 S.E.2d 31, 32 (1983), the court found that a wife could *not* rely on defense of habitation when her husband came home drunk, threatened to kill her, and began beating on the side of the trailer with a crowbar in an effort to get inside. The court so held on the ground that the husband was a co-owner of the trailer and had the right to be on the premises. The supreme court, however, has not considered the balance struck by the court of appeals between the husband's and wife's rights.

### (3) Assailant's Intent

Last, the occupant must reasonably believe that the assailant intends to commit a felony or cause death or serious bodily injury. If the occupant believes only that the assailant intends to commit a misdemeanor such as a simple assault, the rules governing nondeadly force in self-defense apply.[63]

### (4) Other Issues

A person evicting an ordinary trespasser must ask the trespasser to leave before using force.[64] No such requirement exists for defense of habitation.[65] Also, new G.S. 14-51.1 reaffirms the common-law rule that a lawful occupant defending the habitation does not have a duty to retreat.[66]

## § 5.5 Defending against Law-Enforcement Officers

Many actions by law-enforcement officers, if undertaken by private persons, would trigger a right to use defensive force. If a private person unjustifiably sought to restrain another, for example, the person restrained could use reasonable force to free himself or herself. Likewise, if a private person entered another's dwelling without permission, the occupant would have the right to evict the person as a trespasser. In contrast, when a law-enforcement officer properly arrests a person or searches a home or performs some other lawful duty, the subject has no right to use force to resist. He or she must submit "peaceably."[67]

The general requirement that a person must yield to an officer's authority is subject to three main exceptions. A person may use force against a law-enforcement officer when

- the person does not know of the officer's authority;

---

63. *See* State v. McCombs, 297 N.C. 151, 157–58, 253 S.E.2d 906, 911 (1979). Nondeadly force in self-defense is discussed in § 4.3 *supra*.

64. *See supra* § 5.3(b).

65. *See* State v. Baker, 222 N.C. 428, 430–31, 23 S.E.2d 340, 341–42 (1942).

66. *See, e.g., Miller*, 267 N.C. at 411, 148 S.E.2d at 281 (householder need not "flee"), *quoting* State v. Gray, 162 N.C. 608, 610–611, 77 S.E. 833, 834 (1913).

67. State v. Cooper, 4 N.C. App. 210, 214, 166 S.E.2d 509, 513 (1969). *Accord* State v. Miller, 197 N.C. 445, 447, 149 S.E. 590, 592 (1929) (forcible resistance to lawful arrests "will not be sanctioned").

- the person knows of the officer's authority, but the officer is not performing a lawful duty; or
- the person knows of the officer's authority, and the officer is performing a lawful duty, but the officer uses excessive force.

These three exceptions are discussed below.

### (a) When Defendant Does Not Know of Officer's Authority

#### (1) Negating and Justification Defense

If a defendant does not know of an officer's authority, this lack of knowledge may serve both as a *negating defense* and as part of a *justification defense*. The meaning of the phrase "knowledge of an officer's authority" is described further in the next subsection, but first it is important to understand the differences between the two types of defenses in cases involving law-enforcement officers.

Lack of knowledge can serve as a negating defense when knowledge is one of the required elements of the offense charged. For example, both resisting arrest and assault on a law-enforcement officer require the state to show knowledge of the officer's authority. If the state fails to prove the defendant's knowledge beyond a reasonable doubt, the defendant may not be convicted of either offense.[68] When used in this manner, however, lack of knowledge does not provide a complete defense. A person who uses force against an officer, not knowing of the officer's authority, could still be convicted of an offense not requiring proof of knowledge. For example, a person who strikes an undercover officer, not knowing of the officer's authority, could still be convicted of simple assault.[69]

---

68. *See* State v. Avery, 315 N.C. 1, 30–31, 337 S.E.2d 786, 802–03 (1985) (knowledge is essential element of assault with firearm on officer under G.S. 14-34.2); State v. Rowland, 54 N.C. App. 458, 461–62, 283 S.E.2d 543, 545–46 (1981) [knowledge is essential element of assault on officer under former G.S. 14-33(b)(4)]; NORTH CAROLINA CRIMES, *supra* note 59, at 332 (person may not be convicted of resisting officer absent knowledge of officer's authority).

69. *See Rowland*, 54 N.C. App. at 461–62, 283 S.E.2d at 545–46 (trial court erred in failing to submit lesser offense of simple assault where evidence indicated that defendant did not know officer was officer); State v. Mayberry, 38 N.C. App. 509, 512, 248 S.E.2d 402, 404 (1978) (trial court did not err in failing to submit lesser offense of assault where all of evidence showed defendant knew of officer's authority).

When lack of knowledge is part of a justification defense, a person has a complete defense if he or she complies with the applicable rules of defensive force. For example, if a person does not know of an officer's authority and strikes the officer in proper self-defense, the person would have a complete defense to any charge.[70]

### (2) Meaning of "Knowledge"

The phrase "knowledge of an officer's authority" has been used above to describe the role knowledge plays in cases involving law-enforcement officers, but the concept potentially involves two separate issues. The first issue is whether the defendant is aware of the officer's identity—in other words, that the officer is an officer. The law is clear that when the defendant lacks such knowledge, he or she may use defensive force as if the officer were a "private person."[71] A second issue is whether the defendant knows that the officer is performing a law-enforcement duty. In limited circumstances the defendant may know that an officer is an officer but not know that the officer is performing a law-enforcement duty. Whether the defendant would have the right in these circumstances to use force against the officer is unclear.[72]

---

70. *See* State v. Belk, 76 N.C. 10, 14 (1877) (if officer is not known to be an officer and does not notify person to be arrested of authority, person may lawfully resist arrest as if it were made by a private person); State v. Polk, 29 N.C. App. 360, 361–62, 224 S.E.2d 272, 273 (1976) (trial court erred in failing to instruct on defendant's right of self-defense where off-duty officer approached defendant in parking lot, defendant did not know of officer's authority, and defendant thought officer was attempting to steal defendant's car). A person also would be justified in taking other actions when he or she does not know of the officer's authority. *See, e.g.*, State v. Borland, 21 N.C. App. 559, 566, 205 S.E.2d 340, 345 (1974) (defendant who did not know that car pursuing him was law-enforcement car had right to flee; jury should have been instructed on defendant's theory as ground for acquittal of speeding and reckless driving).

71. *Belk*, 76 N.C. at 14.

72. *See generally* NORTH CAROLINA CRIMES, *supra* note 59, at 82 (finding that defendant must know that person he or she assaults is officer for conviction of assault on officer, but that it is unclear whether defendant need know that officer is discharging duty of office). Some sources suggest that such knowledge may be required, but they are not conclusive. See G.S. 15A-401(f)(1) (person may not use deadly force against officer if person knows that officer is officer *and* that officer is effecting arrest); *Mayberry*, 38 N.C. App. at 512, 248 S.E.2d at 404 (court of appeals finds that since evidence showed that defendant knew sheriff was law-enforcement officer *and* was acting in performance of duties, trial court did not err in failing to submit lesser offense of assault).

A related question is whether the test of a person's knowledge is an objective or subjective one. An objective test of knowledge would be: Does the person know *or* have reason to know of the officer's authority? A subjective test would be: Does the person actually know of the officer's authority? North Carolina appears to favor the objective test.[73]

### (3) Rules of Defensive Force

If a person does not know of an officer's authority, he or she may use defensive force as follows. First, as in a case involving defensive force against a private person, the defendant must comply with the principles embodied in the *Norris* test.[74] Second, the defendant may rely on any defensive-force defense supported by the circumstances.[75] Third, a defendant may use *deadly* force but only when the applicable defensive-force defense permits it.[76]

---

73. *See generally* G.S. 15A-401(f)(1) (person may use deadly force against law-enforcement officer if person does not know, or have reason to know, of officer's identity or purpose, which is objective test); State v. Avery, 315 N.C. 1, 30–31, 337 S.E.2d 786, 802–03 (1985) (court states that knowledge is essential element of assault with a deadly weapon on an officer, citing pattern jury instruction on the offense; although court did not specifically decide whether test of knowledge is objective or subjective, cited instruction provided that knowledge element was satisfied if state proved that defendant knew, or had reasonable grounds to know, of officer's authority). *But cf.* NORTH CAROLINA CRIMES, *supra* note 59, at 3 (as general rule, when knowledge is required element of offense, actual knowledge must be shown); 1 ROBINSON, *supra* note 12, at 571 (objective criteria for determining whether defendant had knowledge of officer's status may improperly shift to defendant burden of persuasion to disprove knowledge required for conviction of offense).

74. The *Norris* test is discussed in general in § 2.2(c) *supra*; the four parts of the test are analyzed in detail in §§ 3.1 through 3.4 *supra*; and the potential differences in the application of the test in homicide and nonhomicide cases are discussed in § 4.1 *supra*.

75. *See, e.g.,* State v. Bryant, 65 N.C. 327, 329 (1871) (person making arrest on another's property should make known his purpose, "else he may be treated as a trespasser"); State v. Polk, 29 N.C. App. 360, 361–62, 224 S.E.2d 272, 273 (1976) (where evidence indicated that defendant lacked knowledge of officer's authority, error not to instruct on right to defend against bodily injury or offensive physical contact).

76. *See* State v. Miller, 282 N.C. 633, 642–43, 194 S.E.2d 353, 358–59 (1973) (defendant's evidence indicated that he believed that officers, who burst into house with guns drawn and without announcing purpose, were there to rob occupants; trial court erred in excluding the evidence, which supported defendant's claim that

## (b) When Officer Is Not Performing Lawful Duty

### *(1) Negating and Justification Defense*

The second circumstance in which a person may use defensive force against a law-enforcement officer is when a person knows of an officer's authority, but the officer is not performing a lawful duty.[77] A person may have both a *negating defense* and a *justification defense* in this situation.

An officer's failure to perform a lawful duty can serve as a negating defense against offenses such as resisting arrest and assault on an officer. A person may not be convicted of such offenses unless the state proves beyond a reasonable doubt that the officer was performing a lawful duty. For example, if an officer illegally arrests a person and the person uses nondeadly force to resist, the person may not be convicted of either resisting arrest or assault on an officer.[78] The person could still be convicted of an offense such as simple assault, which does not require proof of a lawful duty, if the person does not comply with the applicable rules of defensive force.

When an officer acts outside his or her lawful duties and the defendant complies with the rules of defensive force, the defense is one of justification, a complete defense. For example, if an officer illegally arrests a person and the person resists with a degree of force considered appropriate under the rules on defensive force, the person would not be guilty of any offense.[79]

---

he killed one of officers in self-defense); G.S. 15A-401(f)(1) (defendant may not use deadly force to resist arrest by officer using reasonable force if defendant knows of officer's identity and purpose).

77. *See generally* Jeffrey F. Ghent, Annotation, *Status of Rules as to Right to Forcefully Resist Illegal Arrest*, 44 A.L.R. 3d 1078 (1972).

78. *See, e.g.*, State v. Mobley, 240 N.C. 476, 478, 83 S.E.2d 100, 102 (1954) (offense of resisting arrest requires lawful arrest); State v. Burton, 108 N.C. App. 219, 224–25, 423 S.E.2d 484, 487–88 (1992) (offense of assault on law-enforcement officer requires that officer be performing lawful duty), *rev. denied*, 333 N.C. 576, 429 S.E.2d 574 (1993); NORTH CAROLINA CRIMES, *supra* note 59, at 84 (assault on officer with deadly weapon requires that officer be performing lawful duty).

79. *See, e.g.*, State v. Allen, 166 N.C. 265, 267, 80 S.E. 1075, 1075–76 (1914); State v. Belk, 76 N.C. 10, 14–15 (1877). A person also may take other actions to avoid an officer's unlawful action, such as barring entry or fleeing. *See, e.g.*, State v. Hewson, 88 N.C. App. 128, 130–32, 362 S.E.2d 574, 575–77 (1987) (defendant had right to close and lock door to prevent officer's illegal entry); State v. Williams, 32 N.C. App.

## (2) Meaning of "Lawful Duty"

The courts have said that when an officer acts outside his or her lawful duties, the officer stands in the position of a "wrongdoer," and a person has the right to defend against the officer's wrongful action.[80] The principal type of unlawful action that appears in the cases is an unlawful arrest. When an arrest is unlawful, it constitutes an interference with liberty in itself, and a person has the right to defend against it regardless of whether bodily injury or any other harm is threatened.[81] Actions short of an unlawful arrest, such as an unlawful stop of a

---

204, 206–08, 231 S.E.2d 282, 283–85 (defendant had right to resist unlawful arrest by fleeing; flight did not give officer probable cause to arrest), *rev. denied*, 292 N.C. 470, 233 S.E.2d 924 (1977).

80. *Mobley*, 240 N.C. at 478, 83 S.E.2d at 102; *accord* State v. Jefferies, 17 N.C. App. 195, 198, 193 S.E.2d 388 (1972), *rev. denied*, 282 N.C. 673, 194 S.E.2d 153 (1973).

81. For cases in which the court found an arrest to be *unlawful*, or at least sufficient evidence to warrant instructions on the defendant's right to resist an unlawful arrest, *see, e.g.*, *Mobley*, 240 N.C. 476, 83 S.E.2d 100 (officer arrested defendant without warrant for misdemeanor not committed in officer's presence; defendant entitled to nonsuit on resisting arrest charge); *Williams*, 32 N.C. App. at 206–08, 231 S.E.2d at 282–85 (officer made warrantless arrest without probable cause; defendant permitted to withdraw guilty plea); State v. Bradley, 32 N.C. App. 666, 669–70, 233 S.E.2d 603, 605–06 (1977) (evidence in conflict over whether officer had probable cause to believe defendant was driving under influence; jury should have been instructed that defendant would not be guilty of assaulting officer if arrest was unlawful); State v. Allen, 14 N.C. App. 485, 491–92, 188 S.E.2d 568, 572–73 (1972) (since defendant was merely criticizing officer who was attempting to arrest another, officer had no ground to arrest defendant for obstructing officer; defendant entitled to nonsuit on charge that he assaulted officer after illegal arrest).

For cases in which the court found sufficient evidence that an arrest was *lawful* to warrant denial of the defendant's motion for nonsuit, *see, e.g.*, State v. Summerell, 282 N.C. 157, 171, 192 S.E.2d 569, 578 (1972) (in assessing lawfulness of warrantless arrest for misdemeanor committed in officer's presence, question is whether officer had reasonable grounds for arrest, not whether defendant actually had committed crime; nonsuit properly denied); State v. Lightner, 108 N.C. App. 349, 350–52, 423 S.E.2d 827, 828–29 (1992) (on facts of case, off-duty officers making arrest were performing duties of office; nonsuit properly denied); State v. Raynor, 33 N.C. App. 698, 699–700, 236 S.E.2d 307, 308–09 (1977) (state produced sufficient evidence that defendant committed offense of disorderly conduct in officer's presence; nonsuit properly denied).

person, also may interfere with a person's liberty and give rise to a limited right to resist.[82] A person also has the right to prevent unlawful actions that do not necessarily interfere with liberty, such as an illegal entry into the home or illegal seizure of property.[83]

A nagging issue remains: May a person use force against an officer acting under an invalid warrant, such as one not supported by probable cause? Some North Carolina decisions hold that a person ordinarily may not use force to prevent the execution of an invalid warrant.[84] Other cases, however, treat actions under an invalid warrant like

---

82. *See* State v. Swift, 105 N.C. App. 550, 554, 414 S.E.2d 65, 67–68 (1992) (defendant had right to flee if investigatory stop was illegal; since stop was legal, trial court properly denied nonsuit on charge of resisting officer); State v. Harrell, 67 N.C. App. 57, 63–64, 312 S.E.2d 230, 235 (1984) (assuming investigatory stop was illegal, defendant had right to use such force as was reasonably necessary to prevent restraint; striking officer in face was not reasonably necessary).

83. *See, e.g.,* State v. Sparrow, 276 N.C. 499, 511–13, 173 S.E.2d 897 (1970) (defendant entitled to instructions on right to resist illegal entry into home); State v. Briggs, 25 N.C. 357 (1843) (right to resist illegal seizure of property); State v. Hewson, 88 N.C. App. 128, 362 S.E.2d 574 (1987) (defendant who resisted illegal entry into home entitled to nonsuit).

84. A few older supreme court decisions lend support to this view, although they could be construed as standing merely for the proposition that a person may not use deadly force to defend against an unlawful arrest absent the threat of some additional harm. *See* State v. Gupton, 166 N.C. 257, 261–64, 80 S.E. 989, 990–92 (1914) (in reversing manslaughter conviction of officer who killed arrestee, court states that arrestee had no right to use deadly force to resist arrest under allegedly invalid warrant); State v. Jones, 88 N.C. 671, 679–81 (1883) (defendant had no right to kill officer who was trying to arrest defendant under allegedly invalid warrant); *cf.* State v. Black, 109 N.C. 856, 857–59, 13 S.E. 877, 878 (1891) (defendant not entitled to use force to retake property previously taken under warrant based on invalid ordinance). The court of appeals decisions that support this proposition are: State v. Truzy, 44 N.C. App. 53, 54–55, 260 S.E.2d 113, 115 (1979), *rev. denied,* 299 N.C. 546, 265 S.E.2d 406 (1980); State v. Hammock, 22 N.C. App. 439, 441, 206 S.E.2d 773, 775 (stating principle in dicta), *rev. denied,* 285 N.C. 665, 207 S.E.2d 759 (1974); State v. Miller, 16 N.C. App. 1, 9, 190 S.E.2d 888, 893 (1972) (stating principle in dicta), *aff'd on other grounds,* 282 N.C. 633, 194 S.E.2d 353 (1973); State v. Sparrow, 7 N.C. App. 107, 115, 171 S.E.2d 321, 326–27 (1969), *rev'd,* 276 N.C. 499, 173 S.E.2d 897 (1970); State v. Wright, 1 N.C. App. 479, 488–89, 162 S.E.2d 56, 62, *aff'd on other grounds,* 274 N.C. 380, 163 S.E.2d 897 (1968). The Pattern Jury Committee takes the position that a person generally does not have the right to resist an arrest under an invalid warrant and that the cases cited in note 85 *infra* only create exceptions to this general rule (essentially, when the warrant is void on its face, improperly executed, or outrageous). North Carolina Pattern Jury Instructions for Criminal Cases, Notes on Law to Instructions in 208.81 Series (North Carolina Superior Court Judges Conference, Committee on Pattern Jury Instructions, March 1981).

other unlawful actions, permitting a person to use force to resist in accordance with the applicable rules on defensive force.[85]

### (3) Rules of Defensive Force

If an officer's action is unlawful, a person may use defensive force as follows. First, the person may use such force as reasonably appears to be necessary to prevent or avoid the unlawful action, as required by the *Norris* test.[86] The courts appear not to have considered the aggressor doctrine, however, in cases in which officers were acting outside their lawful duties.[87]

Second, a person ordinarily may use only *nondeadly* force in defending against an officer's unlawful action. An unlawful arrest, for example, constitutes an interference with liberty. Since the principle of proportionality requires that the force used be proportional to the harm

---

85. More recent as well as older supreme court decisions support this view. *See* State v. Sparrow, 276 N.C. 499, 511–13, 173 S.E.2d 897, 905–06 (1970) (officers had arrest warrant, but failed to knock and announce their purpose before entering defendant's home; defendant had right to resist); State v. McGowan, 243 N.C. 431, 90 S.E.2d 703 (1955) (defendant had right to resist warrant signed by officer, not by judge); State v. Queen, 66 N.C. 615, 617–18 (1872) (defendant had right to resist entry into dwelling under expired warrant); State v. Curtis, 2 N.C. 471 (1797) (if warrant lacks any circumstance essential to its legal form, it is void and will not justify officer in making arrest; defendant acquitted of resisting arrest). The court of appeals decisions supporting this proposition include: State v. Hagler, 32 N.C. App. 444, 446–48, 232 S.E.2d 712, 714–15 (following supreme court's decision in *Sparrow*), *rev. denied*, 292 N.C. 642, 235 S.E.2d 63 (1977); State v. Carroll, 21 N.C. App. 530, 532, 204 S.E.2d 908, 909–10 (officers obtained arrest warrant in retaliation for defendant's refusal to allow officers on his property; arrest warrant was invalid, and defendant had right to resist arrest), *rev. denied*, 285 N.C. 759, 209 S.E.2d 283 (1974).

86. *See, e.g.*, State v. Morrisey, 257 N.C. 679, 680, 127 S.E.2d 283, 284–85 (1962) (force must be reasonably necessary). The *Norris* test is discussed in general in § 2.2(c) *supra*; the four parts of the test are analyzed in detail in §§ 3.1 through 3.4 *supra*; and the potential differences in the application of the test in homicide and nonhomicide cases are discussed in § 4.1 *supra*.

87. The aggressor doctrine is more often an issue in excessive-force cases, discussed in § 5.5(c)(3) *infra*. It is not clear how the doctrine would apply in a case in which an officer fails to perform a lawful duty. If a defendant's actions are insufficient to justify an arrest, for example, then those same actions would seem insufficient to make the defendant an aggressor and deprive him or her of the right to use defensive force. *Cf.* State v. Allen, 14 N.C. App. 485, 491–92, 188 S.E.2d 568, 572–73 (1972) (since defendant was merely criticizing officer who was attempting to arrest another, officer had no ground to arrest defendant for obstructing officer; defendant entitled to nonsuit on charge that he assaulted officer after illegal arrest).

to be prevented, a person may use only *nondeadly* force in such a case.[88] A person would have the right to use *deadly* force only when the officer's unlawful action is accompanied by a threat of some additional harm triggering that right.[89]

Third, some older cases suggest that a person may have the right to defend *another* from an unlawful arrest, but it is difficult to glean a clear holding from these cases.[90] More recently, the court of appeals has held that a person may defend another against the use of *excessive force* by an officer. Although the court did not specifically address the issue, this result suggests that a person may have the right to defend another against an *unlawful arrest*.[91]

---

88. *See* State v. Sanders, 303 N.C. 608, 622, 281 S.E.2d 7, 15, *cert. denied*, 454 U.S. 973, 102 S. Ct. 523, 70 L. Ed. 2d 392 (1981); State v. King, 20 N.C. App. 390, 393, 201 S.E.2d 563, 565 (1974) (firing shotgun at officer was not reasonable in response to officer's unlawful arrest of defendant for misdemeanor not committed in officer's presence). *See also* G.S. 15A-401(f)(1) (specifically prohibiting use of deadly weapon or deadly force to resist arrest by known officer using reasonable force). The principle of proportionality is discussed generally in § 2.1(b) *supra*.

89. *See* State v. Avery, 302 N.C. 517, 527, 276 S.E.2d 699, 705–06 (1981) (suggesting that person would have right to use deadly force if officers illegally entered home and defendant satisfied rules applicable to defense of habitation); State v. Bridges, 178 N.C. 733, 739–40, 101 S.E. 29, 32–33 (1919) (right to use deadly force to defend self if officer sought to arrest defendant unlawfully *and* defendant reasonably feared death or great bodily injury); State v. Medlin, 60 N.C. 488, 492–93 (1864) (defendant had right to use deadly force against armed group of men who without authority came to his home at night for purpose of seizing him).

90. *See* State v. Armistead, 106 N.C. 639, 643, 10 S.E. 872, 873 (1890) (assuming defendant had right to intervene, he first had to request officer to desist from illegally holding prisoner); State v. Hedrick, 95 N.C. 624, 626 (1886) (assuming defendant had right to intervene, defendant first should have requested officer to desist from unlawful action and then should have laid hold of officer in a firm but gentle manner); *see also* State v. Rollins, 113 N.C. 722, 733, 18 S.E. 394, 398 (1893) (finding on one hand that third parties had no right to assault officer or take away prisoner held illegally, but on other hand that officer was guilty of affray in attempting to hold prisoner by force against efforts of prisoner and his friends).

91. *See infra* § 5.5(c)(3).

## (c) When Officer Uses Excessive Force

### (1) Justification Defense

The third exception arises when a person knows of the officer's authority and the officer is performing a lawful duty, but the officer uses excessive force.[92] In those circumstances, the person's defense is one of *justification* only. For example, suppose a uniformed officer lawfully arrests a person for a misdemeanor. The officer uses excessive force in the process, and the arrestee uses force in compliance with the rules of self-defense. The arrestee would have a complete defense to any charge involving his or her use of force, including resisting arrest, assault on an officer, and simple assault.[93]

The officer's use of excessive force would not give the arrestee a negating defense, however. The North Carolina courts have held that an officer's use of excessive force, although improper, does not take the officer outside the performance of his or her duties for purposes of resisting arrest and like offenses. Thus, when a person is charged with an offense such as resisting arrest, the officer's use of excessive force would not "negate" a required element of the state's case. If an arrestee does not comply with the applicable rules on defensive force in defending against an officer's use of excessive force, the arrestee could be convicted of resisting arrest or one of the other specialized offenses involving officers.[94]

### (2) Meaning of "Excessive Force"

What constitutes *excessive force* is the subject of litigation in a variety of contexts and will not be explored in depth here.[95] In brief, an officer's use of *nondeadly* force is governed by the general standard of

---

92. *See generally* Dag E. Ytreberg, Annotation, *Right to Resist Excessive Force Used in Accomplishing Lawful Arrest*, 77 A.L.R. 3d 281 (1977).

93. State v. Mensch, 34 N.C. App. 572, 574, 239 S.E.2d 297, 298–99 (1977), *rev. denied*, 294 N.C. 443, 241 S.E.2d 845 (1978).

94. State v. Irick, 291 N.C. 480, 500–01, 231 S.E.2d 833, 846 (1977); *Mensch*, 34 N.C. App. at 574–75, 239 S.E.2d at 298–99. The differences between negating and justification defenses in cases involving law-enforcement officers are discussed further in §§ 5.5(a), (b) *supra*.

95. *See generally* ISIDORE SILVER, POLICE CIVIL LIABILITY (1990); MICHAEL AVERY & DAVID RUDOVSKY, POLICE MISCONDUCT: LAW AND LITIGATION (2d ed. 1995).

reasonableness. In the context of an arrest, for example, an officer may use such force as is reasonably necessary to take a person into custody or to defend himself, herself, or another from bodily injury.[96] An officer's use of *deadly* force is subject to additional restrictions. For example, an officer may use deadly force to prevent the escape of an arrestee if such force is reasonably necessary to prevent the escape *and* the arrestee poses an imminent threat of death or serious physical injury.[97]

### (3) Rules of Defensive Force

If an officer uses excessive force, a person may use defensive force as follows. First, the person must comply with the principles embodied in the *Norris* test.[98] Thus, the person may use such force as reasonably appears to be necessary to defend against the officer's excessive force.[99] Also, a person must comply with the aggressor doctrine. The aggressor doctrine is typically at issue when a person unjustifiably uses nondeadly force to resist a lawful arrest and the officer uses excessive force in response. In those circumstances, the arrestee would be considered an aggressor *without* murderous intent, having unjustifiably initi-

---

96. *See* Graham v. Connor, 490 U.S. 386, 109 S. Ct. 1865, 104 L. Ed. 2d 443 (1989) (claims of excessive force under Fourth Amendment are to be analyzed under standard of reasonableness); G.S. 15A-401(d)(1) (applying standard of reasonableness under state law); *see also* SILVER, *supra* note 95, at §§ 5.02[2], 6.03[2] (noting that local regulations may further restrict officer's use of force).

97. Both federal and state law place limits on the use of deadly force. *See* Tennessee v. Garner, 471 U.S. 1, 105 S. Ct. 1694, 85 L. Ed. 2d 1 (1985); G.S. 15A-401(d)(2); *see also* SILVER, *supra* note 95, at §§ 5.02(2), 6.03(2) (noting that local regulations may further restrict officer's use of force). For a further discussion of the use of deadly force by law-enforcement officers, *see generally* ROBERT L. FARB, ARREST, SEARCH & INVESTIGATION IN NORTH CAROLINA 45–46 (1993).

98. The *Norris* test is discussed in general in § 2.2(c) *supra*; the four parts of the test are analyzed in detail in §§ 3.1 through 3.4 *supra*; and the potential differences in the application of the test in homicide and nonhomicide cases are discussed in § 4.1 *supra*.

99. *See* State v. Jones, 52 N.C. App. 606, 611, 611–12, 279 S.E.2d 9, 12 (1981) (defendant has right to use reasonable force to defend against excessive force by officer; trial court erred in instructing jury that force had to be actually, not just reasonably, necessary); State v. Mensch, 34 N.C. App. 572, 574–75, 239 S.E.2d 297, 298–99 (1977) (when there is evidence that officer used excessive force in effecting lawful arrest, trial court should instruct jury that defendant is justified in using reasonable force to defend against officer's excessive force), *rev. denied*, 294 N.C. 443, 241 S.E.2d 845 (1978).

ated the conflict. The arrestee's criminal liability would then depend on whether he or she withdrew in compliance with the rules applicable to aggressors *without* murderous intent. In the context of an arrest, *withdrawal* ordinarily would consist of some effort by the arrestee to submit to the arrest or some other action indicating that the arrestee no longer posed a threat of harm or escape.[100]

A second issue is whether a person may use *deadly* force to resist an officer's excessive force. A person may do so but only when he or she reasonably believes that the officer will inflict some harm that the person has a right to prevent by means of deadly force.[101]

A third issue is whether a person may defend *another* from an officer's use of excessive force. In *State v. Anderson*, the court of appeals held that a bystander may intervene to protect an arrestee from an officer's use of excessive force. The court emphasized, however, that the bystander does so at his or her peril. If the arrestee does not have the right to resist, the bystander may not justify the intervention on the ground that he or she reasonably believed the arrestee had such a right.[102]

---

100. The withdrawal requirements applicable to aggressors without murderous intent are discussed generally in § 3.3(d) *supra*. In homicide cases where an officer is the victim, the courts have applied the usual rule that a defendant who does not meet applicable withdrawal requirements loses the right of perfect, but not imperfect, self-defense. *See* State v. Durham, 141 N.C. 741, 53 S.E. 720 (1906) (trial judge did not err in instructing jury that defendant would be guilty of at least manslaughter where defendant resisted arrest, officer responded with deadly force, and defendant killed officer); State v. Horner, 139 N.C. 603, 609–12, 52 S.E. 136, 138–39 (1905) (to same effect). In assault cases where an officer is the victim, the courts have applied the usual rule that a defendant who does not comply with withdrawal requirements loses the right of self-defense altogether. *See* State v. Robinson, 40 N.C. App. 514, 519–20, 253 S.E.2d 311, 314–15 (1979) (applying aggressor principles to misdemeanor assault charges against defendant, court finds that defendant did not have right to use force in self-defense against officer); State v. Gatewood, 23 N.C. App. 211, 213, 208 S.E.2d 425, 427 (to same effect in case involving felony assault charges against defendant), *rev. denied*, 286 N.C. 338, 210 S.E.2d 59 (1974).

101. *See* G.S. 15A-401(f)(1) (prohibiting deadly force when known officer is using *reasonable* force).

102. 40 N.C. App. 318, 321–25, 253 S.E.2d 48, 50–53 (1979). *Compare supra* § 5.2(a)(3) (discussing right to intervene in cases not involving law-enforcement officers).

# 6 Other Applications of Self-Defense

# 6   Other Applications of Self-Defense

❦❦❦   In most criminal cases, it is self-evident that a person has the right to defend against the charges on the ground of self-defense or some other defensive-force defense. When the state claims that the defendant's actions amounted to a homicide or assault, the defendant has the right to defend against the charges on the ground that his or her actions were justified by a particular defensive-force defense. The availability of defensive-force defenses against the charges discussed below may not be immediately apparent, however.

## § 6.1  Felony Murder

May a defendant rely on self-defense or another defensive-force defense when charged with felony murder? The issue has caused some confusion in North Carolina. In *State v. Maynor,* the court found the issue to be an open one but assumed for purposes of the case that the defendant could claim self-defense.[1] In *State v. Bell,* the court directly addressed the question and held that self-defense (and presumably other defensive-force defenses) could serve as defenses to felony-murder charges in certain circumstances.[2] Then, in *State v. James Carl Richardson* (hereinafter *J. C. Richardson*), the court stated that self-defense was not a direct defense to felony murder but could still defeat a felony murder charge by serving as a defense to the underlying felony.[3] The court did

---

1. 331 N.C. 695, 699, 417 S.E.2d 453, 455 (1992). In two felony murder cases decided shortly after *Maynor,* the court appeared to accept that defendants could rely on self-defense but did not explicitly decide the issue. *See* State v. Palmer, 334 N.C. 104, 114, 431 S.E.2d 172, 177 (1993); State v. Ligon, 332 N.C. 224, 240–41, 420 S.E.2d 136, 145–46 (1992).

2. 338 N.C. 363, 385–87, 450 S.E.2d 710, 722–24 (1994). *See also* State v. Moore, 339 N.C. 456, 467–68, 451 S.E.2d 232, 237–38 (1994) (citing *Bell* with approval).

3. 341 N.C. 658, 462 S.E.2d 492 (1995). The full name of the defendant is given

not overrule *Bell*, however. Taken together, *Bell* and *J. C. Richardson* stand for the proposition that self-defense is not a direct defense to felony murder but may properly play a part in felony murder cases in three basic situations.

Self-defense is generally not a defense to felony murder because of the nature of the felonies underlying felony murder. G.S. 14-17 defines felony murder as a murder committed in the perpetration or attempted perpetration of certain enumerated felonies, including arson, rape, robbery, kidnapping, burglary, and other felonies with a deadly weapon. A perpetrator of one of these felonies ordinarily occupies the same status as an aggressor with murderous intent. He or she generally forfeits the right of self-defense during the course of his or her aggressive behavior. Thus, if A attempts to kidnap B and B forcefully resists, A has no legal right to defend himself or herself during the course of the incident. Like an aggressor with murderous intent, A must abide by the consequences of his or her original aggression—that is, the attempted kidnapping of B.[4]

The three situations in which self-defense may play a part in felony murder cases are as follows. The first situation, recognized in *J. C. Richardson,* is when self-defense serves as a defense to the underlying felony. For example, suppose the victim shoots at the defendant from a car, and the defendant shoots back and kills the victim. Under North Carolina law, the defendant could be charged with felony murder based on the commission of a felony with a deadly weapon, namely, discharging a firearm into occupied property.[5] *J. C. Richardson* recognizes, however, that a defendant may rely on self-defense as a defense to the underlying felony and thereby defeat a charge of felony murder.[6] Unlike a felony such as rape or robbery, discharging a firearm into occupied property may be a purely defensive action, reasonably necessary to prevent the assailant from inflicting some serious harm.

---

to distinguish the case from *State v. Clarence Richardson*, which modified the *Norris* test. *See supra* §§ 3.2(b)(4), 3.4(c)(3).

4. *See supra* § 3.3(c) (describing aggressors with murderous intent).

5. *See generally* State v. Wall, 304 N.C. 609, 612–15, 286 S.E.2d 68, 70–72 (1982).

6. *J. C. Richardson,* 341 N.C. at 666–69, 462 S.E.2d at 498–99. *See also* State v. Ligon, 332 N.C. 224, 240–41, 420 S.E.2d 136, 145–46 (1992) (underlying felony was shooting firearm into occupied property; court finds that defendant failed to produce sufficient evidence of self-defense to warrant instructions, but does not question defendant's right to rely on self-defense); State v. Ataei-Kachuei, 68 N.C. App. 209, 314 S.E.2d 751 (defendant charged with shooting firearm into occupied

Similarly, under North Carolina law, the state may charge a defendant with felony murder for the murder of one person in the course of a felonious assault with a deadly weapon on another person.[7] Again, self-defense could serve as a defense to the underlying felony assault and thereby defeat a felony murder charge.[8] For example, the defendant might be able to justify his or her use of force against both persons on the ground that both had attacked the defendant. As noted in *J. C. Richardson,* this theory of self-defense is available against certain underlying felonies only. Although the court did not elaborate, a defendant presumably could not rely on self-defense to justify an inherently aggressive felony such as rape.

Is imperfect self-defense available when a defendant relies on self-defense as a defense to the underlying felony? At least for the felonies charged in *J. C. Richardson*—discharging a firearm into occupied property and a felonious assault with a deadly weapon—the court said no. Although not clearly spelled out in the decision, the court apparently relied on the notion that imperfect self-defense serves to displace malice.[9] Malice is not an element of the underlying felonies with which the defendant was charged. The defendant therefore could not rely on imperfect self-defense against those felonies.[10]

---

vehicle; court does not question that defendant could rely on right to detain as defense), *rev. denied,* 311 N.C. 763, 321 S.E.2d 146 (1984); State v. Musselwhite, 54 N.C. App. 68, 283 S.E.2d 149 (1981) (defendant charged with shooting firearm into occupied dwelling; court does not question that defendant could rely on self-defense), *aff'd per curiam,* 305 N.C. 295, 287 S.E.2d 897 (1982); State v. Evans, 19 N.C. App. 731, 733–34, 200 S.E.2d 213, 214 (1973) (error not to instruct on self-defense as defense to firing into occupied vehicle; jury could find that defendant reasonably believed it necessary to fire at victim, who had been looking for defendant and who was seated in parked vehicle outside defendant's house with pistol); NORTH CAROLINA PATTERN JURY INSTRUCTIONS FOR CRIMINAL CASES 208.90A & n.4 (North Carolina Conference of Superior Court Judges, Committee on Pattern Jury Instructions, Feb. 1990) (noting that when there is evidence of self-defense, instruction on discharging firearm into occupied property should be modified to reflect defense).

7. *See generally* State v. Abraham, 338 N.C. 315, 331–32, 451 S.E.2d 131, 139 (1994).

8. *J. C. Richardson,* 341 N.C. at 666–69, 462 S.E.2d at 498–99.

9. *See supra* § 3.1.

10. This approach may prove harsh in some instances. For example, a defendant would gain the mitigating effect of imperfect self-defense if he or she shoots and kills a person located outside occupied property but not a person just inside the property. A formal analysis of offense elements arguably does not justify the

A second situation in which self-defense may play a part in a felony murder case, identified in *Bell,* is one in which there is a reasonable basis on which the jury could disbelieve that the underlying felony occurred.[11] Here, the nature of the underlying felony alleged by the state is of no consequence because the defendant disputes having committed it. *State v. Palmer,* decided shortly before *Bell,* illustrates this circumstance. In *Palmer,* the defendant claimed that he did not kill the victim in the course of an armed robbery, the underlying felony alleged in the case; he claimed to have killed the victim in defending against the victim's assault on him.[12]

The purpose of this second theory of self-defense is to provide an alternative explanation of the defendant's conduct and call into question that the defendant committed the underlying felony. Thus, self-defense does not operate as a defense to felony murder (and so does not conflict with the court's general statement in *J. C. Richardson* that self-defense is not a defense to felony murder). Rather, it is a way of raising a reasonable doubt about the state's proof of the underlying felony. Since the defendant's purpose is simply to dispute that the underlying felony occurred, he or she would not have to meet the formal requirements of the defense of self-defense.[13] The defendant still would need to meet those requirements, however, to defeat other charges in the case, such as premeditated and deliberate murder.[14]

---

difference in criminal liability. Although malice is not an element of felony murder, the commission of a dangerous felony performs the same function as malice. *See* ROLLIN M. PERKINS & RONALD N. BOYCE, CRIMINAL LAW 71 (3d ed. 1982) (intent to engage in one of felonies underlying felony murder is equivalent of malice). It is therefore not clear why a defendant who meets the requirements of imperfect self-defense would not gain the mitigating effect of that doctrine (assuming that self-defense is a defense to the underlying felony in the particular case).

11. *Bell,* 338 N.C. at 387, 450 S.E.2d at 723. *See also* Layne v. State, 542 So.2d 237, 244 (Miss. 1989) (self-defense is appropriate defense when there is reasonable basis upon which jury may disbelieve that underlying felony occurred).

12. 334 N.C. 104, 112–13, 431 S.E.2d 172, 176–77 (1993) (evidence was sufficient to support underlying felony of armed robbery; motion to dismiss properly denied).

13. *Cf.* State v. Lunsford, 229 N.C. 229, 49 S.E.2d 410 (1948) (defendants presented evidence that they grabbed victim and took away his pistol to prevent victim from shooting them; jury could find defendants not guilty of robbery on ground that they took pistol without intent to steal, but guilty of assault on ground that they did not meet requirements of self-defense).

14. A defendant also could mitigate premeditated and deliberate murder to voluntary manslaughter if he or she satisfied the elements of imperfect self-defense. Voluntary manslaughter based on imperfect self-defense may be an

The third situation that may involve self-defense and felony murder, identified in *Bell*, is one in which there is a factual showing that the defendant clearly articulated an intent to withdraw from the situation or that the dangerous situation posed by the felony no longer existed.[15] In other words, a defendant who ceases his or her aggressive conduct is restored to the right of self-defense. Like the second theory of self-defense described above, this third theory appears to be a way for a defendant to raise a reasonable doubt about an essential element of felony murder—namely, that the defendant killed the victim in the commission or attempted commission of the underlying felony. For example, a defendant might present evidence that he or she had surrendered before trying to defend himself or herself and so was not engaged in the commission of a felony at the time of the victim's death.[16]

---

appropriate verdict even when the prosecution proceeds at trial solely on a felony murder theory. When the defendant disputes that the underlying felony occurred (or that the killing occurred during the commission of the underlying felony, discussed next), a jury may find that the prosecution has failed to prove the required elements of felony murder. In those circumstances, the defendant is entitled to have submitted to the jury any lesser homicides of first-degree murder that are supported by the evidence. *See* State v. Camacho, 337 N.C. 224, 446 S.E.2d 8 (1994) (in prosecution for murder by lying in wait pursuant to general murder indictment, defendant entitled to submission of second-degree murder and voluntary manslaughter based on heat of passion); State v. Thomas, 325 N.C. 583, 386 S.E.2d 555 (1989) (in felony murder prosecution pursuant to general murder indictment, defendant entitled to submission of involuntary manslaughter).

15. *Bell*, 338 N.C. at 387, 450 S.E.2d at 723. *See also* State v. Celaya, 660 P.2d 849, 855 (Az. 1983) (defendant was initial aggressor by commission of felony and could not claim self-defense; court distinguishes case from situation in which defendant had completed burglary and was attempting to surrender); Gray v. State, 463 P.2d 897, 909 (Alaska 1970) (if dangerous situation no longer exists, defendant may rely on self-defense). The court in *Bell* actually broke this third situation into two circumstances (defendant must clearly articulate intent to withdraw *or* dangerous situation must no longer exist). Because the two circumstances have a similar effect, they are treated together.

16. This third theory can be analogized to the standard of withdrawal applicable to aggressors with murderous intent. *See supra* $\S$ 3.3(c)(2) (aggressor with murderous intent must remove any reasonable apprehension from victim). There may be little practical difference between saying that the perpetrator of a felony underlying felony murder must withdraw before acting in self-defense and saying that the perpetrator must cease committing the felony. Assuming there is a difference, however, the North Carolina courts may be unwilling to recognize that a person has the right to act in self-defense while still engaged in the commission of the underlying felony. *See generally* State v. Dennison, 801 P.2d 193, 196–98 (Wash.

## § 6.2  Involuntary Manslaughter

Some decisions hold that self-defense and other defensive-force defenses are not available against charges of involuntary manslaughter.[17] Taken at face value, this proposition is too broad. Except for imperfect defensive-force defenses, the various defenses involving defensive force are fully exculpatory. Thus, if a defendant successfully claims self-defense against a charge of first-degree murder, he or she would be entitled to acquittal on that charge and any lesser included offense, including involuntary manslaughter.[18]

The real issue presented by the above holding is whether certain elements of involuntary manslaughter are incompatible with self-defense and other defensive-force defenses. On the one hand, involuntary manslaughter is defined as the "unlawful killing of a human being without malice, without premeditation and deliberation, *and without intention to kill or inflict serious bodily injury*."[19] On the other hand, some cases have held that a killing is justified in self-defense only if the defendant believed in the need to kill or use deadly force.[20] As so defined, involuntary manslaughter and self-defense are potentially in conflict. Arguably, a jury could not find simultaneously that the defendant had no intent to kill or inflict serious injury (as required for involuntary manslaughter) *and* that the defendant entertained a belief in the need to kill or use deadly force (as purportedly required for self-defense).

Other cases indicate, however, that a belief in the need to kill or use deadly force is *not* required for a killing to be justified in self-defense. Under these cases, if a person uses nondeadly force against an assailant, and in the process inadvertently kills the assailant, the person may still be entitled to claim self-defense.[21]

---

1980) (comparing withdrawal requirement under law of self-defense and statutory requirement that killing must occur during commission of felony).

17. *See, e.g.,* State v. Daniels, 87 N.C. App. 287, 290, 360 S.E.2d 470, 471 (1987); State v. Teel, 65 N.C. App. 423, 424, 310 S.E.2d 31, 32 (1983).

18. *See generally* State v. Thomas, 325 N.C. 583, 591, 386 S.E.2d 555, 559 (1989) (involuntary manslaughter is lesser included offense of murder).

19. State v. Wilkerson, 295 N.C. 559, 577–78, 247 S.E.2d 905, 915 (1978), *quoting* State v. Wrenn, 279 N.C. 676, 681–82, 185 S.E.2d 129, 132 (1971) (emphasis in original).

20. *See supra* § 3.2(b)(3).

21. *Id.* The supreme court's recent decision in State v. Richardson, 341 N.C. 585, 461 S.E.2d 724 (1995), also may bear on the relationship of self-defense and involuntary manslaughter, although the court did not directly address the problem.

Assuming that a defendant may not rely on self-defense to justify an unintentional killing, a defendant would still be entitled to instructions on both self-defense and involuntary manslaughter when the evidence concerning the defendant's intent conflicts. For example, if some evidence shows an intentional killing in self-defense and other evidence shows an unintentional killing, the jury could acquit the defendant of all charges on the ground of self-defense or accident, find the defendant guilty of voluntary manslaughter based on imperfect self-defense, or return a verdict of involuntary manslaughter.[22]

## § 6.3  Assaults and Other Offenses

The various defensive-force defenses may serve as defenses to the various assault offenses recognized in North Carolina. Thus defensive-force defenses may be used against more specialized assault charges, such as assault by pointing a gun or assault on a female.[23]

---

On the one hand, the decision eliminates from the *Norris* test a requirement that the defendant believe in the need to use a specific level of force. That part of the opinion supports the view that self-defense may justify an unintentional killing that otherwise results from an act of self-defense. On the other hand, the court stated that self-defense involves an admitted, intentional act. The meaning of this latter statement remains unclear. *See supra* § 3.2(b)(4).

22. *See* State v. Todd, 264 N.C. 524, 530, 142 S.E.2d 154, 159 (1965) ("The defendant's plea of not guilty entitled him to present evidence that he acted in self-defense, that the shooting was accidental, or both. Election is not required. The defendant may rely on more than one defense."), *quoting* State v. Wagoner, 249 N.C. 637, 639, 107 S.E.2d 83, 85 (1959); State v. Hayes, 88 N.C. App. 749, 751–52, 364 S.E.2d 712, 713 (1988) (when evidence could support finding either of intentional killing in self-defense or unintentional killing, defendant entitled to instructions on both self-defense and involuntary manslaughter). Instructions on involuntary manslaughter may not always be warranted, however, in cases in which the defendant is entitled to self-defense instructions. *See* State v. Ray, 299 N.C. 151, 261 S.E.2d 789 (1980) (in case in which defendant was convicted of involuntary manslaughter, neither state nor defendant presented evidence that killing was accidental; court finds prejudicial error in submission of involuntary manslaughter because there was reasonable possibility that defendant's claim of self-defense would have resulted in acquittal had trial court not submitted unwarranted instruction).

23. *See, e.g.,* State v. Gullie, 96 N.C. App. 366, 368, 385 S.E.2d 556, 557–58 (1989) (self-defense and assault by pointing a gun); State v. Grant, 57 N.C. App. 589, 591–92, 291 S.E.2d 913, 915 (self-defense and assault on a female), *rev. denied*, 306 N.C. 560, 294 S.E.2d 225 (1982). *See also* § 5.5 *supra* (discussing self-defense and related defenses in cases of assaults on law-enforcement officers).

Self-defense and other defensive-force defenses also may apply to charges other than homicide or assault. For example, the cases allow a person to rely on a defensive-force defense against a charge of shooting into occupied property.[24] One case involved a claim of self-defense against a charge of felony riot.[25] Some courts have allowed defendants charged with possession of a firearm by a felon to claim self-defense when the evidence shows that they obtained possession of the firearm in the process of defending themselves or others.[26] These cases suggest that the nature of the charged offense does not necessarily determine whether a defendant has the right to rely on a defensive-force defense. The deciding factor may be whether the defendant's actions satisfy the requirements of the defensive-force defense asserted.

------

24. *See* cases cited *supra* note 6.

25. *See* State v. Platt, 85 N.C. App. 220, 227, 354 S.E.2d 332, 336 (defendant charged with felony riot and assault with deadly weapon with intent to kill inflicting serious injury), *rev. denied*, 320 N.C. 516, 358 S.E.2d 529 (1987).

26. *See* United States v. Newcomb, 6 F.3d 1129 (6th Cir. 1993) (defendant claimed that he took firearm from another person to prevent that person from injuring someone else; court allowed defendant to claim the equivalent of defense of another to a charge of possession of a firearm by a felon); *see generally* Sara L. Johnson, Annotation, *Fact that Weapon Was Acquired for Self-Defense or to Prevent Its Use against Defendant as Defense in Prosecution for Violation of State Statute Prohibiting Persons under Indictment for, or Convicted of, Crime from Acquiring, Having, Carrying, or Using Firearms or Weapons*, 39 A.L.R. 4th 967 (1985).

# 7 Evidentiary Issues

# 7  Evidentiary Issues

☙☙☙  In many ways, the evidentiary issues that arise in defensive-force cases mirror those in other criminal cases. Defensive-force cases involve such common problems as the admissibility of character evidence, exceptions to the hearsay rule, and methods of impeachment, all of which have received ample treatment elsewhere.[1] Nevertheless, it is useful to examine the ways in which those issues typically arise in defensive-force cases.

Sections 7.1 and 7.2 below are organized according to whether the evidence concerns the defendant or the victim. Those sections contain a discussion of the typical kinds of evidence offered about the defendant and victim and the circumstances under which the evidence is admissible. Each of the first two sections includes a chart summarizing the applicable principles of evidence. Section 7.3 deals with evidence that does not fit neatly within the categories described in the preceding sections, but relates generally to the defendant's state of mind.

Generally speaking, the evidence rules discussed in this chapter apply equally to all defensive-force defenses.[2] Since it is not possible to cover all of the different kinds of evidence that may be relevant in defensive-force cases, the reader should be alert to other evidentiary issues not discussed here.[3]

---

1. *See generally* Kenneth S. Broun, Brandis & Broun on North Carolina Evidence (4th ed. 1993) [hereinafter Brandis & Broun]; John W. Strong, McCormick on Evidence (4th ed. 1992) [hereinafter McCormick].

2. *See, e.g.,* State v. Faison, 330 N.C. 347, 354–55, 411 S.E.2d 143, 147 (1991) (applying "first aggressor" exception of Rule 404(a)(2) to case in which defendant claimed he was defending against sexual assault); State v. Graves, 18 N.C. App. 177, 181–82, 196 S.E.2d 582, 585 (1973) (finding that rules of evidence applicable to self-defense also apply to defense of others).

3. *See, e.g.,* State v. Miller, 282 N.C. 633, 642, 194 S.E.2d 353, 358 (1973) (in case in which defendant claimed self-defense, defendant had right to cross-examine officers about injuries that officers allegedly inflicted on defendant after incident; evidence had logical tendency to show officers' bias and interest in case).

## § 7.1  Defendant's Character and Conduct

This section primarily concerns evidence that the state may be able to bring out about the defendant. It also discusses opinion and reputation testimony offered by the defendant. See Figure 4, pages 160–61, for a review of the discussion in this section.

### (a)  Opinion and Reputation Testimony about Defendant

### *(1)  Defendant's Evidence*

Rule 404(a) of the North Carolina Rules of Evidence sets forth the general rule on the admissibility of character evidence: "Evidence of a person's character or a trait of character is not admissible for the purpose of proving that he acted in conformity therewith on a particular occasion." For example, it would not be permissible to introduce evidence that the defendant had a bad temper to show that he or she had a propensity to commit crime.[4]

Rule 404(a)(1) creates an exception to this general rule. It allows defendants in criminal cases to introduce evidence of a pertinent trait of their own character to show that they acted in conformity with that trait. Rule 405(a) specifies that a defendant may prove a pertinent character trait through either opinion or reputation evidence.

These rules work a slight change in the common-law treatment of character evidence. Under the common law, the defendant could offer evidence of his or her general "good" character, but such evidence had to be in the form of reputation testimony. Under the current rules, evidence may be in the form of opinion *or* reputation testimony, but the testimony must relate to a "pertinent" trait of character.[5] In *State v. Squire*, the court held that this change precluded a defendant from offering evidence of his or her "undifferentiated" good character. To be admissible, the evidence had to concern a trait "relevant" to an issue in the case.[6] The court in *Squire* also found, however, that a character trait may

---

4. *See generally* 1 BRANDIS & BROUN, *supra* note 1, at 265–66.

5. Commentary to Evidence Rules 404, 405.

6. 321 N.C. 541, 545–49, 364 S.E.2d 354, 356–59 (1988).

be general in nature and still be relevant. The court concluded that the defendant, who was claiming to have acted in self-defense, could offer evidence that he was peaceful and law abiding.

Offering such evidence, however, gives the state the right to counter with its own opinion or reputation evidence about the defendant (discussed in the next subsection). Also, the state gains the opportunity to cross-examine the defendant's character witnesses about prior bad acts of the defendant (discussed in § 7.1(b), below).

### (2) State's Evidence

Evidence Rule 404(a)(1) creates a second exception to the general rule prohibiting character, or "propensity," evidence. That rule, in conjunction with Rule 405(a), allows the state to offer opinion or reputation evidence about the defendant's character to rebut evidence presented by the defendant about his or her character. It is improper, however, for the state to introduce such evidence when the defendant has not yet done so.[7]

### (b) Prior Bad Acts by Defendant

Evidence Rule 404(b) bars evidence of prior crimes, wrongs, or acts by a person when such evidence is offered to prove the person's character and thereby show that the person acted in conformity with his or her character on a particular occasion. For example, the state may not introduce evidence that the defendant assaulted John, and thus had a violent character, to prove the defendant assaulted Mary. The rule bans evidence of any prior crimes, wrongs, or acts—often called "prior bad acts"—that occurred before trial, not just those that occurred before the date of the offense.[8] However, the state may bring out prior bad acts of the defendant, without violating this prohibition, through three main avenues.

---

7. *See* State v. Sanders, 295 N.C. 361, 373, 245 S.E.2d 674, 682–83 (1978) (trial court erred in allowing state to introduce in its case in chief evidence of defendant's gang membership since defendant had not yet testified or presented evidence of his good character).

8. *See* State v. Faison, 330 N.C. 347, 356–57, 411 S.E.2d 143, 148–49 (1991) (trial court erred in allowing evidence that defendant had fashioned weapon in jail while awaiting trial; evidence was impermissible character evidence).

**Figure 4. Evidence Relating to Defendant's Character and Prior Conduct**

| Type of Evidence | Offering Party | Purpose | Comments |
|---|---|---|---|
| Opinion and reputation testimony about defendant | Defendant | To show defendant acted in conformity with character [Rule 404(a)(1)] | Defendant may offer opinion or reputation testimony about pertinent trait of character. |
| Opinion and reputation testimony about defendant | State | To rebut evidence about defendant's character [Rule 404(a)(1)] | State may offer opinion or reputation testimony about pertinent trait of defendant's character, but only to rebut defendant's evidence. |
| Prior bad acts by defendant | State | To impeach defendant's character witness [Rule 405(a)] | State may cross-examine defendant's character witness about relevant prior bad acts of defendant, but may not offer extrinsic evidence of acts for this purpose. |
| | | To impeach defendant [Rule 608(b)] | State may cross-examine defendant about prior bad acts if they bear on credibility *or* if defendant opens door, but may not offer extrinsic evidence of acts for this purpose. |
| | | To show other purpose [Rule 404(b)] | State may offer extrinsic evidence of prior bad acts if relevant to one of purposes under Rule 404(b), but alleged purpose scrutinized more closely in defensive-force cases. |

**Figure 4. Evidence Relating to Defendant's Character and Prior Conduct (continued)**

| Type of Evidence | Offering Party | Purpose | Comments |
|---|---|---|---|
| Criminal convictions of defendant | State | To impeach defendant [Rule 609] | If defendant testifies, state may elicit criminal convictions covered by Rule 609 (either on cross-examination of defendant or by public record), but evidence limited to time and place of conviction and punishment imposed; however, if defendant opens door, state may have right to cross-examine defendant about acts underlying conviction. |
| Threatening statements by defendant against victim | State | To show defendant's intent and counter defensive-force claim | State may introduce threats for this purpose through witness with personal knowledge of threats; in appropriate case, state may introduce testimony of witness who learned of threats from victim to show victim's state of mind under Rule 803(3). |

## *(1) Impeachment of Character Witness*

If a defense witness testifies about the defendant's character, Rule 405(a) allows the state to cross-examine the witness about prior bad acts of the defendant. The purpose of such cross-examination is to impeach the character witness's testimony about the defendant.[9]

This method of proof is subject to certain limitations, however. First, it is available only if the defendant has placed his or her character in issue.[10] The state may not impeach a defense witness by asking about prior bad acts of the defendant if the witness has not testified to the defendant's character. Second, the questions posed on cross-examination must be in proper form; must have a good-faith factual basis; must be relevant to the character trait to which the witness testified on direct examination; and must not be unduly prejudicial.[11] Third, the state's impeachment of a character witness is limited to cross-examination of the witness. The state may not introduce extrinsic evidence of prior bad acts for the purpose of rebutting the witness's testimony about the defendant's character. Even if a character witness denies on cross-examination knowing about the "prior bad act," the state may not call other witnesses to prove that the act occurred. The rationale for this limitation is that collateral battles over whether the defendant did or did not commit a particular act can be unduly time-consuming, confusing, and prejudicial.[12] The state may, however, be able to offer extrinsic

---

9. Evidence Rule 405(a); State v. Maynor, 331 N.C. 695, 700, 417 S.E.2d 453, 456 (1992) (trial court erroneously barred state from cross-examining witness about specific instances of violence when witness had testified on direct to defendant's nonviolent character); State v. Gappins, 320 N.C. 64, 68–70, 357 S.E.2d 654, 657–59 (1987) (trial court properly allowed state to cross-examine witness, who had testified to defendant's peaceful character, about acts of domestic cruelty and rowdy and abusive conduct by defendant when he was drinking). The state may impeach the witness in other ways as well. *See, e.g.,* State v. Dove, 156 N.C. 653, 658–59, 72 S.E. 792, 794–95 (1911) (state could cross-examine defendant's character witness about prior statements of witness that defendant was a "bad man, dangerous when drunk, and might kill [the victim]"); State v. Fisher, 149 N.C. 557, 558–59, 63 S.E. 153, 153 (1908) (to same effect).

10. *See* Commentary to Evidence Rule 405.

11. Commentators suggest that the questions ordinarily should be phrased in terms of whether the witness has heard or knows of the particular instances of conduct. *See* 1 Brandis & Broun, *supra* note 1, at 323–25; 1 McCormick, *supra* note 1, at 816–17.

12. Evidence Rule 405(a); 1 McCormick, *supra* note 1, at 182–84.

evidence of prior bad acts under a different theory (see discussion of Rule 404(b), below).

### (2) Impeachment of Defendant

If the defendant testifies, the state may impeach the defendant under Evidence Rule 608(b). This rule governs the impeachment of witnesses, including the defendant, through prior bad acts other than convictions. It permits impeachment under the following conditions. First, impeachment of the defendant is limited to cross-examination about the prior acts; extrinsic evidence is prohibited.[13] (Rule 404(b), discussed below, may still permit extrinsic evidence.) Second, the questions must not be unduly prejudicial and must have a good-faith factual basis.[14] Third, and most important, the prior acts must be probative of the truthfulness or untruthfulness of the defendant. The supreme court has held that prior acts of violence generally are *not* probative of truthfulness or untruthfulness.[15]

If the defendant opens the door on direct examination, however, the state may be able to cross-examine the defendant about prior violent acts. For example, in one case the defendant testified on direct examination that he had never injured anyone. The supreme court held that the trial court did not abuse its discretion in allowing the state to cross-examine the defendant about prior violent acts. In that context, the court reasoned, the state's inquiry into prior violent acts tested the accuracy of the defendant's assertion that he had never injured anyone; therefore, the inquiry was probative of truthfulness or untruthfulness under Rule 608(b).[16]

---

13. Evidence Rule 608(b); 1 BRANDIS & BROUN, *supra* note 1, at 310–11 & n.252.

14. *See* Commentary to Evidence Rule 608 (noting that trial court has discretion to preclude questions based on considerations such as remoteness in time, danger of prejudice, and confusion of issues); 1 BRANDIS & BROUN, *supra* note 1, at 309.

15. *See* State v. Harris, 323 N.C. 112, 128–29, 371 S.E.2d 689, 698–99 (1988) (error to allow state to cross-examine defendant about fight defendant had been involved in during competency evaluation; fight was not probative of truthfulness); State v. Morgan, 315 N.C. 626, 633–35, 340 S.E.2d 84, 89–90 (1986) (prior attack on third party, although similar to current attack on victim, could not be used to impeach; evidence must relate to truthfulness).

16. State v. Darden, 323 N.C. 356, 358–59, 372 S.E.2d 539, 540–41 (1988). *See also* State v. Wills, 110 N.C. App. 206, 212–13, 429 S.E.2d 376, 379–80 (defendant testified on direct about prior incident; trial court properly allowed state to explore

In another case, the defendant testified on direct examination that he was a "peaceful" individual who constantly had to fend off verbal and physical attacks from the victim. The state then cross-examined the defendant about the details of three prior assaults, all of which had resulted in convictions. The defendant argued on appeal that under Rule 609, which deals with impeachment by evidence of conviction of crime, the state could inquire only into the time and place of conviction and the punishment imposed. The supreme court held that the defendant had placed his character in evidence through his direct testimony and thereby had become subject to Rule 405(a). Under that rule, the prosecution could inquire into relevant specific instances of conduct, such as the prior assaults, in cross-examining the defendant about his alleged peaceful character. The prosecution also could go into greater detail about the prior assaults than would have been permissible under Rule 609.[17]

### (3) Rule 404(b)

Rule 404(b) provides that prior bad acts may not be used to prove a person's character and thereby show the person's conduct on a particular occasion. Evidence Rule 404(b) states further, however, that prior bad acts are admissible if offered for a purpose other than to prove character. The rule sets forth several illustrative purposes, such as proof of motive, opportunity, and identity. When the state can show that evidence of prior bad acts tends to prove one of these purposes, it may cross-examine the defendant *and* offer extrinsic evidence about the acts. The evidence remains subject to Rule 403's general stricture that the probative value of the evidence must outweigh its prejudicial effect.

In general the North Carolina courts have liberalized the circumstances in which evidence of prior bad acts may be introduced under Rule 404(b).[18] In cases involving defensive force, however, the courts continue to take a relatively strict view of the rule. In several cases, the courts have found that the state's real purpose in offering evi-

---

details of that incident on cross-examination), *rev. denied*, 334 N.C. 438, 433 S.E.2d 184 (1993).

17. State v. Garner, 330 N.C. 273, 287–90, 410 S.E.2d 861, 869–70 (1991).

18. *See* State v. Coffey, 326 N.C. 268, 278–79, 389 S.E.2d 48, 54 (1990) (stating generally that Rule 404(b) is rule of inclusion and that evidence is excluded under this rule only if its purpose is to show defendant's propensity to commit charged crime).

dence of the defendant's prior bad acts was the impermissible one of using character evidence to show conduct. In *State v. Morgan*, for example, the court ruled it improper to allow evidence of a prior attack by the defendant on a third party. The court reasoned that the state offered the prior attack to show the defendant's propensity for violence, which in turn was intended to show that the defendant was the aggressor in the altercation and could not have been acting in self-defense. The court held that this purpose is "precisely what is prohibited by Rule 404(b)."[19] In several other defensive-force cases, the court likewise found the evidence of the defendant's prior acts inadmissible under Rule 404(b).[20] The courts have been more willing to find evidence of prior bad acts permissible when the acts concerned the current victim and took place fairly recently.[21]

---

19. 315 N.C. 626, 638, 340 S.E.2d 84, 92 (1986).

20. *See* State v. Faison, 330 N.C. 347, 356–57, 411 S.E.2d 143, 148–49 (1991) [evidence that defendant had fashioned weapon while in jail was effort to characterize defendant as violent person and therefore was inadmissible under Rule 404(b)]; State v. Sanders, 295 N.C. 361, 373–74, 245 S.E.2d 674, 683 (1978) (evidence that defendant had previously stabbed another person had no logical relevance other than to show tendency on part of defendant to commit criminal offenses, which is impermissible purpose); State v. Irby, 113 N.C. App. 427, 435–39, 439 S.E.2d 226, 232–34 (1994) (evidence that defendant had shot at another person's truck had no connection to current offense other than to show defendant's character and alleged propensity for violence); State v. Mills, 83 N.C. App. 606, 609–14, 351 S.E.2d 130, 132–35 (1986) (Rule 404(b) did not permit evidence that defendant had pointed gun at victim three years earlier). *See also* United States v. Sanders, 964 F.2d 295, 298–99 (4th Cir. 1992) (since the defendant admitted that he stabbed the victim, the only issue was whether he did so in self-defense; interpreting federal counterpart of Rule 404(b), court finds that prior assault had no probative value other than to show defendant's propensity to commit violent crimes, which is improper purpose).

21. *See Morgan*, 315 N.C. at 639, 340 S.E.2d at 92–93 (attack on third party three months earlier was inadmissible; court states that evidence would more likely be relevant to permissible purpose if prior attack had been on victim); State v. Mixion, 110 N.C. App. 138, 146–47, 429 S.E.2d 363, 368 (evidence of prior assaults and threats by defendant against victim during marriage admissible to prove malice and intent), *rev. denied*, 334 N.C. 437, 433 S.E.2d 183 (1993); *Mills*, 83 N.C. App. at 609–12, 351 S.E.2d at 132–34 (evidence that defendant pointed gun at victim three years ago was too remote to be admissible); State v. Blalock, 77 N.C. App. 201, 203–04, 334 S.E.2d 441, 443 (1985) (evidence of prior assaults on victim and other members of victim's family were relevant to show intent and motive).

### (c) Criminal Convictions of Defendant

Evidence Rule 609 allows impeachment of a witness, including the defendant, by evidence of conviction of a crime. The conviction must first meet the criteria set forth in the rule—for example, it must have been punishable by more than sixty days' confinement. Then the state may elicit evidence of the conviction from the witness on cross-examination or may establish the fact thereafter by public record. Rule 609 limits the inquiry into such a conviction to the time and place of the conviction and the punishment imposed.[22]

### (d) Threatening Statements by Defendant

Threatening statements by a defendant present two evidentiary problems. First, the statements must be relevant to an issue in the case. When the defendant has threatened to harm the victim, for example, the courts have had little difficulty finding that the threats tend to show the defendant's intent and tend to negate the defendant's claim of self-defense.[23]

Second, the statements must not be hearsay or must come within an exception to the rule prohibiting hearsay (Evidence Rule 802). If the witness personally heard the defendant make the threat, the hearsay rule presents little obstacle to introduction of the threat. The statement would generally be admissible under Rule 801(d), which exempts from the hearsay rule a party's statement when offered against the party (an "admission of a party-opponent").

The more difficult hearsay problem is with the admissibility of a third person's testimony about statements by the victim describing threats allegedly made by the defendant. For example, suppose the state alleges that the defendant threatened to harm the victim and that the victim told X about the threat. May X testify about what the victim said? For such testimony to be admissible, the victim's statement to X must qualify under an exception to the hearsay rule. The supreme court has held that the victim's statement is admissible under Rule 803(3) in certain circumstances. This rule serves to exempt from the hearsay rule a

---

22. *See* State v. Garner, 330 N.C. 273, 288–89, 410 S.E.2d 861, 869–70 (1991).

23. *See, e.g.,* State v. Groves, 324 N.C. 360, 368–70, 378 S.E.2d 763, 768–70 (1989) (defendant had threatened to kill victim; evidence not barred by Rule 404(b) because it tended to show premeditation and deliberation and to negate self-defense); *Sanders*, 295 N.C. at 366–67, 245 S.E.2d at 679 (to same effect).

victim's statement about his or her then-existing mental, emotional, or physical condition if: (a) the statement shows the victim's then-existing state of mind; (b) the victim's state of mind is relevant to an issue in the case; and (c) the possible prejudicial impact of the evidence does not outweigh its probative value.[24] In a number of homicide cases, including ones involving defensive-force claims, the court has found that the victim's statement to a third person met these conditions and so was admissible.[25] The liberality with which the courts have admitted such evidence has been questioned, however.[26] If such statements are admitted, the defense would appear to have the right to impeach the credibility of the victim as if the victim were testifying at trial.[27]

---

24. *See, e.g.,* State v. Walker, 332 N.C. 520, 535, 422 S.E.2d 716, 725 (1992) (discussing conditions for admissibility), *cert. denied,* __ U.S. __, 113 S. Ct. 2364, 124 L. Ed. 2d 271 (1993).

25. *See* State v. Faucette, 326 N.C. 676, 683, 392 S.E.2d 71, 74–75 (1990) (court finds that statements of victim to third party, which included threats allegedly made by defendant, showed victim's fear of defendant; victim's fear was relevant because it tended to show that victim would not have done anything to provoke the defendant and thus tended to negate defendant's claim of self-defense); *Mixion,* 110 N.C. App. at 147–48, 429 S.E.2d at 368–69 (court finds that statements of victim to third party, which included threats allegedly made by defendant, showed victim's state of mind; however, since other evidence showed that *victim* and not defendant initiated fatal confrontation, court bases finding of relevance on ground that statements showed victim's general "state of mind," which in turn showed "relationship" between the parties).

26. The criticism has primarily been directed at cases not involving claims of defensive force by the defendant. Nevertheless, the same concerns may arise in defensive-force cases. *See generally* State v. Hardy, 339 N.C. 207, 227–28, 451 S.E.2d 600, 611 (1994) (court states that it intends to "recede" from its more expansive holdings on state-of-mind statements); *Walker,* 332 N.C. at 541–44, 422 S.E.2d at 728–30 (1992) (Webb, J., dissenting) (dissent argues first that victim's statement was not probative of victim's state of mind because statement, which only recited prior assaults by defendant, lent itself to any number of inferences about the victim's then-existing state of mind; dissent argues second that, even assuming statements showed victim's state of mind, state of mind was not relevant to any issue in case); 2 BRANDIS & BROUN, *supra* note 1, at 86 n.348 (author questions correctness of some of cases holding that victim's state of mind was relevant to issues in case); 2 McCORMICK, *supra* note 1, at 243–45 (author notes that victim's extrajudicial declarations of fear of the defendant are often admissible in defensive-force cases; author also notes generally that such declarations may include statements about what the defendant allegedly said or did and that, even with a limiting instruction, a jury may be unable to consider the declarations only for the purpose of showing the victim's state of mind and not for some other, impermissible purpose).

27. *See* Evidence Rule 806 (when hearsay statement has been admitted in

## § 7.2  Victim's Character and Conduct

This section primarily addresses evidence that the defendant may wish to bring out about the victim. It also discusses opinion and reputation testimony offered by the state. See Figure 5, pages 170–71, for a review of the discussion in this section.

### (a)  Opinion and Reputation Testimony about Victim

#### (1)  Defendant's Evidence

It is generally impermissible to offer evidence of a person's character to show that the person acted in conformity therewith on a particular occasion. Rule 404(a)(2) creates another exception to this prohibition, allowing the defendant to offer "[e]vidence of a pertinent trait of character of the victim of the crime" to show that the *victim* acted in conformity with that trait. Rule 405(a) specifies that such character evidence must be in the form of opinion or reputation evidence.

What traits of the victim are pertinent in a defensive-force case? On the one hand, the courts have disallowed evidence that the victim was of bad or immoral character, which is consistent with the court's exclusion of evidence of the defendant's undifferentiated "good" character.[28] On the other hand, the courts have allowed evidence about the victim's violent nature. Such evidence is pertinent in a defensive-force case because it tends to show that the victim and not the defendant was the aggressor.[29]

---

evidence, credibility of declarant may be attacked by evidence that would be admissible if declarant had testified as witness); Anthony M. Brannon, *Successful Shadowboxing: The Art of Impeaching Hearsay Declarants*, 13 Campbell L. Rev. 157 (1991); State v. Adams, 90 N.C. App. 145, 367 S.E.2d 362 (1988) (raising, but not ruling upon, possibility of using Rule 806 to impeach declarant).

28. *See* State v. Stewart, 292 N.C. 219, 222–23, 232 S.E.2d 443, 446 (1977) (defendant could not elicit testimony that victims operated illegal liquor business and house of prostitution); State v. Hodgin, 210 N.C. 371, 376, 186 S.E. 495, 499 (1936) (defendant may not prove victim's general bad character or immorality).

29. *See* State v. Watson, 338 N.C. 168, 186–88, 449 S.E.2d 694, 705–06 (1994) (evidence of victim's violent character admissible to show victim was aggressor), *cert. denied*, __ U.S. __, 115 S. Ct. 1708, 131 L. Ed. 2d 569 (1995); State v. Winfrey, 298 N.C. 260, 262, 258 S.E.2d 346, 347–48 (1979) (to same effect).

The defendant need not have known of the victim's violent nature at the time of the encounter for opinion and reputation testimony to be admissible. Such testimony tends to show that the victim was the aggressor whether or not the defendant knew of the victim's violent tendencies.[30] If the defendant had such knowledge, however, opinion and reputation testimony would be admissible for an additional purpose: to show the defendant's apprehension concerning the victim and the reasonableness of that apprehension.[31] Regardless which theory of admissibility applies, opinion and reputation testimony may concern the victim's violent and dangerous character in general.[32] It also may show the victim's violent nature in specific situations, such as when intoxicated.[33]

Before adoption of the current rules of evidence, the North Carolina courts imposed greater restrictions on evidence of the victim's violent nature. A defendant who did not know of the victim's violent character could offer character evidence to show that the victim was the aggressor, but only if the evidence of the encounter was wholly circumstantial or the nature of the encounter in doubt.[34] Rule 404 eliminated this requirement.[35]

---

30. *Watson*, 338 N.C. at 186–88, 449 S.E.2d at 705–06.

31. *Id.*; *Winfrey*, 298 N.C. at 262, 258 S.E.2d at 347–48; State v. Spaulding, 298 N.C. 149, 159, 257 S.E.2d 391, 397 (1979) (victim was inmate in prison cell block known to house particularly violent inmates; error to exclude testimony about reputation for violence of that group, which showed defendant's apprehension concerning victim). When evidence is offered to show the defendant's state of mind, it is not governed by Rule 404(a)(2), which concerns the use of character evidence to prove the victim's conduct. *See* 1 Brandis & Broun, *supra* note 1, at 275 (cited with approval in *Watson*).

32. *See* State v. Champion, 222 N.C. 160, 161, 22 S.E.2d 232, 232–33 (1942) (defendant could show general character of deceased as violent and dangerous); State v. Lefevers, 221 N.C. 184, 185, 19 S.E.2d 488, 489 (1942) (to same effect).

33. *See* State v. Reed, 324 N.C. 535, 537–38, 379 S.E.2d 828, 829–30 (1989); State v. Rummage, 280 N.C. 51, 54–55, 185 S.E.2d 221, 223–24 (1971); State v. Carraway, 181 N.C. 561, 565–66, 107 S.E. 142, 144 (1921).

34. *See, e.g.,* State v. Cooke, 306 N.C. 117, 121–22, 291 S.E.2d 649, 651–52 (1982); State v. Price, 301 N.C. 437, 450, 272 S.E.2d 103, 112 (1980); State v. Blackwell, 162 N.C. 672, 680–82, 78 S.E. 316, 319–20 (1913).

35. Commentary to Evidence Rule 404(a)(2); 1 Brandis & Broun, *supra* note 1, at 273 n.119.

**Figure 5. Evidence Relating to Victim's Character and Prior Conduct**

| Type of Evidence | Offering Party | Purpose | Comments |
|---|---|---|---|
| Opinion and reputation testimony about victim | Defendant | To show victim acted in conformity with character [Rule 404(a)(2)] | Defendant may offer opinion or reputation testimony about pertinent trait of victim's character, whether known or unknown to defendant. |
| | | To show defendant's apprehension concerning victim was reasonable | Defendant may offer opinion or reputation testimony for this purpose if character trait is known to defendant and pertinent. |
| Opinion and reputation testimony about victim | State | To rebut evidence about victim's character [Rule 404(a)(2)] | State may offer opinion or reputation testimony about pertinent trait of victim's character, but only to rebut defendant's evidence. |
| | | To rebut that victim was first aggressor in a homicide case [Rule 404(a)(2)] | State may offer opinion or reputation testimony about victim's character for peacefulness, but only to rebut defendant's evidence. |
| Prior bad acts by victim | Defendant | To impeach victim's character witness [Rule 405(a)]; to impeach victim [Rule 608(b)]; to show other purpose [Rule 404(b)] | Defendant may use prior bad acts of victim for indicated purposes in same manner as state may use prior bad acts of defendant. See Figure 4, pages 160–61 (prior bad acts of defendant). |
| | | To show defendant's apprehension concerning victim was reasonable | Defendant may offer prior bad acts if known to defendant and relevant to defendant's apprehension concerning victim. |

**Figure 5. Evidence Relating to Victim's Character and Prior Conduct (continued)**

| Type of Evidence | Offering Party | Purpose | Comments |
|---|---|---|---|
| Criminal convictions of victim | Defendant | To impeach victim [Rule 609] | Defendant may use criminal convictions to impeach victim who testifies in same manner as state may use criminal convictions to impeach defendant who testifies. See Figure 4, pages 160–61 (criminal convictions of defendant). |
| | | To show defendant's apprehension concerning victim was reasonable | Defendant may offer prior convictions if known to defendant and relevant to defendant's apprehension concerning victim, whether or not victim testifies. |
| Threatening statements by victim against defendant | Defendant | To show victim's intent | Defendant may offer threatening statements for this purpose, whether or not threats were known by defendant. |
| | | To show defendant's apprehension concerning victim was reasonable | Defendant may offer threatening statements if known to defendant and relevant to defendant's apprehension concerning victim. |

Another pre-rules requirement was that the defendant had to make some showing of self-defense (or another defensive-force defense) before the court would admit evidence of the victim's character.[36] This requirement may have survived adoption of the rules.[37]

### (2) State's Evidence

Ordinarily the state may not offer evidence of the victim's character. Evidence Rule 404(a)(2) creates two exceptions to this prohibition. First, it allows the state to offer evidence of a pertinent trait of the victim's character to rebut defense evidence about the victim's character. Second, it allows the state to offer evidence of the victim's peacefulness in a homicide case to rebut evidence that the victim was the first aggressor.[38]

These exceptions are subject to certain limitations, however. First, the state may not introduce evidence of the victim's character if

---

36. State v. McCray, 312 N.C. 519, 533, 324 S.E.2d 606, 616 (1985) (stating general rule; case tried before adoption of current evidence rules); State v. Culberson, 228 N.C. 615, 617, 46 S.E.2d 647, 648 (1948) (trial court disallowed question about victim's violent character because at time question was asked there was no evidence of self-defense); State v. McIver, 125 N.C. 645, 646–48, 34 S.E. 439, 439 (1899) (trial court erred in disallowing questions about victim's character; defendant's evidence of self-defense was sufficient to warrant questions); State v. Tann, 57 N.C. App. 527, 531–32, 291 S.E.2d 824, 827 (1982) (preclusion of cross-examination of state's witness about victim's violent character did not preclude questioning on subject at later time).

37. *See generally* 1 BRANDIS & BROUN, *supra* note 1, at 273 n.119; State v. Ransome, 342 N.C. 847, 467 S.E.2d 404 (1996) (uncommunicated threats by victim against defendant admissible where defendant presented other evidence of self-defense); State v. Goodson, 341 N.C. 619, 623–24, 461 S.E.2d 740, 742–43 (1995) (court holds that character of deceased is not relevant when defendant contends only that killing was accidental). If the requirement remains in effect, it would need to be a minimal one. Otherwise, the defendant would be faced with somewhat of a Catch-22, unable to introduce evidence about the victim's character because he or she had not made a showing of self-defense, and impeded in making a showing of self-defense because he or she could not introduce evidence about the victim's character.

38. The state may not offer evidence of the *defendant's* character to rebut evidence about the victim's character or to rebut evidence that the victim was the first aggressor in a homicide case. The state may offer evidence of the *defendant's* character only to rebut evidence about the *defendant's* character. 1 BRANDIS & BROUN, *supra* note 1, at 274 & n.124.

the defendant has not yet introduced evidence of the victim's character or evidence that the victim was the first aggressor in a homicide case.[39]

Second, the evidence given by the state's character witness must be in the form of opinion or reputation testimony; the witness may not testify to specific instances of conduct.[40] Further, Rule 405(a) disallows *expert* opinion testimony on character as circumstantial evidence of behavior. A recent court of appeals decision applying Rule 405(a) in a defensive-force case found it error to admit expert testimony on the victim's character—to the effect that the victim was not homicidal—to show that the defendant could not have been acting in self-defense.[41]

Third, if the defendant offers evidence of the victim's character, the state may offer rebuttal evidence only to prove a pertinent trait of the victim's character. The state may not offer evidence of the victim's general "good" character.[42] If the defendant offers evidence

---

39. State v. Faison, 330 N.C. 347, 355–56, 411 S.E.2d 143, 147–48 (1991) (opening statement by defendant does not constitute evidence, so it was error to allow state to introduce evidence of victim's character in its case in chief); State v. Quick, 329 N.C. 1, 25–26, 405 S.E.2d 179, 194 (1991) (state may bring out evidence of victim's character only to rebut defendant's evidence calling it into question).

40. The state may, however, inquire into relevant instances of the victim's conduct for impeachment purposes when cross-examining a *defense* witness who testifies to the victim's character. *See* 1 BRANDIS & BROUN, *supra* note 1, at 323–24. This right parallels the state's right to inquire into relevant instances of the defendant's conduct for impeachment purposes when cross-examining a witness who testifies to the defendant's character. *See supra* § 7.1(b)(2).

41. State v. Mixion, 110 N.C. App. 138, 145–46, 429 S.E.2d 363, 367–68, *rev. denied*, 334 N.C. 437, 433 S.E.2d 183 (1993). This rule does not, however, prohibit expert testimony for other purposes. As discussed in § 7.3(b) *infra*, the defendant may be able to introduce expert testimony to show his or her apprehension concerning the victim. *See generally* 1 McCORMICK, *supra* note 1, at 927 (noting that expert testimony about defendant's apprehension in connection with claim of self-defense is not subject to prohibition on use of character evidence to show conduct); 1 BRANDIS & BROUN, *supra* note 1, at 303–04 (discussing Rule 405(a) in general).

42. *See* State v. Johnson, 270 N.C. 215, 220–22, 154 S.E.2d 48, 52–53 (1967) (error to admit testimony of general reputation of deceased in community); State v. Champion, 222 N.C. 160, 22 S.E.2d 232 (1942) (rebuttal limited to showing deceased's character for peace and quiet); State v. Temples, 74 N.C. App. 106, 108, 327 S.E.2d 266, 267 (error to admit evidence of victim's general good character), *rev. denied*, 314 N.C. 121, 332 S.E.2d 489 (1985).

that the victim was the first aggressor in a homicide case, the state may offer only proof of the victim's character for peacefulness.[43]

### (b) Prior Bad Acts by Victim

Section 7.1(b), above, discusses the ways in which the state can introduce evidence of the prior bad acts of the defendant. The defendant may use the same methods to bring out prior bad acts of the *victim*. The defendant may use the victim's prior bad acts to impeach the victim; to impeach a character witness for the victim; or to show one of the purposes identified in Rule 404(b).[44]

Defendants have a broader opportunity, however, to bring out prior bad acts of the victim because in defensive-force cases the defendant's belief in the need for defensive action is directly at issue. As stated in an early defensive-force case noting the relevance of such evidence, "One cannot be expected to encounter a lion as he would a lamb."[45] Thus the law allows evidence of prior violent acts of the victim, if *known* by the defendant at the time of the encounter, to show that the defendant honestly and reasonably believed that the victim posed some threat of harm. The evidence also may bear on the reasonableness of the force used by the defendant to avert the perceived threat. The law does not require the defendant to have personally suffered or witnessed these prior acts of violence because the defendant's purpose in offering such evidence is simply to show why he or she was apprehensive of the victim.[46]

---

43. Evidence Rule 404(a)(2); *Faison*, 330 N.C. at 354–55, 411 S.E.2d at 147.

44. *See, e.g.,* State v. Smith, 337 N.C. 658, 664–67, 477 S.E.2d 376, 379–81 (1994) (defendant sought to rely on Rule 404(b) to justify admission of prior bad acts of victim that were *unknown* to defendant; court finds unknown acts inadmissible on facts of case); State v. Burton, 108 N.C. App. 219, 229–30, 423 S.E.2d 484, 490–91 (1992) [trial court erred in precluding defendant from inquiring into prior misconduct on cross-examination of witness to test veracity of witness under Rule 608(b)], *rev. denied*, 333 N.C. 576, 429 S.E.2d 574 (1993); Evidence Rule 405(a) (permitting inquiry into specific instances of person's conduct on cross-examination of witness who testifies to person's character).

45. State v. Floyd, 51 N.C. 392, 398 (1859).

46. *See Smith*, 337 N.C. at 664–67, 477 S.E.2d at 379–81 (prior acts of victim, if known by defendant, are admissible to show defendant's apprehension concerning victim; evidence inadmissible for this purpose because defendant did not know of acts at time of encounter); State v. Barbour, 295 N.C. 66, 72–73, 243 S.E.2d 380, 384 (1978) (error to preclude defendant from testifying that he once saw deceased hit a man with brass knuckles); *Johnson*, 270 N.C. at 218–20, 154 S.E.2d at 51–52 (error for trial judge to limit defendant's testimony to defendant's own experiences with

Must the defendant make some showing of self-defense or another defensive-force defense before introducing prior bad acts of the victim known to the defendant? Some cases that were decided before adoption of the current rules of evidence required such a showing.[47] This requirement may still hold.[48]

### (c) Criminal Convictions of Victim

Section 7.1(c), above, discusses the general requirements for impeaching a witness with criminal convictions under Rule 609. In defensive-force cases, however, the defendant has a broader opportunity to introduce the victim's convictions because the defendant's perception of the victim is at issue. Whether or not the victim testifies, the defendant may introduce the victim's convictions if known to the defendant at the time of the encounter and relevant to the defendant's apprehension concerning the victim.[49]

---

deceased; defendant should have been allowed to relate specific acts of violence that occurred in defendant's presence or of which he had knowledge before conflict); State v. Hall, 31 N.C. App. 34, 38–39, 228 S.E.2d 637, 639–40 (1976) (error to exclude evidence that victim had told defendant that victim had shot at somebody with pistol; telling of incident to defendant was sufficient to show defendant's knowledge of incident and apprehension concerning victim); State v. Graves, 18 N.C. App. 177, 181–82, 196 S.E.2d 582, 585 (1973) (trial court erred in excluding evidence that defendant had seen victim assault another person); State v. Brice, 17 N.C. App. 189, 193–94, 193 S.E.2d 299, 302 (1972) (evidence of prior assault by victim inadmissible where there was no evidence that defendant was present *or* that act was ever communicated to defendant), *rev. denied*, 283 N.C. 258, 195 S.E.2d 690 (1973). Some court of appeals decisions state that the defendant must have had "personal" knowledge of the acts, but those cases do not actually require personal knowledge in the sense that the defendant must have been present when the acts occurred. *See, e.g.,* State v. Hodges, 35 N.C. App. 328, 331–32, 241 S.E.2d 365, 368–69 (1978) (trial court did not err in refusing to allow testimony by defendant that victim had assaulted others and that defendant was, therefore, afraid of victim; excluded answer did not show that defendant had *any* knowledge of assaults at time of encounter).

47. *See* State v. Allmond, 27 N.C. App. 29, 30–31, 217 S.E.2d 734, 736–37 (1975) (court holds that there must be some evidence of self-defense before specific acts of violence of victim are admissible); *accord* State v. Jones, 83 N.C. App. 593, 599–600, 351 S.E.2d 122, 126 (1986) (court follows *Allmond*; case tried in 1982, before adoption of current rules), *rev. denied*, 319 N.C. 461, 356 S.E.2d 9 (1987).

48. *See supra* note 37.

49. *See* State v. Corn, 307 N.C. 79, 85, 296 S.E.2d 261, 265–66 (1982) (since defendant did not have knowledge of prior convictions, convictions were not admissible to show that defendant had reasonable apprehension concerning victim);

## (d) Threatening Statements by Victim

If the defendant knows of threatening statements by the victim, these statements are admissible under the same theory that prior bad acts of the victim are admissible. They tend to show that the defendant honestly and reasonably believed that the victim posed some threat of harm and that the defendant responded in a reasonable manner.[50]

The cases also recognize that threats by the victim against the defendant are admissible even if the defendant doesn't know about them. The theory of admissibility is essentially twofold. First, the courts have found that evidence of uncommunicated threats by the victim against the defendant tend to corroborate communicated threats. Second, the courts have found that uncommunicated threats by the victim against the defendant tend to support the defendant's claim that he or she acted in self-defense. This second theory of admissibility treats threatening statements by the victim against the defendant like threats by the defendant against the victim—namely, as statements of intent

---

Government of Virgin Islands v. Carino, 631 F.2d 226, 229–30 (3d Cir. 1980) (prior conviction for manslaughter admissible to demonstrate defendant's fear of victim). The court has so far rejected efforts to characterize criminal convictions as evidence of the victim's reputation, which would be admissible whether known or unknown to the defendant. *See* State v. Leazer, 337 N.C. 454, 458, 446 S.E.2d 54, 56 (1994) (court states that it is doubtful whether character can be proved by convictions); *Corn*, 307 N.C. at 85, 296 S.E.2d at 265–66 (noting that evidence of the victim's reputation for violence is admissible in defensive-force case to show that victim was aggressor, but finding that criminal convictions do not constitute reputation evidence); State v. Adams, 90 N.C. App. 145, 146–47, 367 S.E.2d 362, 362–63 (1988) (to same effect). *Adams* raises the possibility that the defense may be able to introduce the victim's criminal convictions under Rule 806 in an appropriate case. *See supra* note 27 (discussing right to impeach hearsay statements of victim as if victim were testifying at trial).

50. *See* State v. Rice, 222 N.C. 634, 635, 24 S.E.2d 483, 483–84 (1943) (error to exclude evidence of threat by victim that had been communicated to defendant); State v. Carraway, 181 N.C. 561, 565–66, 107 S.E. 142, 144 (1921) (error to exclude threat by deceased communicated to defendant by third person); *Allmond*, 27 N.C. App. at 30–31, 217 S.E.2d at 736–37 (jury entitled to hear evidence of communicated threats in appropriate case); *Graves*, 18 N.C. App. at 181–82, 196 S.E.2d at 585 (trial court erred in excluding evidence of prior threat defendant heard victim make against another person); G.S. 14-33.1 (in assault cases in which the defendant's plea is self-defense, evidence of threats by victim against defendant, if communicated to defendant before the altercation, are admissible to show reasonableness of defendant's apprehension and reasonableness of force used).

tending to show how the person making the threat later acted.[51] If, however, the defendant neither knows about nor is the subject of the threat, the threat ordinarily would not tend to show that the victim initiated the encounter with the defendant or that the defendant acted out of fear of the victim.[52]

Some pre-rules cases refused to admit evidence of threats by the victim unless the defendant first made some showing of self-defense or another defensive-force defense.[53] This requirement may still remain in effect.[54]

## § 7.3 Defendant's State of Mind

This section addresses a body of evidence that does not fit neatly within the categories of evidence described above, but bears on the defendant's belief in the need to defend against some threat of harm. It focuses on the defendant's perceptions during the encounter with the victim and on expert testimony.[55]

---

51. *See* State v. Goode, 249 N.C. 632, 633, 107 S.E.2d 70, 71 (1959) (error to exclude evidence of uncommunicated threats made a brief time before homicide); State v. Minton, 228 N.C. 15, 17, 44 S.E.2d 346, 348 (1947) (uncommunicated threats tend to show that killing may have been done in self-defense); State v. Dickey, 206 N.C. 417, 419–20, 174 S.E. 316, 317–18 (1934) (uncommunicated threats are admissible if they tend to corroborate communicated threats or tend to show defendant may have acted out of self-defense); State v. Turpin, 77 N.C. 473, 479–80 (1877) (in one of first cases on issue, court identified purposes of uncommunicated threats: to corroborate communicated threats; to show state of feeling of victim toward deceased; and to support defendant's claim that he was defending himself from victim's attack); *Allmond*, 27 N.C. App. at 30–31, 217 S.E.2d at 736–37 (jury entitled to hear evidence of uncommunicated threats in appropriate case); State v. Hurdle, 5 N.C. App. 610, 612–13, 169 S.E.2d 17, 19 (1969) (error not to admit evidence of uncommunicated threats).

52. *See* State v. Edmondson, 283 N.C. 533, 539, 196 S.E.2d 505, 508 (1973) (trial court properly excluded testimony that deceased said to third person, "I will blow your head off"; no evidence that defendant knew of episode).

53. *See* State v. Byrd, 121 N.C. 684, 686–88, 28 S.E. 353, 353–54 (1897); State v. Allmond, 27 N.C. App. 29, 30–31, 217 S.E.2d 734, 736–37 (1975).

54. *See supra* note 37.

55. The victim's character and prior conduct, when known by the defendant at the time of the encounter, also may bear on the defendant's belief in the need for defensive force. *See supra* § 7.2.

### (a) Defendant's Perceptions

Any number of things may be relevant to the defendant's belief in the need to defend against harm and the reasonableness of his or her response. In two recent cases, for example, the supreme court held that the trial court erred in precluding the defendant from testifying directly about his state of mind. In both cases the defendant would have testified that he feared for his life. Recognizing that the defendant's belief in the need to defend himself is an essential element of self-defense, the court held that the testimony was relevant and should have been allowed.[56]

Also admissible are the impressions formed by the defendant about the victim during the encounter. For example, in one case the court held that the defendant should have been permitted to testify that he thought that the victim was about to shoot him.[57] In another case the court held that the defendant could testify that the victim looked as if he were angry and had been drinking. In that case, the court held that such evidence was permissible opinion testimony by a lay witness because it constituted the "instantaneous conclusions of the mind as to the appearance, condition, or mental or physical state" of the other person.[58]

The defendant's impressions of the victim during the encounter also may be based on information relayed by others. For example, in one case the defendant heard someone yell, "Run, . . . Ben is going to kill us." The court held that the statement was not hearsay because it was not offered for the truth of the matter asserted (that is, that Ben was actually trying to kill the defendant), but rather was properly offered to

---

56. State v. Webster, 324 N.C. 385, 389–93, 378 S.E.2d 748, 751–54 (1989) (error to disallow question, "State whether or not you felt your life was threatened"); State v. Reed, 324 N.C. 535, 537–38, 379 S.E.2d 828, 829–30 (1989) (involving similar questions). *Cf.* State v. Price, 301 N.C. 437, 449–50, 272 S.E.2d 103, 111–12 (1980) (defendant's statement to officers that he had acted in self-defense was inadmissible as substantive evidence because of its hearsay character and was inadmissible as corroborative evidence because defendant had not yet taken stand).

57. State v. Robinson, 181 N.C. 552, 553–54, 107 S.E. 131, 132 (1921).

58. State v. Holland, 193 N.C. 713, 720, 138 S.E. 8, 12 (1927). *See also* 1 BRANDIS & BROUN, *supra* note 1, at 607–08 (to same effect); Evidence Rule 701 (lay witness may testify to opinion and inferences if rationally based on perception of witness and helpful to jury); State v. Sanders, 295 N.C. 361, 369–70, 245 S.E.2d 674, 680–81 (1978) (trial court properly excluded opinion of third persons that officers approached defendant with purpose of beating him up; court notes that witnesses could have described the words, acts, and demeanor of the officers).

show the effect that the statement had on the defendant.[59] A number of cases consider other circumstances that may bear on a defendant's perceptions or actions.[60]

### (b) Expert Testimony

Evidence Rule 702 permits expert testimony if it will assist the trier of fact in understanding the evidence or determining a fact in issue. Although few North Carolina decisions discuss the admissibility of expert testimony in defensive-force cases, expert testimony about the defendant's state of mind would appear to be admissible in an appropriate case. For example, since an essential issue in a self-defense case is whether the defendant "honestly" believed in the need to defend himself or herself from harm, expert testimony may help the jury understand the defendant's state of mind.[61]

---

59. State v. Crump, 277 N.C. 573, 584–85, 178 S.E.2d 366, 373–74 (1971). *See also* State v. Miller, 282 N.C. 633, 642–43, 194 S.E.2d 353, 358–59 (1973) (while defendant was engaged in card game, a number of unidentified persons broke in; error to preclude defendant from testifying that others had told him about recent robberies of gambling games in area, which bore on defendant's belief that game was being robbed).

60. *See, e.g., Webster*, 324 N.C. at 392–93, 378 S.E.2d at 753 (defendant had recently been released from hospital and was still sick and weak); State v. Spaulding, 298 N.C. 149, 156–60, 257 S.E.2d 391, 396–98 (1979) (error to exclude evidence that most inmates had weapons, that weapons were hidden in the recreation yard, that others had been previously injured with knives, that a pervasive fear of physical harm existed among the inmates, and other evidence bearing on reasonableness of defendant's perceptions and actions); State v. Erby, 56 N.C. App. 358, 359–61, 289 S.E.2d 86, 87–88 (1982) (defendant should have been permitted to explain why he had loaded gun).

61. *See generally* Kerry A. Shad, Note, State v. Norman: *Self-Defense Unavailable to Battered Women Who Kill Passive Abusers*, 68 N.C. L. Rev. 1159, 1165 n.44 (1990) (collecting cases dealing with expert testimony on battered woman syndrome and finding that majority of jurisdictions allow such testimony); James O. Pearson, Jr., Annotation, *Admissibility of Expert or Opinion Testimony on Battered Wife or Battered Woman Syndrome*, 18 A.L.R. 4th 1153 (1982). *Cf.* State v. Clark, 107 N.C. App. 184, 187–88, 419 S.E.2d 188, 190–91 (1992) (trial court could exclude expert testimony on ground that probative value of particular testimony was weak and outweighed by danger of unfair prejudice, confusion of issues, or misleading of jury); State v. Bennett, 67 N.C. App. 407, 412–13, 313 S.E.2d 277, 280–81 (court finds no error in exclusion of expert testimony about defendant's organic brain syndrome; court states that testimony was offered only for purpose of showing that defendant was capable of perceiving life-threatening situations accurately), *rev. denied*, 311 N.C. 764, 321 S.E.2d 147 (1984).

The question remains whether an expert may give an opinion on whether the defendant's belief was "reasonable." In a pre-rules case, the court held that the trial court properly excluded expert testimony that the circumstances encountered by the defendant could have produced in a person of ordinary firmness an apprehension of death or great bodily injury. The court reasoned that the jury was in as good a position as the expert to evaluate the reasonableness of the defendant's apprehension.[62] Current Rule 704 allows greater leeway for expert testimony in that it permits an expert to give an opinion on an issue ultimately to be decided by the jury. Thus it would seem permissible for an expert to give testimony bearing on the issue of reasonableness in a self-defense case.[63] Even under Rule 704, however, an expert's opinion may not be in the form of a "legal conclusion." It still appears to be objectionable for an expert to testify specifically about whether a person of "ordinary firmness" would or would not have formed a similar belief under the circumstances because that term is one of the legal standards employed in the *Norris* test itself.[64]

---

62. *Spaulding*, 298 N.C. at 160, 257 S.E.2d at 398.

63. *See* Shad, *supra* note 61, at 1172 n.99 (1990) (noting that since Rule 704 allows expert testimony on ultimate issue to be decided by jury, expert could give testimony bearing on issue of reasonableness). *See also* 2 Brandis & Broun, *supra* note 1, at 640 n.172 (current evidence rules on expert testimony allow greater admissibility because their emphasis is on helpfulness rather than on a comparison of the expert's and jury's qualifications).

64. *Compare* State v. Rose, 323 N.C. 455, 459–60, 373 S.E.2d 426, 429–30 (1988) (in case involving defense of diminished capacity, court rules inadmissible medical expert's opinion on whether legal standards of *premeditation* and *deliberation* had or had not been met) *with* State v. Shank, 322 N.C. 243, 247–49, 367 S.E.2d 639, 642–43 (1988) (medical expert could give opinion on whether defendant had capacity to plan, which was relevant to elements of premeditation and deliberation; such testimony did not violate proscription on testimony in form of legal conclusion).

# 8  Burdens, Presumptions, and Instructions

# 8 Burdens, Presumptions, and Instructions

🖉🖉🖉 That the prosecution bears the burden of proving the defendant's guilt beyond a reasonable doubt is a basic principle of criminal law. Although this principle applies in cases involving defensive-force defenses, more complex burdens come into play. This chapter considers the burdens applicable in defensive-force cases as well as the instructions to be given to the jury.

## § 8.1 Pleading Requirements

Unlike defendants in civil cases, defendants in criminal cases ordinarily do not have any "burden" to plead, or otherwise give notice of, the defenses they intend to assert at trial. In *State v. Ross*,[1] the North Carolina Supreme Court considered the propriety of a trial court order requiring the defendant to give notice of whether he intended to claim self-defense. Although the court found that the order was not so prejudicial as to warrant a new trial in the case under review, it strongly disapproved such a requirement. The court recognized that the only legislative authorization for requiring defendants to give notice of their defense is G.S. 15A-959(a), and that requirement applies only to the insanity defense.

## § 8.2 Burdens of Proof

### (a) In General

The term *burden of proof* refers to two separate burdens—the burden of production and the burden of persuasion. Generally speaking, the party with the *burden of production* on a particular issue must

---

1. 329 N.C. 108, 112–14, 405 S.E.2d 158, 161 (1991).

present sufficient evidence to warrant submitting the issue to the jury for decision. The party with the *burden of persuasion* on a particular issue must present sufficient evidence to justify a finding by the jury in the party's favor.[2]

In a case in which the defendant simply denies the state's allegations, the burdens of both production and persuasion rest with the state. To meet its burden of persuasion before the jury, the state must prove beyond a reasonable doubt all facts necessary to establish the defendant's guilt of the charged offense.[3] The state must meet a parallel burden of production to have the charged offense submitted to the jury—that is, the trial court must find that a rational fact finder could accept the evidence as proof of the defendant's guilt beyond a reasonable doubt.[4] The state is aided in meeting its burden of production by the principle that the court must consider the evidence in the light most favorable to the state.[5] If the prosecution fails to meet its burden of production, the court must grant the defendant's motion for dismissal or nonsuit.

### (b) Prosecution's Burden of Persuasion

In defensive-force cases the prosecution still has the burden of proving beyond a reasonable doubt all facts necessary to establish the defendant's guilt. As part of this burden, the prosecution also must prove to the jury beyond a reasonable doubt that the defendant was *not*

---

2. *See* 1 Kenneth S. Broun, Brandis & Broun on North Carolina Evidence 115–16 (4th ed. 1993) [hereinafter Brandis & Broun]; 1 Wayne R. LaFave & Austin W. Scott, Jr., Substantive Criminal Law 67 (1986).

3. *See* Mullaney v. Wilbur, 421 U.S. 684, 95 S. Ct. 1881, 44 L. Ed. 2d 508 (1975); *In re* Winship, 397 U.S. 358, 90 S. Ct. 1068, 25 L. Ed. 2d 368 (1970).

4. *See* Jackson v. Virginia, 443 U.S. 307, 318–19, 99 S. Ct. 2781, 2788–89, 61 L. Ed. 2d 560, 573 (1979); 1 Brandis & Broun, *supra* note 2, at 134; 2 John W. Strong, McCormick on Evidence 434 (4th ed. 1992) [hereinafter McCormick].

5. *See, e.g.,* State v. Carter, 335 N.C. 422, 429, 440 S.E.2d 268, 271–72 (1994); State v. McAvoy, 331 N.C. 583, 589, 417 S.E.2d 489, 493–94 (1992). In ruling on a motion for nonsuit, the court may consider evidence offered by a defendant that explains or clarifies the state's evidence as well as exculpatory features of the state's own evidence. *See* State v. Bates, 309 N.C. 528, 535, 308 S.E.2d 258, 262–63 (1983) (defendant's evidence may be considered if not inconsistent with state's evidence); State v. Bruton, 264 N.C. 488, 499, 142 S.E.2d 169, 176 (1965) (state is bound by exculpatory features of its own evidence if not disproved by other evidence).

entitled to use defensive force. The prosecution has this burden because a fact necessary for conviction of offenses such as murder and assault is that the defendant *unlawfully* killed or assaulted the victim. In other words, when a defendant has the right to use defensive force, his or her actions are not unlawful.[6] Consequently, in defensive-force cases, the prosecution must prove beyond a reasonable doubt that the defendant did *not* have the right to use defensive force.[7]

Since self-defense and the other defensive-force defenses have multiple elements, the state can meet its burden of persuasion by disproving any of the required elements of the particular defense asserted.[8] For example, to defeat a claim of self-defense in an assault case, the state would have to prove beyond a reasonable doubt that the defendant did not honestly believe in the need to defend himself or herself from some harm; *or* that the defendant's belief was unreasonable; *or* that the defendant was the aggressor; *or* that the defendant used excessive force. The state's evidence would have to be more focused in a murder case because of the availability of both perfect and imperfect self-defense. To defeat a claim of both perfect and imperfect self-defense, the state would have to prove beyond a reasonable doubt that the defendant did not honestly or reasonably believe in the need to defend himself or herself *or* that the defendant was the aggressor with murderous intent. If the state proves only that the defendant was an aggressor without murderous intent or used excessive force, the defendant at most would be guilty of voluntary manslaughter.

---

6. *See* 1 LaFave, *supra* note 2, at 75 ("where the law of criminal homicide is defined in terms of an 'unlawful' killing, the burden of proof as to the 'defense' of self-defense may not be placed on the defendant, for a killing in self-defense is not unlawful").

7. At one time the North Carolina courts differentiated between assault and homicide cases, placing the burden of persuasion on the prosecution in the former but not in the latter context. *See* State v. Fletcher, 268 N.C. 140, 141–42, 150 S.E.2d 54, 56 (1966). Now, the state clearly bears the burden of persuasion in both contexts. *See* State v. Hankerson, 288 N.C. 632, 641–52, 220 S.E.2d 575, 583–89 (1975), *rev'd on other grounds*, 432 U.S. 233, 97 S. Ct. 2339, 53 L. Ed. 2d 306 (1977).

8. *See* State v. Potter, 295 N.C. 126, 143–44, 244 S.E.2d 397, 408–09 (1978) (state need only prove beyond reasonable doubt that one of four elements did not exist to deprive defendant of perfect self-defense; it was error to place burden of persuasion on defendant with respect to any of elements). The required elements of self-defense and other defensive-force defenses are discussed generally in § 2.2(c) *supra* (discussing *Norris* test).

### (c) Defendant's Burden of Production to Obtain Instructions

Although the prosecution bears the burden of persuasion before the jury, the defendant first bears the burden of producing evidence that he or she acted in self-defense or pursuant to another defensive-force defense. When a defendant meets this burden, he or she becomes entitled to have the judge submit instructions to the jury on the particular defensive-force defense asserted. Meeting the burden of production also can be said to trigger the prosecution's burden of persuading the jury that the defendant did not have the right to use defensive force.[9] The defendant's burden of production thus is a mechanism for controlling the issues presented to the jury for decision.[10]

What evidence must the defendant produce to meet this burden? The question involves two subsidiary questions. First, on which elements of self-defense (or other defensive-force defense) must the defendant produce evidence? Second, how much evidence must the defendant produce on the required elements? For the sake of clarity, the second question is addressed first.

The threshold of proof is low in defensive-force cases. If the defendant comes forward with "any evidence" on the required elements, he or she is entitled to instructions to the jury.[11] The defendant is aided

---

9. *See, e.g.,* State v. Jones, 299 N.C. 103, 107, 261 S.E.2d 1, 5 (1980) (when there is competent evidence to raise issue of defense of home, jury must be instructed on defense; burden of persuasion remains on state); State v. Boone, 299 N.C. 681, 687, 263 S.E.2d 758, 761 (1980) (state must prove that defendant did not act in self-defense only when there is some evidence of self-defense in the case).

10. Some have argued that placing a burden of production on the defendant on any issue relating to culpability relieves the state of its burden of persuasion on all essential facts and invades the province of the jury. *See* Ronald J. Allen, *Structuring Jury Decisionmaking in Criminal Cases: A Unified Constitutional Approach to Evidentiary Devices,* 94 Harv. L. Rev. 321, 329, 358–60 (1980). It is generally accepted, however, that some burden of production may be placed on the defendant for defenses such as self-defense. *See generally* 1 Paul H. Robinson, Criminal Law Defenses 20–26, 130–36 (1984) (accepting that burden of production may be placed on defendant for certain defenses, but noting that too-rigorous burden may effectively relieve prosecution of burden of persuasion and deny defendant right to trial by jury).

11. State v. Clark, 324 N.C. 146, 161–63, 377 S.E.2d 54, 63–64 (1989) (contrasting "any evidence" standard for self-defense with higher evidentiary thresholds for defenses of voluntary intoxication and diminished capacity); State v. Bush, 307 N.C. 152, 160, 297 S.E.2d 563, 569 (1982) (setting forth "any evidence" test); State v. Marshall, 105 N.C. App. 518, 522, 414 S.E.2d 95, 97 (following "any evidence" stan-

in meeting this burden by the principle that the court must consider all of the evidence, both the state's and the defendant's, in the light most favorable to the defendant.[12]

The first question—on which elements must the defendant produce evidence?—does not have such a clear answer. In *State v. Bush*, the court held that the defendant is entitled to instructions on defensive force in a homicide case if he or she produces evidence on the first two elements of the *Norris* test. The court in *Bush* stated that instructions on self-defense must be given if the answer to the following two questions is yes: "(1) Is there evidence that the defendant in fact formed a belief that it was necessary to kill his adversary in order to protect himself from death or great bodily harm, and (2) if so, was that belief reasonable?"[13]

A number of cases followed the rule announced in *Bush*, holding in both homicide and assault cases that the defendant was entitled to instructions on defensive force if he or she produced sufficient evidence of the first two *Norris* elements.[14] Other cases after *Bush*, however, relied on the third element of the *Norris* test—the aggressor requirement—in denying instructions on defensive force.[15] Still other cases suggest that a

---

dard for defense of habitation), *rev. denied*, 332 N.C. 150, 419 S.E.2d 576 (1992). *See also* State v. Patterson, 297 N.C. 247, 255–56, 254 S.E.2d 604, 610 (1979) (defendant does not have burden to produce evidence sufficient to raise reasonable doubt; burden is simply to produce some evidence from which jury *could* find existence of self-defense).

12. *See Bush*, 307 N.C. at 159, 297 S.E.2d at 568; State v. Jones, 299 N.C. 103, 107, 261 S.E.2d 1, 5 (1980).

13. 307 N.C. at 160–61, 297 S.E.2d at 569. The *Norris* test is discussed generally in § 2.2(c) *supra*; the first two elements are discussed in § 3.2 *supra*.

14. *See* State v. Lyons, 340 N.C. 646, 661–62, 459 S.E.2d 770, 778 (1995) (reciting *Bush* rule with approval); *Clark*, 324 N.C. at 162, 377 S.E.2d at 64 (to same effect); State v. Kinney, 92 N.C. App. 671, 675–76, 375 S.E.2d 692, 695 (1989) (applying two-part test from *Bush* in case involving charge of assault with a deadly weapon with intent to kill inflicting serious injury); State v. Hughes, 82 N.C. App. 724, 727, 348 S.E.2d 147, 150 (1986) (recognizing in homicide case that *Bush* articulated a two-question test for judging the sufficiency of the evidence to support an instruction on self-defense).

15. In some homicide cases, the court denied defensive-force instructions because the evidence established that the defendant was an aggressor *with* murderous intent and had not withdrawn. *See, e.g.,* State v. Baldwin, 330 N.C. 446, 464–65, 412 S.E.2d 31, 42 (1992) (defendant not entitled to instruction on imperfect self-defense where evidence showed that defendant instigated conflict with murderous intent); State v. Mize, 316 N.C. 48, 53, 340 S.E.2d 439, 442 (1986) (to same effect). In

trial court could deny instructions on the ground that the defendant's force was excessive under the fourth *Norris* element.[16]

Assuming that all of these cases remain good law, they suggest the following approach. Per *Bush* and the cases following it, the defendant initially bears a burden of production on the first two *Norris* elements alone. Evidence of those elements is sufficient by itself to require instructions on defensive force. If the state offers evidence (or points to evidence already in the record) that the defendant was the aggressor under the third *Norris* element or that the defendant used excessive force under the fourth element, the defendant would have to come forward with further evidence to counter the state's theory. For example, a defendant could counter evidence that he or she was the aggressor by offering evidence (or pointing to evidence already in the record) that he or she withdrew from the encounter. If the defendant comes forward with such additional evidence, he or she remains entitled to defensive-force instructions. If the state's evidence is conclusive that the defendant was the aggressor or used excessive force—that is, there is no evidence or inference to the contrary—the defendant may lose the right to instructions on defensive force.

This analysis is somewhat complicated by the existence of *imperfect* defensive-force defenses. In a homicide case, if the evidence conclusively establishes that the defendant was the aggressor *with* murderous intent and did not withdraw, the defendant would appear to lose the right to instructions on both perfect and imperfect defensive-force

---

some assault cases, the court denied defensive-force instructions because the evidence established that the defendant was an aggressor (with or without murderous intent) and had not withdrawn. *See, e.g.,* State v. Hunter, 315 N.C. 371, 374, 338 S.E.2d 99, 102 (1986) (in upholding denial of self-defense instructions in assault case, court relied in part on evidence that defendant was the aggressor); State v. Hall, 89 N.C. App. 491, 493–94, 366 S.E.2d 527, 528 (1988) (in case involving charge of assault with a deadly weapon inflicting serious injury, court found instructions on self-defense were not warranted because evidence established that defendant was aggressor); State v. Brewer, 89 N.C. App. 431, 434–35, 366 S.E.2d 580, 582–83 (to same effect), *rev. denied*, 322 N.C. 482, 370 S.E.2d 229 (1988).

16. *See, e.g.,* State v. Richardson, 341 N.C. 585, 461 S.E.2d 724 (1995) (stating generally that evidence must be presented on all four elements of self-defense); State v. Wallace, 309 N.C. 141, 148–49, 305 S.E.2d 548, 553 (1983) (relying on *Bush*, court states in one part of opinion that instruction on imperfect self-defense required if defendant meets first two elements of *Norris*; yet court states in another part of opinion that defendant is entitled to instructions on perfect self-defense only when there is evidence of all four *Norris* elements).

defenses. If the evidence conclusively establishes that the defendant was the aggressor *without* murderous intent (and did not withdraw) or that the defendant used excessive force, the defendant arguably would lose instructions on the *perfect* form of a defensive-force defense but not on the *imperfect* form.[17]

### (d) Prosecution's Burden of Production to Avoid Nonsuit

The prosecution always bears a burden of production to justify submitting the charged offense to the jury. To meet that burden, the prosecution must come forward with sufficient evidence of each element of the offense. In cases in which the defendant offers evidence of defensive force, the prosecution also may need to offer evidence (or point to evidence already in the record) showing that the defendant did not have the right to use defensive force. When the defendant's evidence on defensive force is sufficiently strong, the prosecution's failure to produce countervailing evidence may result in dismissal or nonsuit of the charged offense.[18] The state must produce sufficient evidence (taken in the light most favorable to the state) for a rational fact finder to find beyond a reasonable doubt that at least one of the required elements of the particular defensive-force defense is not present. This burden parallels the prosecution's burden of persuasion before the jury (discussed in § 8.2(b), above).

---

17. *See generally* § 2.2(c) *supra* (discussing difference between perfect and imperfect forms of defensive-force defenses). Although the excessive force element is included in the above analysis, the element actually may play little role in assessing whether the defendant has met his or her burden of production. The reason lies in the similarity between the second and fourth elements of the *Norris* test. To satisfy the second element, a defendant must reasonably believe in the need to protect himself, herself, or some other interest from harm; to satisfy the fourth element, a defendant must use a reasonable amount of force to avert the perceived harm. *See generally* § 3.4 *supra*. Evidence showing reasonableness under the second element often will tend to show reasonableness under the fourth element. Consequently, by producing evidence to satisfy the second element, the defendant may satisfy any burden to produce evidence on the fourth element.

18. *See* State v. Johnson, 261 N.C. 727, 136 S.E.2d 84 (1964) (nonsuit granted; state did not produce evidence contradicting that defendant killed deceased in self-defense); State v. Carter, 254 N.C. 475, 119 S.E.2d 461 (1961) (nonsuit granted; state did not produce evidence showing that defendant did not act in proper defense of others).

## § 8.3 Presumption of Malice

The term *presumption* can have several meanings.[19] This section considers how the term is used in connection with the element of malice in homicide cases.

In past homicide cases, the North Carolina Supreme Court has said that a mandatory presumption of *malice* and *unlawfulness* arises when the trial court determines that the evidence would permit a jury to find beyond a reasonable doubt that the defendant intentionally inflicted a wound upon the deceased that proximately resulted in death. The defendant then has the burden of producing evidence to rebut the presumption, such as evidence of heat of passion or self-defense. If the trial court determines that the defendant has failed to produce any such evidence, the trial court must instruct the jury essentially as follows. The court must instruct the jury that if it finds beyond a reasonable doubt that the defendant intentionally used a deadly weapon in the manner described above, the jury must find the defendant guilty of second-degree murder. Such an instruction effectively directs the jury to *presume* the elements of malice and unlawfulness required for conviction of second-degree murder. If, however, the trial court determines that the defendant has produced any evidence that would rebut malice and unlawfulness, this presumption "disappears." The trial court then instructs the jury that it may but is not required to infer that the killing was unlawful and done with malice in light of all of the evidence.[20]

It is unclear whether the North Carolina courts continue to employ this presumption of malice. The Pattern Jury Committee does not include the presumption in any of its pattern instructions. And, in its commentary to the instructions on murder, the Committee questions the validity of a mandatory presumption of malice and unlawfulness. The commentary notes that recent cases by the United States Supreme Court suggest that a mandatory presumption on a required element of the state's case, such as malice, may impermissibly lessen the state's burden to prove beyond a reasonable doubt all facts necessary for

---

19. *See generally* 1 BRANDIS & BROUN, *supra* note 2, at 149–69; 2 McCORMICK, *supra* note 4, at 449–54.

20. *See* State v. Reynolds, 307 N.C. 184, 188–92, 297 S.E.2d 532, 535–37 (1982); State v. Patterson, 297 N.C. 247, 252–57, 254 S.E.2d 604, 608–11 (1979); State v. Hankerson, 288 N.C. 632, 649–52, 220 S.E.2d 575, 588–89 (1975), *rev'd on other grounds*, 432 U.S. 233, 97 S. Ct. 2339, 53 L. Ed. 2d 306 (1977).

conviction.[21] If the presumption remains good law, however, the defendant's burden to produce evidence to rebut the presumption could be no greater than his or her burden to produce evidence to obtain instructions on defensive force (see § 8.2(c), above).[22]

## § 8.4  Jury Instructions

If the defendant fails to meet his or her burden of production, the result is clear under North Carolina law: the defendant is not entitled to any instructions on defensive force.[23] The course is not so clear when the defendant satisfies the burden. The trial court must correctly instruct the jury on the law relating to any applicable defensive-force defense even in the absence of a request for such instructions.[24] As shown in other parts of this book, however, the law on which the court must instruct the jury is not always clear or simple.

This section does not attempt to describe in detail the wording of possible instructions. Rather, it seeks to isolate the basic components of the instructions required in defensive-force cases.

---

21. North Carolina Pattern Jury Instructions for Criminal Cases 206.10 n.5 (North Carolina Superior Court Judges Conference, Committee on Pattern Jury Instructions, Aug. 1994) [hereinafter N.C.P.I.—Crim.], *citing* Francis v. Franklin, 471 U.S. 307, 105 S. Ct. 1965, 85 L. Ed. 2d 344 (1985). *See also* 2 McCormick, *supra* note 4, at 493–94 (because of rigid requirements for validity of mandatory presumptions, few presumptions in criminal cases are properly mandatory).

22. *See generally* 1 Brandis & Broun, *supra* note 2, at 206–07 and accompanying notes.

23. *See, e.g.,* State v. Davis, 289 N.C. 500, 508–09, 223 S.E.2d 296, 301–02, *vacated on other grounds*, 429 U.S. 809, 97 S. Ct. 47, 50 L. Ed. 2d 69 (1976); State v. Brewer, 89 N.C. App. 431, 434–35, 366 S.E.2d 580, 582, *rev. denied*, 322 N.C. 482, 370 S.E.2d 229 (1988). In cases involving assault charges, the court of appeals also has said that when the defendant fails to meet his or her burden of production, the instructions to the jury need not state that the assault must have been "without justification or excuse." *See* State v. Gullie, 96 N.C. App. 366, 367–68, 385 S.E.2d 556, 557–58 (1989); State v. Hall, 89 N.C. App. 491, 495–96, 366 S.E.2d 527, 529–30 (1988). *But cf. supra* § 8.2(b) (required element of state's case is that defendant unlawfully assaulted victim) and § 8.3 (discussing propriety of mandatory presumption of malice and unlawfulness in homicide cases).

24. Defensive-force defenses are considered substantial features of a case, requiring instructions even without a special request. *See* State v. Jones, 299 N.C. 103, 107, 261 S.E.2d 1, 5 (1980); State v. Dooley, 285 N.C. 158, 163, 203 S.E.2d 815, 818 (1974). Generally, absent a request for instructions, a failure to instruct is reviewed

## (a) Perfect and Imperfect Self-Defense

In most homicide cases, if the trial court finds sufficient evidence to warrant instructions on perfect self-defense, it also must instruct on imperfect self-defense. The reason lies in the similarity between the second and fourth elements of the *Norris* test. To warrant instructions on perfect self-defense, a defendant must produce evidence that he or she reasonably believed it necessary to protect himself or herself from death or great bodily injury, as required by the second element of the *Norris* test. To avoid nonsuit, the state ordinarily will produce evidence contradicting the defendant's claim of reasonableness. In most instances, each side's showing will bolster that side's respective position on the fourth element of the *Norris* test, which considers whether the defendant used an excessive, or unreasonable, amount of force to avert the perceived harm. Thus, in most homicide cases in which the jury is authorized to determine whether the defendant acted in perfect self-defense, the jury also must decide whether the defendant used excessive force and is liable for voluntary manslaughter.[25]

---

on appeal under the "plain error" standard. *See generally* State v. Odom, 307 N.C. 655, 300 S.E.2d 375 (1983). The failure to give an instruction on an applicable defensive-force defense may, however, be such fundamental error as to meet the "plain error" standard of review in some cases. *Cf.* State v. Marshall, 105 N.C. App. 518, 524–25, 414 S.E.2d 95, 99 (due process requires trial court to instruct jury on defense of habitation when evidence supports instruction), *rev. denied*, 332 N.C. 150, 419 S.E.2d 576 (1992).

25. *See supra* § 3.4 (discussing application of excessive-force element); *see also* State v. Rummage, 280 N.C. 51, 58, 185 S.E.2d 221, 226 (1971) (error in failing to explain that excessive force mitigates second-degree murder to manslaughter); State v. Best, 79 N.C. App. 734, 737, 340 S.E.2d 524, 527 (1986) ("[i]t is difficult to imagine a homicide case in which the evidence supports an instruction on self defense but not an instruction on voluntary manslaughter based upon an excessive force theory"); State v. Hutchison, 26 N.C. App. 290, 292, 215 S.E.2d 820, 822 (trial court properly instructed jury on voluntary manslaughter based on excessive-force theory), *rev. denied*, 288 N.C. 247, 217 S.E.2d 671 (1975). Isolated cases have upheld the denial of instructions on *imperfect* self-defense even though it was proper to give instructions on *perfect* self-defense. These cases reasoned that if the jury accepted the defendant's evidence of reasonableness under the second *Norris* element, it could not have found the defendant's force to have been excessive within the meaning of the fourth element of *Norris*. *See* State v. Perry, 338 N.C. 457, 465–68, 450 S.E.2d 471, 476–77 (1994) (recognizing imperfect defense of another but upholding denial of instruction); State v. Burden, 36 N.C. App. 332, 335–36, 244 S.E.2d 204, 206 (upholding denial of instruction on imperfect self-defense), *rev. denied*, 295 N.C. 468, 246 S.E.2d 216 (1978). These cases may not be reliable authority,

## (b) The *Norris* Elements

In any case in which instructions on defensive force are warranted, the trial court must adequately explain to the jury the basic principles embodied in *Norris*, such as the honest-and-reasonable-belief requirement, aggressors, and excessive force.[26] In certain cases, however, it may be inappropriate to give any instruction on the aggressor element. The court has held generally that the trial court should not instruct the jury on a theory not supported by the evidence.[27] In the context of defensive-force cases, the court of appeals has held that when the evidence does not indicate that the defendant was the aggressor, the trial court should not instruct on that element.[28] Conversely,

---

however, on when trial courts should give instructions on imperfect self-defense. First, at the time the cases were decided, it was unclear how the second and fourth *Norris* elements differed. The two elements still concern similar matters, but evidence satisfying element two no longer automatically satisfies element four. *See supra* 3.4(c)(3) (discussing recent changes in phrasing of *Norris* test). Second, even when decided, the cases did not provide trial courts with a reliable way of determining when they should, and when they should not, instruct on imperfect self-defense based on an excessive-force theory.

26. *See, e.g.,* State v. Potts, 334 N.C. 575, 581, 433 S.E.2d 736, 739 (1993) (as long as trial court correctly explained principles of perfect and imperfect self-defense, it was not necessary to label or compare them); State v. Herbin, 298 N.C. 441, 446, 259 S.E.2d 263, 267 (1979) ("When charging on self-defense, a trial judge must correctly define the term self-defense."); *Rummage*, 280 N.C. at 58, 185 S.E.2d at 226 (error in failing to explain that excessive force mitigates second-degree murder to manslaughter); State v. Jennings, 276 N.C. 157, 162–66, 171 S.E.2d 447, 450–53 (1970) (error in instructing jury that defendant had to act out of actual, not apparent, necessity; also error in failing to amplify meaning of "without fault" and "free from blame" in light of facts of case).

27. *See* State v. Porter, 340 N.C. 320, 331, 457 S.E.2d 716, 721 (1995) ("Where jury instructions are given without supporting evidence, a new trial is required."); State v. Moore, 315 N.C. 738, 749, 340 S.E.2d 401, 408 (1986) ("It is generally prejudicial error for the trial judge to permit a jury to convict upon a theory not supported by the evidence.").

28. *See* State v. Temples, 74 N.C. App. 106, 109, 327 S.E.2d 266, 268 (when evidence showed only that victim attacked defendant and defendant responded with force, trial court erred in including aggressor doctrine in its instructions to jury on self-defense), *rev. denied,* 314 N.C. 121, 332 S.E.2d 489 (1985); State v. Tann, 57 N.C. App. 527, 530–31, 291 S.E.2d 824, 827 (1982) (to same effect); State v. Ward, 26 N.C. App. 159, 162–63, 215 S.E.2d 394, 396–97 (1975) (to same effect). *See also* State v. Washington, 234 N.C. 531, 535, 67 S.E.2d 498, 501 (1951) (error to instruct on duty of aggressor to retreat where evidence showed only that victim attacked defendant and defendant then responded with force).

such instructions are appropriate when the jury could find from the evidence that the defendant was the aggressor.[29]

### (c) Multiple Defensive-Force Defenses

The trial court must give instructions on each defensive-force defense supported by the evidence. For example, the appellate courts have found that the defendant is entitled, in an appropriate case, to instructions on: defense of oneself, defense of others, and defense of habitation;[30] defense of others and the crime prevention privilege;[31] and the right to defend oneself from death or great bodily injury *and* mere bodily harm or offensive physical contact.[32] This listing illustrates but does not exhaust the possible combinations of instructions.

### (d) No Duty to Retreat

Many cases hold that the trial court must give no-duty-to-retreat instructions in cases that involve self-defense within the home or

---

29. *See, e.g.,* State v. Terry, 329 N.C. 191, 198–99, 404 S.E.2d 658, 662–63 (1991) (evidence sufficient to warrant instruction on aggressor element); State v. Edmondson, 283 N.C. 533, 539, 196 S.E.2d 505, 508–09 (1973) (evidence sufficient to warrant instruction on duty of aggressor to retreat).

30. *See* State v. Oxendine, 300 N.C. 720, 724–25, 268 S.E.2d 212, 215 (1980) (defendant is entitled to instructions on self-defense and defense of others when facts support both principles; evidence did not support defense of others); State v. Jones, 299 N.C. 103, 107, 261 S.E.2d 1, 5 (1980) (defendant had right to instructions on defense of habitation and defense of others; giving of instruction on one did not cure failure to give instruction on other); State v. Miller, 267 N.C. 409, 411–12, 148 S.E.2d 279, 282 (1966) (failure to instruct on both defense of habitation and self-defense held to be error). *But cf.* State v. Roberson, 90 N.C. App. 219, 222, 368 S.E.2d 3, 5–6 (in case in which defendant claimed defense of habitation and self-defense to justify force against assailant attempting to enter home, court upholds denial of nonsuit on ground that defendant could not claim self-defense until assailant gained entry; principle of law stated by court appears to be contrary to North Carolina law), *rev. denied,* 322 N.C. 484, 370 S.E.2d 237 (1988).

31. *See* State v. Robinson, 213 N.C. 273, 281–82, 195 S.E. 824, 829–30 (1938) (error not to instruct on right to fight in defense of stepfather and right to intervene to prevent felonious assault).

32. *See* State v. Fletcher, 268 N.C. 140, 142, 150 S.E.2d 54, 56 (1966) (error not to instruct on both principles); State v. Anderson, 230 N.C. 54, 55–56, 51 S.E.2d 895, 896–97 (1949) (to same effect); State v. Moore, 214 N.C. 658, 660–61, 200 S.E. 427, 428 (1939) (to same effect); State v. Barnette, 8 N.C. App. 198, 174 S.E.2d 82 (1970) (failure to instruct on right to use nondeadly force not prejudicial where jury returned verdict that defendant assaulted victim with intent to kill).

business.[33] Many cases also indicate that defendants do not have a duty to retreat before using deadly force regardless of whether the conflict occurs inside *or* outside the home or business. Consistent with this line of authority, several cases hold that the defendant is entitled in an appropriate case to instructions that he or she does not have a duty to retreat before using deadly force to repel a "felonious assault"—that is, some action that a reasonable person would perceive as threatening death or great bodily injury.[34]

### (e) Burdens and Presumptions

The trial court must explain that the state bears the burden of proving beyond a reasonable doubt that the defendant did not act in self-defense or pursuant to any other applicable defensive-force defense.[35] In a homicide case, if the evidence warrants instructions on defensive force, the judge may not instruct the jury to presume malice

---

33. *See supra* §§ 3.5(c)(2), 4.4; *see also* State v. Morgan, 315 N.C. 626, 641–47, 340 S.E.2d 84, 94–97 (1986) (failure to give no-duty-to-retreat instruction is error even without request, although error reviewed on appeal under "plain error" standard); State v. Brown, 117 N.C. App. 239, 242, 450 S.E.2d 538, 541 (1994) (court finds in split opinion that failure to give no-duty-to-retreat instruction is constitutional error), *rev. denied*, 340 N.C. 115, 456 S.E.2d 320 (1995).

34. *See supra* § 3.5(c)(1); *see also* State v. Watson, 338 N.C. 168, 186, 449 S.E.2d 694, 705 (1994) (no error in failing to give instruction because evidence did not support it), *cert. denied*, __ U.S. __, 115 S. Ct. 1708, 131 L. Ed. 2d 569 (1995); State v. Washington, 234 N.C. 531, 534–35, 67 S.E.2d 498, 500–01 (1951) (suggesting that trial court should have instructed jury in accordance with principle that a person is not required to retreat if he or she is without fault and is assaulted with murderous intent); State v. Ellerbe, 223 N.C. 770, 772–73, 28 S.E.2d 519, 520–21 (1944) (trial court instructed jury that defendant had no duty to retreat if assault was actually made on him with felonious purpose; supreme court finds error because trial court failed to indicate that defendant should get benefit of this principle if he had reasonable ground to believe assault was made on him with felonious purpose); State v. Nixon, 117 N.C. App. 141, 150–51, 450 S.E.2d 562, 567–68 (1994) (error in failing to instruct); State v. Ward, 26 N.C. App. 159, 162, 215 S.E.2d 394, 396 (1975) (error in failing to instruct). Since there also is no duty to retreat before using *nondeadly* force, a defendant may be entitled to a no-duty-to-retreat instruction in that context as well. *See supra* §§ 3.5(c)(1), 4.3 (discussing right to use nondeadly force without retreating).

35. *See* State v. Herbin, 298 N.C. 441, 446, 259 S.E.2d 263, 267 (1979) (trial court must instruct jury that state has burden to disprove self-defense beyond reasonable doubt); State v. Potter, 295 N.C. 126, 142–44, 244 S.E.2d 397, 408–09 (1978) (error to place burden on defendant to show he was not aggressor, but error was not prejudicial on facts of case).

and unlawfulness from the defendant's intentional use of a deadly weapon to inflict injury. The reason is that the presumption of malice and unlawfulness "disappears" when there is any evidence showing self-defense or any other defensive-force defense.[36]

## (f) Final Mandate

The supreme court has held that the trial court, in its final mandate to the jury, must include as a possible verdict "not guilty by reason of self-defense" (or by reason of some other defensive-force defense). The trial court must so advise the jury even though it has given other instructions on defensive force in earlier parts of the charge. The rationale for this requirement is that, without such a statement, the final mandate may unfairly emphasize verdicts favorable to the state.[37]

## (g) Pattern and Special Instructions

Several pattern jury instructions exist on defensive-force defenses.[38] These instructions are generic in nature, however, and may not be appropriate in all cases.[39]

---

36. *See supra* § 8.3. The Pattern Jury Committee apparently is of the view that the trial court should never instruct the jury to presume malice and unlawfulness. N.C.P.I.—CRIM., *supra* note 21, at 206.10 n.5 (Aug. 1994).

37. *See* State v. Buck, 310 N.C. 602, 607, 313 S.E.2d 550, 553–54 (1984); State v. Dooley, 285 N.C. 158, 165–66, 203 S.E.2d 815, 819–20 (1974); State v. Bevin, 55 N.C. App. 476, 285 S.E.2d 873 (1982) (in assault case, court finds error in failure to explain in final mandate that jury could find defendant not guilty by reason of self-defense); State v. Patterson, 50 N.C. App. 280, 283–85, 272 S.E.2d 924, 926–27 (1981) (trial court must give final mandate explaining effect of defense of others).

38. *See, e.g.,* N.C.P.I.—CRIM., *supra* note 21, at 206.10 (Aug. 1994) (first-degree murder involving deadly weapon); 206.11 (Aug. 1994) (first-degree murder not involving deadly weapon); 206.30 (April 1994) (second-degree murder involving deadly weapon); 206.31 (Nov. 1992) (second-degree murder not involving deadly weapon); 206.40 (April 1992) (voluntary manslaughter); 208.81 A–F (Mar. 1981) (assault on officer); 308.10 (May 1983) (retreat in home or business); 308.40 (Sept. 1986) (self-defense not involving deadly force); 308.41 (Sept. 1986) (detention of offenders); 308.45 (Sept. 1986) (self-defense involving deadly force); 308.60 (Dec. 1986) (defense of others); 308.70 (Dec. 1986) (self-defense against sexual assault); 308.80 (Dec. 1986) (defense of habitation).

39. *See* N.C.P.I.—CRIM., *supra* note 21, at xix (cautioning that pattern instructions should be tailored to case as needed).

Also, trial courts must give at least the substance of instructions that a party requests when the instructions are supported by the evidence and are a correct statement of the law.[40] For example, defendants are entitled to jury instructions, on request, on the relevance of evidence concerning their peaceful character and other pertinent character traits.[41] Defendants also are entitled to jury instructions on the bearing of the *victim's* violent character on the reasonableness of the defendant's apprehension concerning the victim.[42] The North Carolina courts appear to require such instructions, even without a specific request, when the evidence warrants them.[43] If, however, the defendant wants instructions explaining the import of particular types of evidence (such as threats or prior violent acts by the victim), the onus would seem to be on the defendant to request them.

---

40. *See, e.g.,* State v. Rose, 323 N.C. 455, 458, 373 S.E.2d 426, 428 (1988); State v. Corn, 307 N.C 79, 86, 296 S.E.2d 261, 266 (1982).

41. *See* State v. Bogle, 324 N.C. 190, 199–200, 376 S.E.2d 745, 750 (1989) (defendant entitled to instruction on request); State v. Moreno, 98 N.C. App. 642, 644–46, 391 S.E.2d 860, 861–63 (distilling four-part test for determining when such an instruction is appropriate), *rev. denied,* 327 N.C. 640, 399 S.E.2d 331 (1990); N.C.P.I—CRIM., *supra* note 21, at 105.60 (Feb. 1992) (evidence of defendant's character trait).

42. *See, e.g.,* State v. Rummage, 280 N.C. 51, 54–55, 185 S.E.2d 221, 223–24 (1971) (error not to relate reputation of deceased as violent man when intoxicated to reasonableness of defendant's apprehension); State v. Riddle, 228 N.C. 251, 252–53, 45 S.E.2d 366, 367 (1947) (error not to relate reputation of deceased as violent man to reasonableness of defendant's apprehension); State v. Tann, 57 N.C. App. 527, 528–30, 291 S.E.2d 824, 826–27 (1982) (error not to instruct on relevance of prior incidents of violence and prior threats known to defendant); State v. Powell, 51 N.C. App. 224, 226–28, 275 S.E.2d 528, 530–31 (1981) (error not to instruct on relevance of prior assaults by victim against defendant); State v. Hall, 31 N.C. App. 34, 39–40, 228 S.E.2d 637, 640 (1976) (error not to instruct on relevance of victim's violent character, which included prior threat by victim against defendant and prior act of violence by victim known to defendant); State v. Covington, 9 N.C. App. 595, 176 S.E.2d 872 (1970) (error not to relate in instructions reputation of deceased as violent person and defendant's claim of self-defense).

43. *See* 1 BRANDIS & BROUN, *supra* note 2, at 275 & nn.128–29; *Rummage, supra* note 42; *Tann, supra* note 42. A number of pattern jury instructions contain a general provision stating that the jury should consider the victim's reputation for danger and violence in evaluating the reasonableness of the defendant's actions. *See, e.g.,* N.C.P.I.—CRIM., *supra* note 21, at 206.10 (Aug. 1994) (first-degree murder involving deadly weapon).

www.ingramcontent.com/pod-product-compliance
Lightning Source LLC
Chambersburg PA
CBHW070358200326
41518CB00011B/1971